OECD ECONOMIC SURVEYS

1999-2000

New Zealand

OECD

ORGANISATION FOR ECONOMIC CO-OPERATION AND DEVELOPMENT

ORGANISATION FOR ECONOMIC CO-OPERATION AND DEVELOPMENT

Pursuant to Article 1 of the Convention signed in Paris on 14th December 1960, and which came into force on 30th September 1961, the Organisation for Economic Co-operation and Development (OECD) shall promote policies designed:

- to achieve the highest sustainable economic growth and employment and a rising standard of living in Member countries, while maintaining financial stability, and thus to contribute to the development of the world economy;
- to contribute to sound economic expansion in Member as well as non-member countries in the process of economic development; and
- to contribute to the expansion of world trade on a multilateral, non-discriminatory basis in accordance with international obligations.

The original Member countries of the OECD are Austria, Belgium, Canada, Denmark, France, Germany, Greece, Iceland, Ireland, Italy, Luxembourg, the Netherlands, Norway, Portugal, Spain, Sweden, Switzerland, Turkey, the United Kingdom and the United States. The following countries became Members subsequently through accession at the dates indicated hereafter: Japan (28th April 1964), Finland (28th January 1969), Australia (7th June 1971), New Zealand (29th May 1973), Mexico (18th May 1994), the Czech Republic (21st December 1995), Hungary (7th May 1996), Poland (22nd November 1996), Korea (12th December 1996) and the Slovak Republic (14th December 2000). The Commission of the European Communities takes part in the work of the OECD (Article 13 of the OECD Convention).

Publié également en français.

Table of contents

Figures

BASIC STATISTICS OF NEW ZEALAND

THE LAND

Area (thousand sq. km)	268.0	Urban population,[1]	
Percentage of total pasture		percentage of total (June 1999)	77.1
and arable land, 1996	49.5	Population of major urban areas	
		(June 1999, 1 000 persons):	
		Auckland	1 090.5
		Christchurch	341.0
		Wellington	346.6

THE PEOPLE

Population, June 2000 (1 000)	3 831.0	Civilian employment, 1999 (1 000)	1 750.3
Inhabitant per sq. km	14.3	of which:	
		Agriculture, forestry, hunting, fishing	165.5
		Manufacturing	278.4
		Trade (wholesale and retail)	371.5
		Community and personal services	478.6

PARLIAMENT AND GOVERNMENT

Present composition of Parliament:		Present Government: Labour Party/Alliance coalition
Labour Party	49	Next general election: at latest by December 2002
National Party	39	
Alliance	10	
Act New Zealand	9	
Green	7	
New Zealand First	5	
United New Zealand Party	1	

PRODUCTION[2]

Gross Domestic Product 1999-2000		GDP per capita, 1999-2000	
(NZ$ million)	103 681	(NZ$)	27 137

FOREIGN TRADE (1999)

Main exports (percentage of total):		Main imports (percentage of total):	
Manufactures	20.0	Machinery and transport equipment	44.3
Meat and edible offal	12.7	Manufactures	19.2
Dairy produce	16.0	Mineral, chemicals, plastic materials	22.6
Wool	3.1	of which:	
		Mineral fuels, lubricants, etc.	6.0

THE CURRENCY

Monetary unit: New Zealand dollar	Currency unit per US dollar,	
	average of daily figures:	
	Year 1999	1.8917
	October 2000	2.4972

---

1. An international comparison of certain basic statistics is given in an annex table.
2. Year ending 31 March.

Assessment and recommendations

*Following
a strong rebound
from recession,
the economy
has slowed*

The economic recovery in New Zealand that began in the second half of 1998, supported by stimulative monetary and fiscal policies, gathered considerable momentum during the course of the following year, as the situation in Asian markets and climatic conditions at home improved. With strong growth (of nearly 6 per cent) through 1999, economic slack was rapidly absorbed. However, since then, despite strong trading-partner growth and a very competitive exchange rate, economic activity in New Zealand has weakened significantly, reflecting interest rate increases from late 1999 and a slump in business and consumer confidence associated in part with a negative private-sector reaction to policies announced by the new government. Consumer price inflation remained subdued until mid-year but moved to the top of the official 0 to 3 per cent target range in the September 2000 quarter, and input and producer prices as well as surveyed pricing intentions point to rising inflation pressures. At the same time, the large current account deficit, which had temporarily narrowed during the 1998 recession, has widened again, reflecting New Zealand's high marginal propensity to import and persistently unfavourable terms of trade.

*Growth
is projected to
strengthen
again...*

Following the recent growth pause – the economy may have expanded by around 1 per cent during the course of 2000 – the pace of activity is expected to accelerate again, with real GDP growth stabilising at just under 3 per cent by 2002. This projection is based on the assessment that current depressed confidence levels are out of step with some positive fundamentals, which should reassert themselves over time. In particular, New Zealand's very favourable competitive position should allow exporters to take advantage of ongoing robust market growth. It is true that a number of negative influences will weigh on domestic demand, including the lagged effects of higher interest rates in the context of heavy personal sector debt and gradual fiscal tightening. However, the combination of projected income gains resulting from the strength in exports and relative weakness in domestic expenditure should serve to lift the low level of private savings, which is the major factor behind New Zealand's sizeable current account deficit. In the absence of a further deterioration in the terms of trade, the external balance is projected to improve gradually toward levels consistent with a stable albeit rather high foreign-debt-to-GDP ratio. Reflecting the impact of oil price increases and exchange-rate depreciation, consumer price inflation is expected to move beyond the ceiling of the official target range only temporarily before receding progressively from next year.

... although there are considerable risks to the outlook...

While this would seem to be the most likely outcome, the recent volatility in indicators makes for a difficult task in assessing economic prospects. As export demand is expected to drive the expansion, a pronounced downturn in market growth would certainly pose a significant downside risk to activity, although projections for world growth remain relatively favourable at present. In the near term, uncertainties would seem to concern, in particular, the evolution of confidence and wage- and price-setting behaviour, against the backdrop of changes to the industrial relations framework discussed below. If business and consumer confidence stay low for an extended period, domestic demand could continue to weaken. Given substantial cost pressures, which might well be reinforced by further exchange-rate depreciation, this could lead to a period of subdued economic activity together with higher inflation, although resulting excess supply should, over time, restrain price increases. On the other hand, confidence and activity could bounce back more quickly and to a greater extent than expected. In this case, with rising excess demand, the near-term hike in the price level might spill over into more persistent generalised inflation, through mounting inflation expectations, compensatory wage demands and other forms of implicit or explicit indexation.

... requiring skilful monetary management

Although these risks and uncertainties are partially off-setting, they are greater than usual. Hence, supporting growth while avoiding a build-up of generalised inflation pressures will be a challenging task for policymakers. Over the six months to May 2000, the Reserve Bank raised interest rates gradually. This was appropriate, given signs of emerging excess demand and relatively easy overall monetary conditions due to the low exchange rate. Since then, the authorities have left interest rates unchanged despite intensifying cost pressures, deciding to "look through" the upcoming inflation spike associated with recent energy price increases and exchange-rate depreciation. Although slowing activity means that the balance of risks has probably shifted somewhat away from a sustained build-up in inflationary pressures, the central projections presented above would suggest that there will be a need for further official interest-rate increases – the projections build in a rise of ½ percentage point – in the period ahead to prevent the emergence of cost-push inflation. The required extent of such increases will depend on further evolution of the exchange rate, which in the above projections is assumed to remain unchanged at end-October levels. Moreover, while the projections suggest some further tightening, monetary policy settings will need to be continuously reassessed in light of the uncertainty surrounding the momentum of the economic expansion.

The way the monetary policy framework has evolved should help in this respect

The operating framework for monetary policy is now under review. Nevertheless, the current arrangements seem sound and should facilitate the achievement of sustained non-inflationary growth. The inflation targeting approach has evolved with changes in the monetary policy transmission mechanism, alongside the acquisition of policy credibility and increased stability in the inflation process. This evolution is manifest in a number of changes, including the widening of the target range, some de-emphasis of the target's edges, and a lengthening of the time horizon at which policy responses to inflation pressures are directed. Such changes imply that outcomes for the target measure of inflation might vary a little more than in the past, but without raising a threat to medium-term price stability that would require offsetting policy action with its consequential effects on the real economy. More recently, a welcome development has been the Bank's shift from a target for its Monetary Conditions Index – which combines the effect of short-term interest rate and exchange-rate movements – to a cash interest-rate target in implementing monetary policy. By reducing communications problems, this move has lessened the need for frequent official statements while resulting in more interest-rate stability. Altogether, these changes appear to have had positive effects on macroeconomic stability. However, there are limits to how flexible policies can be without compromising the credibility of the framework and allowing inflation expectations to rise. Such concerns are particularly relevant in the current conjuncture.

A fiscal deficit has been avoided...

An appropriate fiscal stance will also be needed to underpin sustained economic expansion in the period ahead. Despite the economic turbulence in recent years, public debt has kept falling and budget deficits have been avoided, consistent with the principles of responsible fiscal management in the *Fiscal Responsibility Act*, which has been maintained by the new government. However, operating surplus outcomes in 1998/99 and 1999/2000 owed a great deal to one-off factors. Abstracting from them, the underlying budget position in 1999/2000 was in only slight surplus, in actual and cyclically-adjusted terms. While less ambitious in its long-term objective for the ratio of expenditure to GDP, the new administration has broadly preserved the fiscal track envisaged by its predecessor, which calls for a gradual rebuilding of budget surpluses. According to its first Budget Policy Statement, the reasons for doing so are threefold. Strengthening the fiscal position should take some pressure off monetary policy, thereby moderating movements in interest rates and the exchange rate. It should also bolster confidence and guard against possible adverse effects associated with New Zealand's large current account deficit and high external debt. In addition, it will allow the government to start pre-funding the future fiscal costs arising from population ageing.

... but rebuilding surpluses will be a challenging task

The projected fiscal policy stance is appropriate in the light of both near-term and longer-term economic challenges. However, there are clear risks surrounding the budget outlook. Downside risks to short-term economic prospects may imply outcomes that are less favourable than currently forecast. In this situation, the authorities have indicated, appropriately, that the fiscal stabilisers would be allowed to operate. In addition, there are risks relating to the front-loading of expenditure plans. Indeed, some two-thirds of the new government's fiscal provision (that is, funding available for new initiatives) for the three-year electoral term starting last November has already been allocated, implying a sharp constraint on new government expenditure in the next two years. Given the strong expenditure pressures inherent in areas like health care and education and emerging demand for faster public-sector pay increases in some areas, achieving the reduction in public spending as a percentage of GDP shown in the current fiscal plans will require a much greater measure of success in managing spending demands than has been seen in recent years. At the same time, meeting these targets will boost the credibility of the government's policies. Its intention to pre-fund future pension costs might serve to enhance spending discipline. In addition, as discussed below, more systematic processes to evaluate the effectiveness of public spending would be of benefit. Finally, while the fiscal stance – provided it can be realised – appears suitable, the fact that it results from both higher spending and revenue levels than earlier envisaged raises some concern from a microeconomic perspective.

Past structural reform has produced positive results, though more needs to be done

With recent economic performance falling short of earlier optimistic expectations, there has been extensive debate on whether structural reform in New Zealand has paid off. The rebound in potential output growth on average in the 1990s indicates that benefits have accrued. Indeed, despite slowing somewhat in the latter part of that period, trend growth has continued to compare favourably with that in the 1970s and 1980s. Nevertheless, there are lingering gaps between various groups in society, undermining the public's faith in government, and the current administration has made it a priority to reduce them. Moreover, the extensive reforms have only halted the trend decline in relative living standards. This stems largely from relatively poor aggregate productivity performance. This may reflect a number of factors, including the long time it takes for economic outcomes to adjust to new policies, inconsistent progress in the past towards a stable macroeconomic environment, implementation difficulties in some areas of structural policy, and persistently high levels of agricultural protection in other OECD countries. Nonetheless, in view of the relatively slow increase in total factor productivity in recent years, there remains a need to improve the quality of factor inputs and the way they are combined. There is therefore no room for policy complacency, and consideration should be given to refining and reinvigorating existing structural policies, and identifying and addressing any areas where reforms have not gone far enough.

The new government has a different policy approach in some areas

The new administration considers that the previous policy approach was, in some respects, not sufficient to improve economic performance and simultaneously strengthen social cohesion. It has broadly maintained the main features of reforms taken to date but seeks to develop a partnership with business and local communities that will see a somewhat greater role for government in product and labour markets. In addition, it places a greater emphasis on social inclusion issues and closing the gaps among various groups in society, especially reducing the disparities in the performance of Maori and Pacific peoples relative to other New Zealanders.

But some of the recent policy moves may hinder the full development of economic potential

Structural reform requires constant attention to keep pace with an evolving economic environment. The new administration has pointed out that recent changes in the structural policy area are only a return to the international mainstream. Yet, arguably, given its relative geographical isolation and resource endowments, New Zealand has to do more than other countries in order to make it an attractive location for both domestic and foreign labour and capital. This may also help to mitigate the net loss of skilled workers seen in migratory flows over the past few years. Against this backdrop, some recent policy developments do not appear to be helpful, for example: boosting the top marginal income tax rate; lowering the obligation of some benefit recipients to seek work; introducing income-related rents for public housing; stopping the privatisation process; re-nationalising accident insurance; and ending unilateral tariff reductions while introducing an export credit scheme. At the same time, some initiatives would not seem to be conducive to achieving the government's social policy objectives, for instance, the more generous student loan scheme.

A new industrial relations framework has probably affected the business climate

Probably the most controversial change occurred in the area of industrial relations with the introduction of the *Employment Relations Act*, which may have been a major factor behind the slump in business confidence. While it will take time before the Act's impact can be ascertained, it seems unlikely that bargaining will return to the centralised and distortionary practices of the more distant past. Nor is it clear, however, that the legislation will improve the functioning of the labour market. To minimise potentially adverse macroeconomic and microeconomic consequences from the strengthening of the role of trade unions, bargaining parties will need to keep wage increases in line with productivity developments, with multi-employer contracts taking account of the different conditions facing firms. Moreover, the new notice and dismissal procedures will need to be carefully monitored to assess any ongoing impact on compliance costs, particularly in small firms, in relation to any employment effects.

Industrial policy has become more activist

Another key element of the new government's policy approach is the creation of Industry New Zealand (INZ). This agency oversees a wide range of existing and new industrial policy programmes and could, in principle, play a valuable role in improving their co-ordination and delivery, promoting coherence in policy making. It does not appear to reflect any specific intent to "pick winners" but does embody the objective of increasing economic activity in depressed regions. The latest budget also provides new funds to boost research and development, which may help spur innovation. Given that the benefits of such programmes are not always clear, they need to be carefully evaluated. Not only would this reduce the risk of rent-seeking behaviour, it would also allow a set of best practices to be developed that could be used to target expenditures appropriately. Similarly, any temptation to use the proposed People's Bank for regional development purposes should be avoided, with the Bank run on a strictly commercial basis, with no question of any public deposit guarantee, either explicit or implicit.

A reassessment
of the regulatory
framework
is also under
way

The government feels that there are some gaps and deficiencies in regulatory structures and has initiated reviews in a number of areas, including the telecommunications, electricity and financial sectors. Each review is timely, given the vast changes that have been witnessed. The basic approach of light-handed intervention, with appropriate self-regulation, has worked reasonably well, while helping to minimise compliance costs. The principles of this approach should therefore be broadly maintained, as the government proposes, while addressing shortcomings that do appear to have emerged.

Careful evaluation
of changes
in the health and
education sectors
is required...

Health care and education are two areas where many OECD countries are struggling to improve outcomes. The current re-organisation of New Zealand's health-care sector represents the third major reform in this domain since the early 1990s, with the move away from the purchaser/provider split and creation of District Health Boards (DHB) being the most fundamental changes. The previous system was considered to be overly complex, with heavy ensuing transaction costs, although it remains to be seen whether the new system reduces them. Indeed, careful planning and attention to the implementation of the DHBs will be necessary. Only a strengthening of the monitoring and evaluation process will ensure that the new arrangements help to contain costs and achieve health-policy objectives. The education sector, particularly primary and secondary schools, has also seen a shift away from market mechanisms (such as bulk funding and student choice) although some of the policy benefits have been retained through other initiatives such as greater flexibility for schools to recruit and remunerate staff above standard entitlements. In any case, establishing clearer goals for schools and students, disseminating best-practice approaches and bolstering the incentives to up-skill are essential to better outcomes. The government's emphasis on providing alternative pathways to the labour market for youths, such as the Modern Apprenticeships, is welcome; its impact on raising qualification levels should be monitored. However, the costly expansion of the student-loan programme is poorly targeted and will not necessarily improve access to tertiary education. Given the high cost of this scheme, the government is urged to carefully evaluate its impact. Although it is not clear that market-based solutions are always superior in social-policy areas, such as health and education, it is not obvious that regulatory measures will be as effective as risk-based premia in areas such as accident insurance, even if they lead to some reduction in administrative costs. The intention to move to actuarially-based full funding for all of the activities of the accident insurance scheme should provide transparency about the likely sustainability of current low premium levels.

... and of public
expenditures
more generally

Across the board, more attention needs to be paid to the quality of government spending. Although aggregate expenditure is assessed under a well-defined framework, there has been no systematic process to evaluate individual programmes. The *Value for Money* initiative is welcome, as is the review of programmes targeted at Maori and Pacific peoples. These should not be *ad hoc* efforts, however, and a requirement to evaluate programmes should become entrenched in the policy-making process.

Pre-funding
of public pensions
should not
exclude
a reassessment
of the generosity
of the system

The government also faces serious challenges in the context of the proposed partial pre-funding of New Zealand Superannuation, that is state pensions. When analysing the potential benefits that might arise from pre-funding (enhanced spending discipline over the next few years and preparing for the future ageing of the population), the authorities should also carefully consider those that could accrue from an alternative financing strategy that would place greater emphasis on tax reductions over the short to medium term. Such reductions might help to boost the productive capacity of the economy; in any event there will be pressures to reduce corporate taxes, given such moves elsewhere in the OECD. Pre-funding raises important governance and operational issues. To address them, as proposed, the Investment Board should be at arm's length from the government and its investment strategy transparent and periodically assessed. Governance would be assisted by allocating some portion of the funds overseas and/or investing passively. Nevertheless, it may be difficult to ring-fence the savings from current expenditure demands. Moreover, such savings could also lead to pressure to increase the generosity of state pensions. In this regard, public pension eligibility and entitlements should be subject to ongoing evaluation, including whether a less generous system would help to boost private savings.

To what extent
tax measures
could enhance
private savings
is uncertain

It might be argued that tax policy could also play a role in raising the low level of private savings in New Zealand. However, targeted tax incentives are likely to result primarily in shifting savings into lower taxed portfolios and any possible impact on private savings will probably be more than offset by reduced government savings as tax revenues decline. A more promising direction would be a revenue-neutral change in the tax mix toward more consumption tax and less income tax, but even though such a move could potentially spur private savings, most available empirical evidence suggests that the effect would likely be moderate.

In most respects,
the tax system
compares
favourably with
other countries...

New Zealand's tax system is still one of the most neutral and efficient in the OECD area, although other countries have been making improvements to their own systems. Bases are generally broad and rates are moderate. The full imputation system for dividend payments works to reduce tax distortions for corporate financing decisions. At the same time, the low level of targeted tax incentives encourages efficiency in investment decisions. The tax system is also more neutral with respect to private savings than in most other countries, in particular because there are no incentives for private pension savings. Finally, the international tax regime is more comprehensive and sophisticated than elsewhere, helping contain the domestic cost of capital while discouraging tax avoidance through a more coercive taxation of capital exports than generally found overseas.

... but a number
of issues could be
addressed...

There is hence no need for major tax reform. However, several second-order issues should be addressed to reap the full benefits of an otherwise well-functioning system. The most important improvement would be a broadening of the income tax base by including capital gains in a more comprehensive way as well as introducing a tax on imputed rental income of owner-occupied housing beyond the local property tax. These two steps would not only reduce horizontal inequities, and hence tax-shifting incentives, but also contribute to a better allocation of private saving, which is currently biased strongly toward housing, resulting in unbalanced household portfolios. Equity and neutrality would also be bolstered by limiting tax-avoidance possibilities for individuals through various corporate structures, such as trusts and "loss-attributing qualifying companies". Moreover, there appears to be some room for improving work incentives for disadvantaged groups, in particular single parents, by lowering marginal effective tax rates that result from the abatement of tax credits and welfare benefits for those seeking less than full-time work. Such a move, however, is likely to require a reduction in the overall coverage of the various tax credits if revenue losses are to be avoided, given the tradeoff between the range and rate over which abatement occurs.

... and stepping backward should be resisted

While such measures would be important steps forward, it is equally important for New Zealand to avoid stepping backward. The recent increase in the top personal income tax rate to 39 per cent has reduced the neutrality of the tax system, creating a wedge between corporate and personal taxation, though probably not to an extent that will have significant adverse economic consequences. However, other initiatives currently under consideration, such as tax incentives for investment (for instance in R&D) or private pension savings, may potentially be much more harmful. Even though the scope of such incentives may be limited, they would nevertheless signal that the "no exception" policy of the past fifteen years is being loosened, thus encouraging lobbying for more significant relaxation measures in the future. As a result, the quite unique existing consensus that tax exemptions are unwarranted could be undermined.

With the economy at a crossroads, it is crucial that policy be set in a far-sighted way

New Zealand weathered the turbulence of the late 1990s relatively well compared with its past experience. After a brief recession associated with the Asian crisis and adverse climatic conditions, growth resumed swiftly. Contrary to what typically happened in the past, fiscal deficits and a run-up in inflation were avoided. Nonetheless, vulnerabilities remain. As the economy continues to rely heavily on agricultural production and processing, it remains exposed to swings in international commodity prices, which have not been in its favour, and to the harmful effects of protectionism in the rest of the world. Because of a lack of domestic savings, the economy is also highly dependent on foreign capital, which is reflected in a chronically large current account deficit, leaving the country open to changes in foreign investor sentiment. Moreover, while improving in the 1990s, growth outcomes have not been sufficient to close the substantial per capita income gap with the OECD average, given relatively poor productivity performance. This highlights the importance of implementing policies that are conducive to both lifting savings and potential output growth. While macroeconomic policies have continued to be broadly supportive of these objectives, some new microeconomic policy measures do not seem to be well tailored to enhancing efficiency and improving growth prospects. An important way to better the situation of disadvantaged groups is to ensure a higher standard of living for all New Zealanders. Increasing per capita incomes relative to other OECD countries by maintaining macroeconomic stability and enhancing structural policies should therefore be a key focus of policymakers.

I. Macroeconomic performance

The New Zealand economy rebounded vigorously from the 1998 recession before losing momentum recently (Figure 1, Panel A). Although the 1998 setback to economic expansion was short-lived, trend growth has slowed somewhat following its marked acceleration toward the middle of the 1990s, and the initial progress made during that period in narrowing New Zealand's substantial per capita income gap against an OECD benchmark has not been sustained (Panel B). Despite indications that economic slack that had re-emerged in 1998 has already been taken up, inflationary pressures have remained relatively subdued so far. However, New Zealand's chronic current account deficit and ensuing foreign indebtedness have reached high levels both by historical and international standards, posing some risks to the economic outlook. The remainder of this chapter reviews, against the backdrop of the major forces shaping activity, recent and prospective economic developments in New Zealand in more detail.

Forces shaping economic activity

Moving into the second half of the 1990s, the New Zealand economy was hit by a number of adverse shocks while it was under the strain of corrective policy action prompted by the emergence of inflation pressures. Export markets contracted (Figure 2, Panel D) as demand from Asia collapsed during the financial crisis in that region (which accounts for about two-fifths of New Zealand's exports). At the same time, the economy was affected by severe drought, which depressed agricultural output and exports. The impact of these shocks was compounded by very firm monetary conditions (Panel B) – manifest in high real interest rates and a strong New Zealand dollar – that had been established on the basis of expectations of continued robust growth. Along with deteriorating household and business confidence (Panel E), these factors served to push the economy into recession at the beginning of 1998.

Aided by an easing in both monetary and fiscal policies (Figure 2, Panels B and C), economic growth resumed in the second half of 1998. Income-tax cuts and lower interest rates boosted domestic demand. With a marked decline in the exchange rate, exporters were in a favourable position to take advantage of

Figure 1. **Growth performance over the long term**

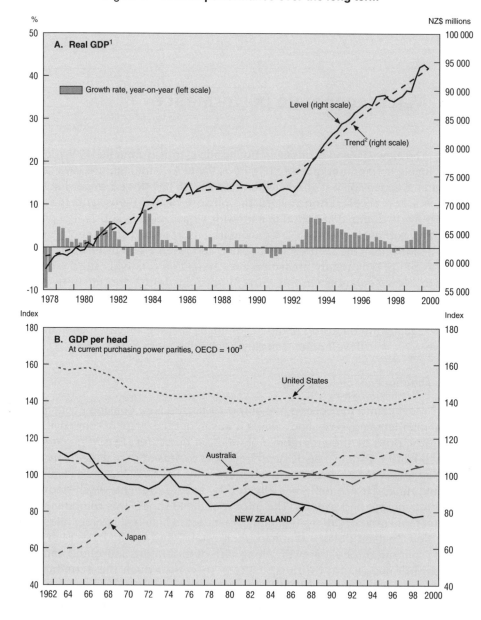

1. Output measure; 1991-92 prices.
2. Hodrick-Prescott filter, λ = 1 600.
3. 25 countries.
Source: Statistics New Zealand and OECD.

Figure 2. **Conditions for growth**

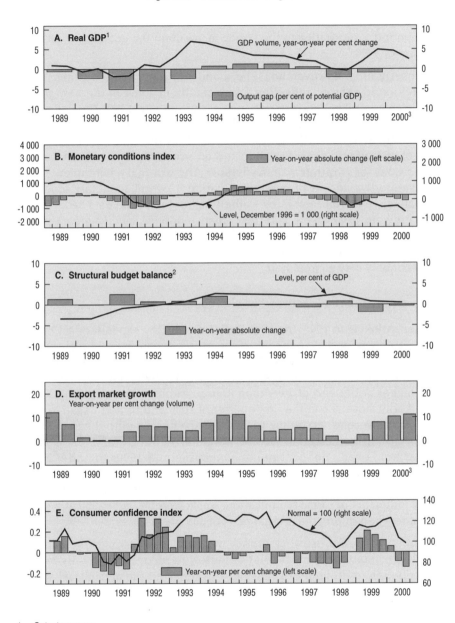

1. Output measure.
2. General government (national accounts basis).
3. Estimates for 2000.
Source: Statistics New Zealand, Reserve Bank of New Zealand and OECD.

the renewed robust expansion of their markets in the aftermath of the Asian crisis. In addition, improving weather conditions entailed a strong recovery in agricultural output and exports.In these circumstances, consumer and business confidence rebounded, contributing to the strong momentum the economy built up by the latter part of 1999.

Subsequently, however, household and – in particular – business confidence deteriorated sharply, reflecting a lack of faith in some of the new government's policies as well as interest-rate increases from late 1999. The collapse in confidence appears to have translated rather quickly and directly into a weakening in economic activity, although part of the slowdown is attributable to an unwinding of one-off influences that boosted growth at the end of 1999. Looking ahead, conditions for growth remain favourable. The external environment seems set to stay supportive and, as discussed in Chapter II, overall monetary conditions are still relatively easy. Interest rates – albeit higher than two years ago – remain well below previous peak levels, and the exchange rate has fallen a great deal further in recent months. Confidence indicators have posted a modest turnaround of late. Still, their continued depressed levels have heightened uncertainty about where the economy may go from here.

Following a strong rebound, activity has slowed

After shrinking in 1998, the New Zealand economy expanded in 1999 as a whole by 3½ per cent and 3¾ per cent, respectively, according to the output and expenditure measures of real GDP (Table 1). Up to mid-1999, the recovery proceeded at a modest pace, but a subsequent spurt in activity left real GDP almost 6 per cent higher at the end of 1999 than four quarters earlier. Economic growth slowed markedly, however, in the first quarter of 2000 and turned negative (at an actual rate) in the second. According to OECD estimates, an output gap of around 2 per cent of GDP had emerged in 1998. As potential output growth is estimated to have slowed from over 3 per cent per annum in the mid-1990s to under 2½ per cent (see Chapter III), the rapid expansion in late 1999 seems to have exhausted spare capacity in the economy (Figure 2, Panel A). This assessment is consistent with survey indicators of capacity utilisation, which were in early 2000 at a similar level to that reached during the cyclical peak of activity in the mid-1990s.

During the recent upswing, growth was widespread across the economy (Table 1). The primary sector was relatively slow to recover but finally made a strong contribution to economic expansion. This reflected the agricultural sector's bounce-back from protracted drought, compounded by a better-than-normal farming season last year. Output in the secondary sector was buoyed by the strength of construction activity and of machinery and equipment manufacturing. Growth in the services sector also picked up markedly, with particularly strong contributions from trade, tourism, transportation and communications industries. Y2K influences

Table 1. **Demand and output**

Volume percentage change at annual rates, calendar years

	1997 NZ$ billion	1970-83[1]	1983-91	1991-98	1996	1997	1998	1999	2000[2]
Private consumption	55.6	1.5	1.7	3.0	4.3	2.8	1.8	2.4	2.2
Government consumption	13.8	3.0	1.3	1.6	2.7	5.2	-1.0	8.7	-0.7
Gross fixed investment	19.8	2.2	-0.8	7.5	7.0	3.8	-1.9	8.4	9.0
Public	3.5	4.2	-5.9	3.6	23.6	21.8	-0.5	3.7	5.2
Residential	4.5	0.0	1.6	3.8	5.4	6.3	-16.9	12.0	17.9
Non-residential	11.9	2.0	1.4	10.4	4.2	-1.5	3.3	8.6	7.4
Final domestic demand	**89.3**	**1.9**	**1.2**	**3.6**	**4.6**	**3.4**	**0.5**	**4.7**	**3.2**
Stockbuilding[3]	0.6	-0.1	0.1	0.1	-0.5	-0.1	-0.7	1.1	-0.1
Total domestic demand	**89.9**	**1.8**	**1.3**	**3.7**	**4.1**	**3.3**	**-0.2**	**5.8**	**3.1**
Exports of goods and services	28.4	3.9	4.5	4.4	3.6	3.0	1.6	6.2	10.7
Imports of goods and services	30.1	2.8	4.4	7.3	8.4	4.2	2.7	12.0	4.8
Foreign balance[3]	**-1.7**	**0.3**	**0.2**	**-0.9**	**-1.5**	**-0.4**	**-0.4**	**-2.2**	**1.7**
GDP (expenditure basis)	**88.1**	**2.0**	**1.4**	**2.8**	**2.6**	**2.9**	**-0.6**	**3.7**	**5.0**
Agriculture and hunting	5.4	4.2	5.0	1.9	8.1	5.3	-2.5	0.9	8.0
Mining, forestry and fishing	2.4	2.2	7.6	0.9	4.3	3.7	-6.6	5.0	0.0
Manufacturing	16.0	2.8	-0.7	2.9	1.0	1.7	-2.8	2.2	4.8
Construction	3.2	1.0	-3.2	2.6	2.8	1.6	-7.6	3.2	12.8
Services	56.9	1.7	1.6	3.4	4.0	2.2	1.8	3.7	4.4
GDP (output basis)	**88.7**	**2.2**	**1.1**	**3.0**	**3.3**	**2.0**	**-0.2**	**3.4**	**4.7**
Memorandum item:									
Per capita GDP	..	1.0	0.4	1.6	1.0	1.6	-1.4	3.2	4.4

1. 1978-83 for components of GDP by industry and GDP output measure.
2. First two quarters over corresponding period.
3. Contribution to GDP volume growth.
Source: Statistics New Zealand and OECD.

seem to have played a role, adding to other one-off factors (in particular, favourable weather conditions) that apparently lifted the economy temporarily at the turn of the year.

In expenditure terms, too, the recovery was broadly based, with external and domestic demand expanding at similar rates in 1999 (Table 1). However, despite the rebound in exports, the real foreign balance continued to act as a drag on economic growth until the end of 1999 (Figure 3). This was attributable to a sharp acceleration in import growth, reflecting both the cyclical recovery in aggregate demand and a number of special factors (see below for further details). With import growth falling back at the beginning of 2000, real net exports have begun to

Figure 3. **Contributions to GDP growth**

Per cent change over 4 quarters

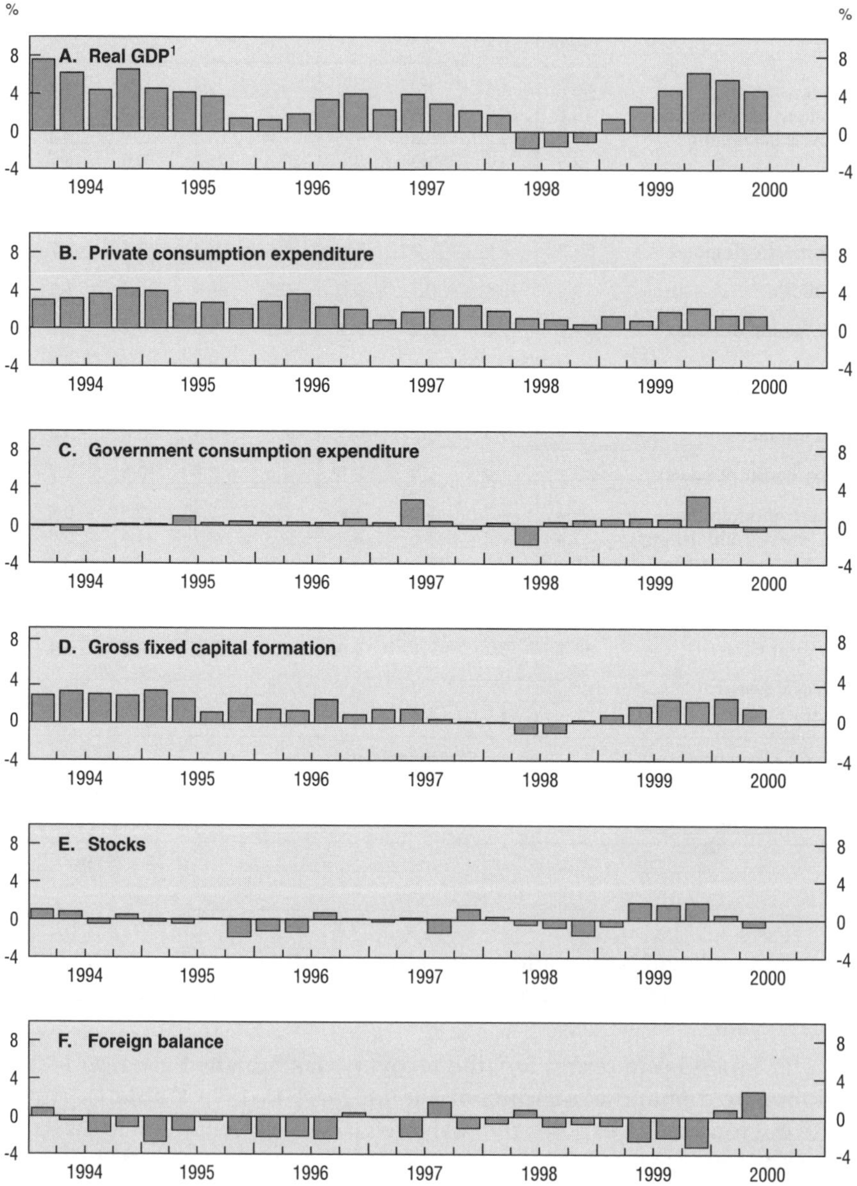

1. Expenditure measure; 1991-92 prices.
Source: Statistics New Zealand and OECD Secretariat.

become supportive of GDP growth. Within domestic demand, reflecting the monetary easing in 1998, interest-sensitive components (in particular, residential investment) posted the strongest revival, although spending strengthened across the board. Stockbuilding made a major contribution to the economic upturn, accounting for about one-third of GDP growth in 1999. A rundown in inventories at the beginning of 2000 would seem to suggest that precautions taken for Y2K played a role, although it could also have been an early reaction to the quite general weakening in final demand at that time.

Private consumption supported the recent economic upturn, but its growth contribution was relatively modest compared with that observed in the mid-1990s (Figure 3). Apart from lower interest rates, the revival in consumer spending through 1999 reflected higher incomes associated with improving labour-market conditions. However, disposable income growth did not re-attain its earlier strong pace, constraining consumer demand despite continued dissaving. The subsequent weakening in private consumption can be traced to a number of factors. The renewed rise in interest rates from late-1999 appears to be already impacting on consumer behaviour, both through increasing the cost of debt servicing and through weakening consumer confidence. Indeed, while other factors have also affected consumer sentiment, a rising proportion of survey respondents attribute their pessimism to higher interest rates. On the income side, negative influences include rising petrol prices and tax increases for high-income consumers, although this has been partially offset by increased transfer payments to lower-income earners and the elderly. Consumers also appear to be starting to pay more attention to their growing debt levels. Household borrowing is slowing, and there is anecdotal evidence that higher farm incomes have been used primarily to repay debt, rather than being spent. In addition, the sluggish housing and stock markets mean that there are no wealth effects supporting consumer spending. This contrasts with the situation in the mid-1990s, at the peak of the previous economic cycle, when a house price boom provided a boost to private consumption. It is difficult to assess to what extent the personal sector's financial position has become a constraint to private consumption. Despite a strong rise over the 1990s, households' debt-to-income ratio remains well within the middle of the range of those in comparable OECD countries. Available estimates for the debt-to-assets ratio suggest that it is relatively high, but net worth statistics underlying these calculations do not include durable goods, affecting international comparability. In any case, debt-service ratios are now historically quite high, probably inducing households to be more circumspect as to their spending decisions.

Residential investment continued to grow into 2000, but the building boom that followed the sharp contraction in 1998 (Figure 4) appears to have come to an end. The slump in investment in 1998 reflected tight monetary policy settings along with net emigration and oversupply of housing in some parts of the country. The subsequent surge can in large part be explained by the marked fall in interest

Figure 4. **Private gross fixed investment**
Year-on-year volume change

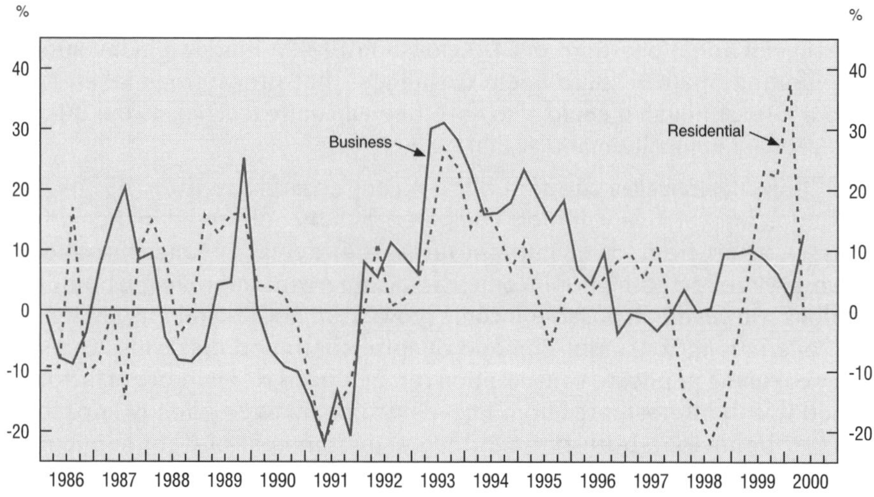

Source: Statistics New Zealand and OECD.

rates and stronger growth in household incomes. While the rise in investment continued, the housing market showed signs of softening from the latter part of 1999. House sales and house prices started to fall off. Building consents began to decline at a rapid pace, being recently about one-third below their levels recorded a year earlier. Following a further strong increase in early 2000, residential investment dropped in the second quarter. The renewed rise in interest rates is one factor behind falling housing demand. Moreover, it appears that, in the absence of a pronounced turnaround in net migration, soaring residential investment quickly led again to some oversupply of housing, putting downward pressure on house prices.

In stark contrast to residential investment, *business fixed investment* has tended to become less cyclical (Figure 4). Since the mid-1990s, it has displayed only limited fluctuations relative to GDP. The fact that business investment held up relatively well during the 1998 recession partly explains its modest contribution to the recent recovery. Still, fixed capital formation has been surprisingly muted, given that it was buoyed by computer investment in anticipation of Y2K and that overall investment conditions would seem rather favourable. As noted, capacity utilisation is at high levels, pointing to the need for investment. At the same time, the outlook for trading-partner growth remains strong, and the exchange rate is very competitive. Although more recently firms have complained about rising cost pressures, solid profit growth over the last year suggests that sufficient funds are available to finance capital spending. Indeed, while there is no comprehensive information on non-bank corporate debt developments over the last year, anecdotal evidence points to relatively low corporate debt-to-equity ratios. Despite these positive fundamentals, a lack of confidence has apparently led to some deferment of new investment, although firms report that investment opportunities are available. With the recent rise in business confidence from its mid-year low, investment intentions have also recovered somewhat, but – except in parts of the agricultural sector – they remain relatively subdued.

Unemployment has kept falling

The pattern of economic activity has been reflected in the labour market. Employment growth accelerated through 1999 and then weakened markedly in the first half of 2000 before picking up again recently (Table 2). Mirroring output developments, agriculture, construction and the services sector (notably trade, transport and communications) have contributed most to renewed job creation

Table 2.   **The labour market**
Annual percentage change over corresponding period

	1995	1996	1997	1998	1999	1999 Q4	2000 Q1	2000 Q2	2000 Q3
Working age population	2.0	2.0	1.3	0.9	0.6	0.6	0.6	0.7	0.6
Labour force	3.1	3.5	1.0	0.3	0.7	1.1	0.5	0.1	1.1
Employment	5.2	3.7	0.4	−0.6	1.4	2.7	1.4	1.0	2.1
Full time	5.3	2.6	0.0	−1.1	1.1	3.3	3.3	2.0	2.4
Part time	5.1	7.6	1.9	1.3	2.8	0.5	−4.8	−2.4	1.3
Unemployment rate[1]	6.3	6.1	6.7	7.5	6.8	6.3	6.4	6.1	5.9
Participation rate[2]	64.9	65.8	65.6	65.2	65.3	65.5	65.2	64.9	65.4
Employment ratio[3]	60.8	61.8	61.3	60.3	60.8	61.4	61.0	60.9	61.6
Labour productivity[4]									
Output basis	−1.2	−0.4	1.6	0.5	1.9	2.9	3.6	3.4	n.a.
Expenditure basis	−1.7	−1.0	2.5	0.1	2.2	3.5	4.1	3.4	n.a.
Memorandum item:									
Net migration[1]	0.4	0.3	0.1	−0.1	−0.1	0.1	−0.2	−0.3	0.0

1. Per cent of labour force.
2. Labour force/population 15 years and over.
3. Employment/population 15 years and over.
4. Per person employed.
Source: Statistics New Zealand.

since the 1998 recession. By contrast, employment in manufacturing industries has changed little, despite a significant advance in production. Job creation initially reflected rising part-time employment and shifted toward full-time employment only when the economic upturn gathered momentum in the second half of 1999. Swings in part-time employment at the turn of the year seem to support the view that the economy was temporarily lifted by some one-off influences at that time, the unwinding of which partly explains the subsequent softening in activity. However, the fact that the level of full-time employment dropped in the second quarter of 2000 for the first time since 1998 points to more generalised economic weakness at that time. The subsequent pickup in full-time employment could be a harbinger of strengthening activity, although around half of the jobs created in the September quarter occurred in the non-market (education, health and community services) sectors.

With employment expanding at a slower pace than output, labour productivity growth, which had come virtually to a halt during the 1998 recession, has picked up markedly (Table 2). Productivity gains are less impressive when measured in terms of full-time equivalent employment (Figure 5). But even on that basis they compare favourably with the performance over the 1991-98 cycle when

Figure 5. **Labour productivity**
Annual average percentage change

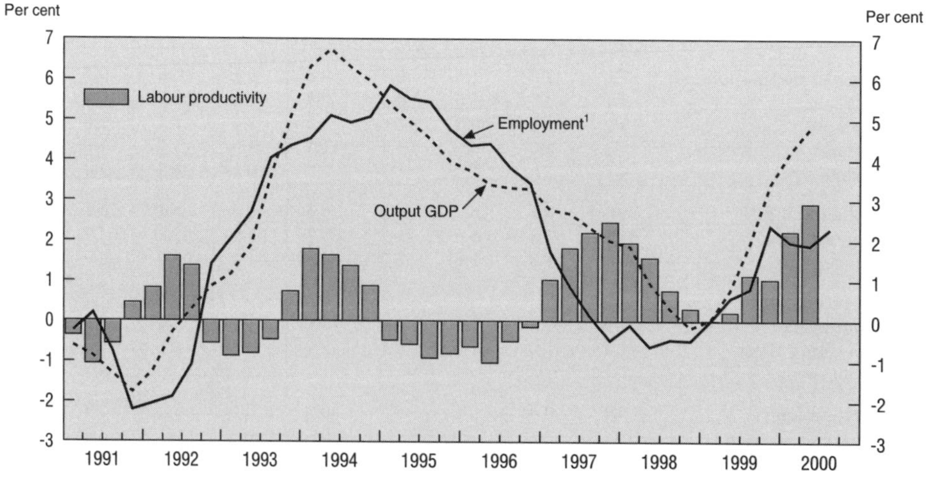

1.   Full-time equivalent.
Source: Statistics New Zealand and OECD.

labour productivity grew on average by less than 1 per cent per annum. However, as discussed in Chapter III, the initial impact of the Employment Contracts Act implemented at the beginning of that period seems to have been to dampen trend productivity growth. While it is possible that the legislation's expected positive effects may have started to enhance performance in recent years, it remains to be seen whether the observed pick-up in labour productivity growth is more than a cyclical phenomenon.

On the supply side, ongoing net emigration has meant that the expansion in the working age population has remained well below its natural rate of around 1¼ per cent per annum (Table 2). Although net outward migration has been less pronounced than in the aftermath of previous cyclical downturns, it has been protracted – ceasing only temporarily in late 1999 – despite an easing in entrance criteria which had been tightened in the mid-1990s when immigration boosted population growth. Nonetheless, the increase in labour supply accelerated noticeably through 1999 as improving job opportunities entailed higher labour force participation. However, the renewed rise in the participation rate was temporarily reversed in the first half of 2000. The deteriorating economic climate and a lack of attractive job opportunities in certain areas – manifest in continued outward migration – may have discouraged people from actively seeking employment.

Renewed net job creation translated into a fall in the unemployment rate as from late 1998 when it had peaked at 7¾ per cent of the labour force. Even though labour demand weakened in the first half of the year, the decline in unemployment has continued because, at the same time, developments in the participation rate have restricted labour supply (Table 2). In the third quarter of 2000, strong employment growth offset a rise in the participation rate and, at just under 6 per cent, the unemployment rate was near the low that it reached at the peak of the previous cycle. Unemployment is, however, still a little above its estimated structural rate of 5¾ per cent. Survey evidence points to emerging skills shortages, though not yet to the extent reported by firms in the mid-1990s.

Inflation is picking up

From 1997, persistent labour market slack (that is, unemployment in excess of its structural component) has put downward pressure on wages. The gradual tightening in labour market conditions more recently is likely to feed into wage movements only with a lag. Indeed, apart from the public sector, where salary increases (notably in the areas of education and health care) have picked up significantly in recent quarters, wage growth has remained quite muted (Table 3). Wage moderation combined with the rebound in productivity growth has curbed unit labour costs, which actually declined somewhat in 1999 and into 2000. This has partly offset rising cost pressures in other areas – especially on

Table 3. **Wages and prices**

Percentage change over corresponding period

	1995	1996	1997	1998	1999	1999 Q4	2000 Q1	2000 Q2	2000 Q3
Wages									
Average weekly earnings	2.6	3.5	3.4	2.6	2.5	1.8	1.7	1.8	2.2
Salary and wage rates									
Private sector	1.5	1.9	2.0	1.6	1.5	1.5	1.4	1.3	1.3
Central government	1.3	2.3	3.2	2.5	1.7	1.8	2.0	2.9	2.0
Unit labour costs	2.1	2.4	1.9	0.9	−0.3	. .	. .	. .	. .
Prices									
Consumer prices	3.8	2.3	1.2	1.3	−0.1	0.5	1.5	2.0	3.0
Excluding credit services (CPIX)	2.4	2.3	1.7	1.5	1.1	1.3	1.8	2.0	3.1
Energy (petrol)	0.0	0.5	0.2	−6.2	0.6	11.8	19.6	24.9	31.1
Food	1.3	1.4	2.2	3.2	1.0	−0.8	−0.2	0.0	1.8
Producer prices									
Inputs	0.8	0.6	0.4	0.7	0.8	2.8	4.9	5.5	8.0
Outputs	1.3	0.5	0.7	0.8	0.7	2.0	3.3	3.9	5.6
GDP price deflator	2.7	1.8	0.0	1.7	0.1	−0.4	0.5	0.4	. .
Import price deflator	−2.3	−4.2	−2.8	4.2	0.3	5.5	9.7	10.7	. .
Export price deflator	−0.3	−3.0	−2.1	4.8	0.7	2.2	8.1	8.8	. .

Source: Statistics New Zealand; OECD, Main Economic Indicators.

the import side – that have emerged over the past year or so but has not prevented an acceleration in price inflation.

Headline consumer price inflation had virtually come to a halt in 1999 before it rebounded this year. However, to a considerable extent this pronounced swing reflects the sharp fall and subsequent rise in interest rates. The twelve-month increase in the index excluding credit services (CPIX) – the authorities' target measure until recently – bottomed out at around 1 per cent and has edged up to 3 per cent since then (Figure 6). Underlying this pattern are both internal and external sources, the importance of which has shifted over time. Inflation in the non-tradeables sector dropped sharply in 1998, picked up through 1999, and has fallen back somewhat of late. It has been driven above all by developments in the output gap (Figure 2) and housing costs. As noted, excess supply, which put downward pressure on inflation in 1998-99, appears to have disappeared, while the recent burst in construction activity temporarily boosted housing-related components of the CPI. By contrast, inflation in the tradeables sector mounted in 1998, but then receded in mid-1999, only to re-accelerate more recently. Its moderation can to some extent be explained by the fact that the trend decline in the New Zealand dollar from 1997 was temporarily interrupted in the first half of 1999. Nonetheless, it is somewhat surprising that exchange-rate depreciation, which has already led

Figure 6. **Inflation indicators**
Annual percentage change

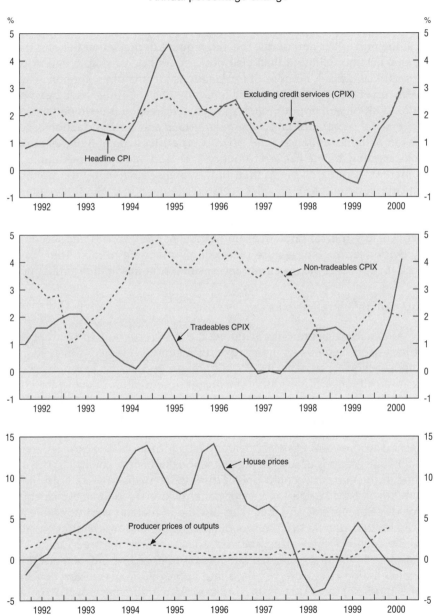

Source: Statistics New Zealand and Reserve Bank of New Zealand.

to a marked acceleration in import and producer prices (Table 3), has not had a greater effect on consumer price inflation.

The dynamics of the exchange-rate pass-through to consumer prices have been puzzling for some time. Both during the appreciation of the New Zealand dollar in the mid-1990s and during the subsequent depreciation the pass-through has been much more limited than historical experience, or simple import-to-GDP ratios, would suggest. A number of explanations for this phenomenon, which has also been observed in some other inflation-targeting countries, have been put forward. Competition and import penetration have increased (due in part to such factors as removal of parallel-importing restrictions and tariff reductions). Surplus capacity in Asia has enhanced the price competitiveness of Asian exports. The inflation-targeting regime has led to better-anchored inflation expectations. "Pricing to market" strategies mean that, in the face of exchange rate movements, foreign suppliers tend to hold prices relatively steady in each of the countries in which they operate. It is unclear, however, whether and to what extent factors of this kind will persist. In any case, some price increases are already being passed on to consumers (petrol price rises, in particular; see Table 3) and, according to survey evidence, businesses are increasingly planning to raise their prices in response to input cost increases and the ensuing squeeze in their profit margins.

The external deficit remains large

After narrowing temporarily during the 1998 recession, the current account deficit increased again as economic growth resumed (Figure 7). In 1999, it once more approached 7 per cent of GDP, slightly exceeding the level recorded two years earlier. Although the extent of the recent deterioration is overstated by special factors (notably the import of a naval frigate, equivalent to ½ percentage point of GDP), the underlying deficit is still high by international standards. With continued external deficits since the mid-1970s, averaging 5 per cent of GDP, gross foreign debt has reached 105 per cent of GDP. At around 84 per cent of GDP, New Zealand's net external liability ratio is easily the highest among industrial countries. The marked widening in the current account deficit during the 1990s reflects both the trend deterioration in New Zealand's terms of trade (Figure 7) – dominated by commodity price developments – and a marked decline in real net exports (Table 1). The latter can be traced in part to the pronounced rise in import penetration, attributable to the country's small size, relative resource endowments and trade liberalisation. Swings in the real exchange rate appear to have had only a modest impact on the penetration rate. However, the sharp appreciation of the New Zealand dollar in the middle of the 1990s, associated both with improving growth expectations and tight macroeconomic policy settings, may have affected export performance and thus contributed to the rise in the current account deficit. More fundamentally, New Zealand's large external deficit reflects the low level of national savings.

Figure 7. **External current account**
Per cent of GDP, four quarters ended

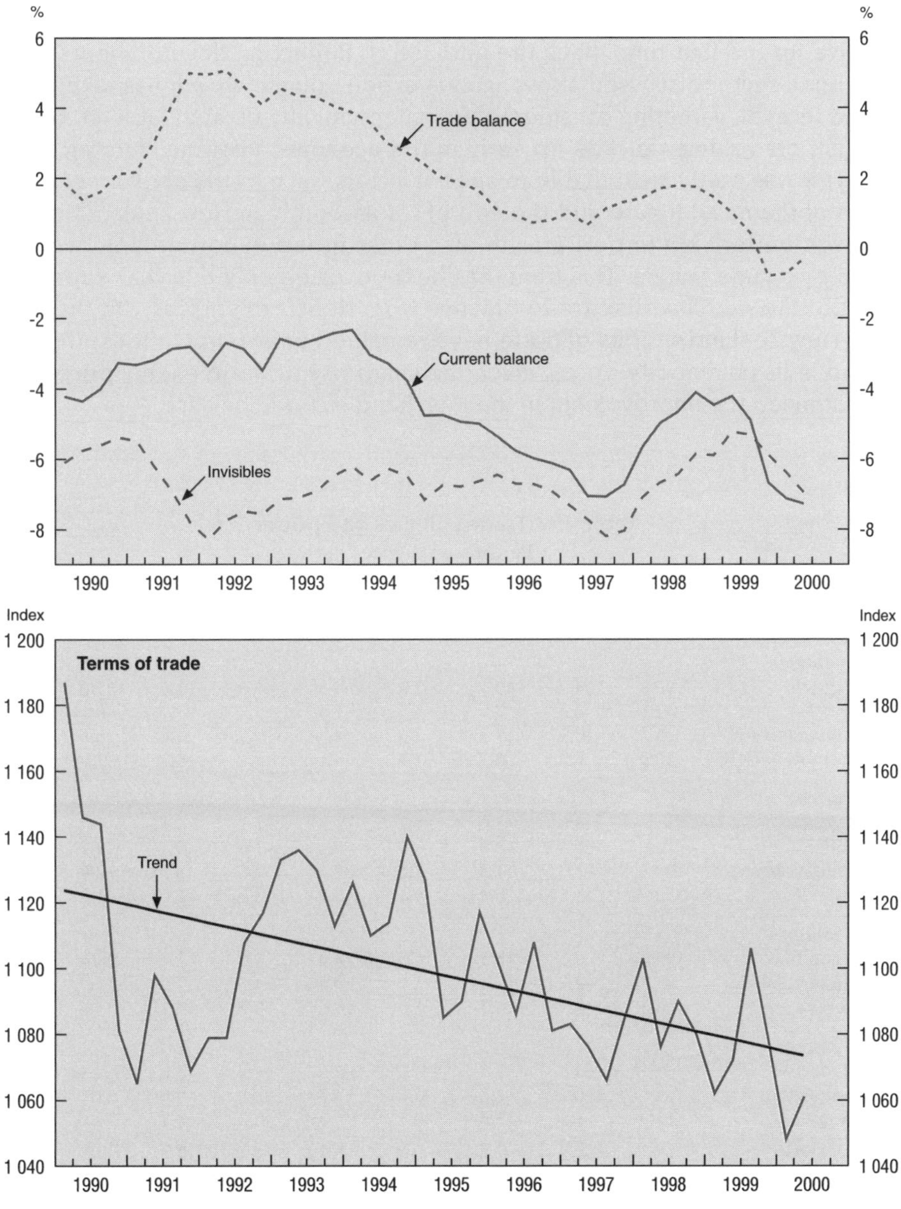

%

6

4   Trade balance

2

0

-2

                                                                                     Current balance
-4

-6   Invisibles

-8

1990   1991   1992   1993   1994   1995   1996   1997   1998   1999   2000

Index

1 200   **Terms of trade**

1 180

1 160

1 140   Trend

1 120

1 100

1 080

1 060

1 040

1990   1991   1992   1993   1994   1995   1996   1997   1998   1999   2000

Source: Statistics New Zealand.

The latter's renewed decline in recent years has implied an increased reliance on foreign savings to finance the sustained rise in investment expenditure.

The renewed widening in the current account deficit over the past year or so stems largely from a deterioration in the trade balance (Figure 7), which turned negative for the first time since the mid-1980s. Reflecting developments in the agricultural sector discussed above, goods export volume growth has taken some time to recover, gathering considerable momentum only of late (Table 4). By contrast, import volumes picked up early in the economic upswing, surging during 1999. This was partly attributable to special factors, such as the above-mentioned import of the naval frigate and the end of car assembly in New Zealand in 1998. However, underlying import growth also outstripped export growth over that period by a large margin. This trend has been reversed only this year, supporting a shift of the merchandise trade balance from deficit to surplus. On the other hand, New Zealand's terms of trade have remained unfavourable, despite some pick-up in its commodity prices, given the sharp rise in world energy prices. This has restrained the improvement in the merchandise trade balance.

Table 4. **Trade volumes and prices**
Percentage change

	1995 shares	1993	1994	1995	1996	1997	1998	1999	2000[1]
Export volumes									
Total goods	100.0	4.2	10.1	2.9	4.8	5.6	−1.0	1.6	7.9
Food	42.3	2.2	8.0	5.2	7.5	4.7	−1.7	−0.1	6.5
Manufactures[2]	35.4	10.5	13.0	3.6	4.3	9.2	1.0	5.8	9.2
Raw materials	20.0	0.0	8.9	−2.3	−0.4	−1.1	−4.2	1.0	14.4
Export prices									
Total goods		2.6	−4.0	−1.7	−3.5	−2.7	4.8	1.4	11.0
Food		0.6	−8.3	−5.3	0.1	−3.0	9.7	3.2	4.3
Manufactures[2]		−1.0	1.4	2.1	−7.1	−2.5	3.5	−2.0	14.3
Raw materials		13.6	0.4	3.4	−8.8	−2.6	−2.6	−1.2	14.3
Import volumes									
Total goods	100.0	4.3	16.3	6.5	3.4	3.6	2.4	13.4	5.1
Manufactures[2]	84.4	2.7	17.4	7.1	3.4	4.3	1.0	15.6	5.9
Energy	5.3	8.3	16.2	1.6	11.8	0.7	13.1	1.0	0.5
Import prices									
Total goods		−0.3	−3.6	−0.1	−2.6	−1.1	3.8	2.2	12.3
Manufactures[2]		0.7	−2.8	−0.1	−3.7	−2.1	5.0	1.4	7.0
Energy		−6.8	−15.6	0.7	6.5	6.2	−14.7	19.7	90.8
Terms of trade		2.9	−0.5	−1.6	−1.0	−1.6	0.9	−0.8	−1.2

1. First two quarters over corresponding period.
2. Non-food manufactures.
Source: Statistics New Zealand.

Table 5. **Balance of payments**

NZ$ million, calendar years

	1993	1994	1995	1996	1997	1998	1999	2000[1]
Exports	19 354	20 189	20 647	20 849	21 515	22 881	23 809	27 546
Imports	16 150	17 880	19 166	20 074	20 228	21 181	24 678	26 836
Trade balance	3 204	2 309	1 481	774	1 288	1 702	−871	710
Non-factor services, net	−1 187	−552	−307	−375	−931	−1 475	−479	−342
Investment income, net	−4 186	−5 508	−6 033	−6 845	−7 289	−4 482	−5 916	−7 464
Transfers, net	245	495	303	700	384	537	394	558
Invisibles, net	−5 128	−5 565	−6 037	−6 520	−7 836	−5 820	−6 001	−7 248
Current balance	−1 926	−3 256	−4 556	−5 746	−6 548	−4 122	−6 872	−6 538
Per cent of GDP	−2.4	−3.8	−5.0	−6.1	−6.7	−4.2	−6.7	−6.2
Memorandum item: Foreign liabilities Per cent of GDP	91.6	89.8	80.8	82.5	85.4	101.1	103.4	105.0

1. First two quarters at annual rates.
Source: Statistics New Zealand.

In contrast to developments in merchandise trade, services export volume growth boomed already in 1999, boosted by strong tourist arrivals, and has remained strong this year. The number of US tourists, in particular, has soared, increasing by nearly 40 per cent over the year to mid-2000. As the low value of the New Zealand dollar has, at the same time, discouraged outward tourism, the deficit in the balance on services has narrowed significantly (Table 5), despite some offset from adverse terms-of-trade movements. The improving services balance has partly compensated for the marked deterioration in the investment income account, limiting the renewed rise in the invisibles deficit. The deficit on investment income, which largely accounts for the overall external imbalance, reflects the substantial cost of servicing New Zealand's sizeable external debt. In the short run, however, it is strongly influenced by cyclical swings in the profits earned by foreign-owned companies in New Zealand. This factor contributed to reduce the investment income deficit temporarily during the 1998 recession. Since then, it has resumed its upward trend and reached new record levels.

Growth should continue at a slower pace

Recent indicators (Figure 8) point to a marked slowdown in demand and output. Against this backdrop, the economy is projected to expand only by about

Figure 8. **Short-term economic indicators**

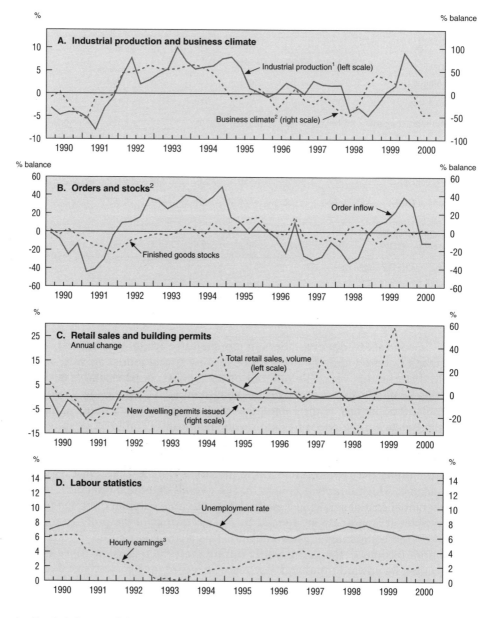

1.   Manufacturing, annual change.
2.   Survey balance.
3.   All industry, annual change.
Source: Statistics New Zealand and OECD, *Main Economic Indicators*.

I per cent through the year 2000. Nonetheless, given the high level of activity reached at the beginning of the year, this still implies economic growth in the 3½ per cent range in 2000 as a whole (Table 6), much the same rate as achieved on average in 1999. In the period ahead, activity is expected to rebound, with growth averaging just below 3 per cent in 2001 and little less in the year thereafter. This reflects the view that current low levels of confidence are out of step with a number of positive fundamentals, which should reassert themselves over time. In particular, robust trading partner growth combined with a very low exchange rate

Table 6.   **Short-term economic prospects**

	Current prices, NZ$ billion		Percentage volume change		
	1997	Per cent of GDP	2000	2001	2002
Private consumption	61.5	63.1	1.8	1.7	1.7
Government consumption	14.6	15.0	−4.8	1.5	1.0
Gross fixed investment	19.9	20.4	6.2	3.5	4.4
Final domestic demand	96.0	98.6	1.8	2.1	2.3
Stockbuilding[1,2]	0.7	0.8	−0.1	0.0	0.0
Total domestic demand	96.8	99.3	1.7	2.1	2.2
Exports of goods and services	27.9	28.7	9.2	7.8	7.4
Imports of goods and services	27.3	28.0	3.3	5.3	5.7
Foreign balance[1]	0.7	0.7	1.8	0.7	0.5
GDP expenditure at constant prices			**3.6**	**2.9**	**2.8**
GDP price deflator			2.2	2.9	2.0
GDP at current prices	97.4	100.0	5.9	5.9	4.9
Memorandum items:					
GDP production at constant prices			**3.5**	**2.9**	**2.8**
Private consumption deflator			1.8	2.9	2.0
Private compensation per employee			3.1	3.7	3.2
Total employment			1.0	1.0	1.0
Unemployment rate			6.1	6.0	6.0
Breakdown of gross fixed investment					
Private non-residential			6.5	5.9	5.5
Private residential			6.4	−3.6	2.0
General government			5.0	3.0	3.0
Short-term interest rate			6.5	6.9	7.0
Long-term interest rate			7.0	7.4	7.5
Current balance as a per cent of GDP			−5.7	−4.7	−4.0

1. As a percentage of GDP in the previous period.
2. Including statistical discrepancy and valuation adjustment.
Source: OECD Secretariat.

should provide a solid foundation for ongoing economic expansion and some correction of the large external deficit. Domestic demand is likely to remain relatively subdued, given a slightly restrictive fiscal stance and the apparent need for further interest-rate increases to fend off inflation pressures. Budget surpluses are projected to rise gradually and short-term interest rates to be raised by another 50 basis points over the next few months. While this would restrain economic growth, the implied shift toward export demand should prevent the external deficit from reaching levels that might be viewed as unsustainable by financial markets.

New Zealand's export markets are projected to expand by about 8 per cent on average over the next two years. At the same time, considerably improved competitiveness – the effective exchange rate is almost 30 per cent lower than in 1997 and is assumed to remain at its recent level – should allow exporters to gain market share. The main components of exports expected to respond to the favourable external environment are manufactured goods and tourism. Higher world market prices and robust international demand should assist commodity exporters, although a return to more normal weather conditions would have a damping influence on agricultural exports. The outlook for continued growth of exports along with the lack of spare capacity resulting from earlier deferral of projects is expected to underpin business investment, which should show the strongest expansion among domestic demand components. Residential investment, however, is likely to remain weak, falling into 2001 and recovering then only gradually, given higher mortgage rates and an oversupply of housing. Private consumption growth is expected to be muted during the projection period, restrained by price increases, higher interest rates and the likely lack of supporting wealth effects. Moreover, high levels of debt and debt servicing are expected to reduce the propensity to consume.

Unemployment is projected to remain relatively stable, in the neighbourhood of its estimated structural rate of somewhat below 6 per cent. While labour demand is expected to pick up a little, labour supply should also strengthen, as outward migration recedes and improving job opportunities lead to some rebound in the participation rate. The virtual disappearance of labour market slack along with rising inflation is nevertheless likely to entail a rise in wage growth, implying a renewed increase in unit labour costs. However, the major source of inflation in the near term will be the sharp rise in energy prices and import prices more generally owing to lagged effects of recent exchange-rate depreciation. Consumer price inflation is likely to overshoot the 0 to 3 per cent target band, even if only temporarily. Subsequently, it is projected to fall back within the band but to remain above its mid-point. The economic slowdown this year should serve to remove excess demand, but the projections do not imply the emergence of significant excess supply and hence downward pressure on inflation. The combination of projected strength in exports and relative weakness in domestic expenditure means that the external deficit will diminish. Yet, in the absence of a substantial improvement of New Zealand's terms of trade, this process is expected to be gradual, with the current account deficit remaining at relatively high levels.

There are considerable risks and uncertainties surrounding this relatively favourable central scenario, however. On the one hand, given positive fundamentals, confidence and activity could bounce back more quickly and to a greater extent than expected. In particular, investment intentions might revert swiftly to the stronger pattern evident at the turn of the year. The external sector could also provide more stimulus than assumed, spilling over into stronger domestic demand. In such an environment, existing cost pressures might be passed through quickly and fully into price increases, and the assumption underlying the central scenario that the near-term hike in price increases does not provoke a more generalised inflation cycle might prove overly optimistic. Employees could seek wage compensation for consumer price increases, and businesses might then respond in order to maintain their profit margins. If inflation expectations were to increase significantly, interest rates risk rising to the high levels seen in the mid-1990s, with adverse consequences for economic expansion thereafter.

On the other hand, confidence surveys may turn out to be early indicators of a sustained weakening in demand. If they stayed lower for an extended period, one might expect investment and employment decisions to be scaled back. In an environment where more debt is being carried by households and house prices are falling, interest-rate increases over the past year or so could turn out to have a greater impact on demand than assumed. It may also be the case that the stimulus from the low exchange rate is overestimated. While exports have picked up, there has not been a uniformly strong export profile across the board, and the overall response to exchange-rate depreciation has been relatively muted so far. This may reflect the usual, quite long lags. However, there could also be more structural factors at work impeding the stimulus one might expect from the exchange rate, notably the restructuring of activity associated with lower protection. A significant slowdown in major markets such as Australia and the United States could exacerbate the situation further. Given existing cost pressures, this might lead to a more sustained period of low growth coupled with relatively high inflation, complicating the task of monetary policy.

A medium-term scenario

Assuming that such risks to the near term outlook will not materialise, an OECD medium-term scenario (Table 7) is that, over the first half of the new decade, the New Zealand economy could grow at an annual rate of around 3 per cent. This is broadly in line with its recent trend but somewhat below the rate projected for the OECD area as a whole. It implies slightly higher potential output growth than achieved in the second half of the 1990s, mainly reflecting greater

Table 7.   **A medium-term scenario**

Average annual percentage change, volumes

	1992-99	1999-2006
Private consumption	3.4	1.7
Government consumption	2.4	0.2
Fixed capital formation	8.4	4.6
Stockbuilding[1]	0.1	0.0
Total domestic demand	4.2	2.2
Exports	4.9	7.5
Imports	7.8	5.3
Real foreign balance[1]	−0.9	0.8
Real GDP	3.3	3.0
Output gap[2]	−0.9	0.1
Potential output	2.7	2.8
Labour productivity	0.9	1.8
Employment	2.5	1.2
Participation rate (per cent)	64.7	64.9
Unemployment rate (per cent)	7.7	6.0
Private consumption deflator	1.7	1.8
GDP deflator	1.5	2.1
Private compensation per employee	1.8	3.0
Current balance[1]	−4.8	−3.6
Real exchange rate	1.0	−2.1
Short-term interest rate (per cent)	7.2	6.0
Long-term interest rate (per cent)	7.3	6.9

1.   Per cent of GDP.
2.   Per cent of potential output.
Source: Statistics New Zealand; OECD.

labour inputs due to migration and participation-rate developments. Growth is still largely driven by export demand, which is expected to expand at a much higher rate than in the 1990s, given robust growth in New Zealand's export markets combined with gains in market share due to sustained favourable price competitiveness (under the assumption of an unchanged real exchange rate). At the same time, domestic demand is expected to grow at much lower rates than before, restrained by somewhat restrictive monetary and fiscal policies as well as high personal-sector indebtedness. As a result, the current account deficit is projected to decline steadily. In about three years it is expected to reach – at around 4 per cent of GDP – levels that would arrest the rise in New Zealand's external debt ratio. The unemployment rate is expected to converge to its (unchanged) structural rate. With growth close to its potential rate, inflation is projected to be broadly stable near the mid-point of the current inflation target range.

Obviously, there are important risks attached to this relatively favourable scenario. Given its strong reliance on external demand, the outlook is largely conditioned by future regional and global developments. Moreover, the economy is projected to operate close to its potential for a protracted period. It will be a challenging task for policy makers to achieve this without the emergence of inflation pressures, the more so since the persistently large external imbalance leaves the economy vulnerable to changes in market sentiment. Finally, there are considerable uncertainties surrounding the strength of potential output growth. Assumptions about migration trends and labour force participation may be too optimistic, as may be investment projections which imply continued robust fixed capital formation. A number of factors will influence productivity growth, including those related to the "new economy" debate (see Chapter III). It has also to be noted that the projections, even if achieved, do not imply any significant narrowing in New Zealand's per capita income gap with the OECD average. This highlights the need for both skilful macroeconomic management and further efforts in the microeconomic area, as discussed in the remainder of the Survey.

II. Macroeconomic policies

Recent economic performance has benefited from the authorities' ability to strike a balance between the need to support recovery from the brief downturn in 1998, while maintaining the credibility of the macroeconomic policy framework, which calls for the preservation of price stability and budget surpluses (until public debt has reached "prudent" levels). Although short-term interest rates have been raised significantly since late-1999, they are still well below the peaks seen during the last economic cycle, and, with the New Zealand dollar falling to record low levels, overall monetary conditions have remained stimulative. Such policy settings have not resulted in a significant lift in core inflation, and the direct effects of the sharp currency fall are considerably more muted than was the case in earlier episodes, suggesting that to date the policy settings have been well judged. At the same time, while surpluses have been reduced, a budget deficit has been avoided, and declines in the public debt-to-GDP ratio have been sustained. The new government has made some adjustments to fiscal plans but has maintained its predecessor's commitment to rebuild the budget surplus gradually over the next few years. The following sections review monetary and fiscal policies in more detail. The chapter concludes with a discussion of the key macroeconomic issues facing policymakers in the period ahead.

Monetary management

The operational framework

The *Reserve Bank Act* 1989 established an unambiguous goal for monetary policy of achieving and maintaining price stability and provided the Reserve Bank with operational autonomy to pursue that goal. An inflation targeting framework was chosen at the outset of the new arrangements, and has been embedded in an evolving Policy Targets Agreement (PTA) between the Governor and the Minister of Finance (Treasurer).[1] Modifications to the PTA in recent years in part reflect the evolution of the inflation process (notably greater anchoring of inflation expectations) and monetary policy transmission mechanism (in particular the weakening of exchange rate pass-through), to which the inflation targeting arrangements needed to adjust in order to minimise damage to economic stability while maintaining price stability. In December 1996, the target band was widened from 0 to 2 per cent to 0 to 3 per cent. The December 1997 PTA introduced less prescriptive language into that part of the PTA that deals with events (such as commodity price shocks) that might temporarily push inflation outside the target range. At the same time, the practice of calculating an underlying inflation rate to represent the effective target measure was dropped. Finally, the latest PTA of December 1999 specified that, in pursuing its price stability objective, the Bank should seek to avoid unnecessary instability in output, interest rates and the exchange rate. This amendment was motivated by the incoming government's concern not to repeat the experience of the mid-1990s when the export sector was placed under immense pressure by a sharp increase in the value of the New Zealand dollar. Overall, these changes imply that near-term shifts in the price level are now somewhat more likely to be accepted without eliciting a policy reaction. For one thing, less can be done to offset such near-term shifts. For another, the medium-term inflation outlook is less likely to be disturbed by them.

Since March 1999, the Reserve Bank's primary policy instrument has been a new overnight interest rate target, the Official Cash Rate (OCR), which is formally reviewed eight times a year. The previous regime was unconventional in that there had been no officially set or targeted interest rate at the heart of the operational structure. Instead, policy had been conducted through periodic announcements about the desired level of the Monetary Conditions Index (MCI), a weighted average of short-term interest rates and the effective exchange rate. However, given the turbulence in the exchange market during the 1997-98 Asian financial crisis and the relatively narrow bands around the announced desired level of the MCI, short-term interest-rate volatility had increased considerably, and official comments on monetary conditions were required on an uncomfortably frequent basis. The shift from an MCI target to an interest-rate instrument aims to address these issues. The OCR is expected to constitute a more effective means of signalling policy intentions than public comments about monetary conditions. There is no longer a presumption that exchange-rate shocks be offset by interest-rate changes (so long as the medium-term inflation outlook is left unaffected). Nonetheless, the MCI remains an important indicator of monetary conditions, although it no longer has a direct role in policy implementation.

The new government has commissioned an independent review of monetary policy to be concluded in February 2001. The goal of the review is to ensure that the monetary policy framework and the Reserve Bank's operations within it are appropriate to the characteristics of the New Zealand economy and best international practice. The government is committed both to maintaining the achievement of price stability as the Bank's primary function and to the Bank's autonomy in pursuing that goal. These aspects are therefore excluded from the review, which will focus on the Bank's operations and governance. For instance, it will consider whether the way monetary policy now implemented is consistent with avoiding undesirable instability in output, interest rates and the exchange rate, as called for in the revised PTA. It will also look into the Bank's decision-making process and accountability structures.

The recent conduct of policy

The marked easing in *overall monetary conditions* during the Asian crisis – by around 1500 basis points (short-term interest-rate equivalent) according to the MCI (Figure 9) – came to a halt in late-1998 when the economy moved out of recession. Some monetary tightening in the early part of 1999, reflecting a temporary firming in the New Zealand dollar, was reversed in the middle of the year as markets reassessed their view of the benefits of the commodity price recovery for the New Zealand economy. Thereafter, a rise in official interest rates over the six months to May 2000 broadly offset the effect of exchange-rate weakening on overall monetary conditions. However, with no further interest-rate increases forthcoming since then, the MCI fell to a historical low during the third quarter, as the New Zealand dollar remained under considerable downward pressure. In terms of this measure the policy stance is now significantly easier than during the recession of the early 1990s. However, the scale of the 1997-98 and 2000 falls in the MCI points to weaknesses in its use as an indicator for assessing the stance of policy. As well, they point to the existence of shocks that warrant a decline in the real exchange rate (the Asian crisis, in the first case; external indebtedness, the terms of trade and greater third-country competition for export markets in the second), falls in the MCI being non-inflationary in such circumstances.

In March 1999, the Reserve Bank set the first Official Cash Rate (OCR) at 4.5 per cent, at the upper end of market expectations. Market rates adjusted swiftly to that level. Subsequently, *short-term interest rates* edged up gradually, reaching 5 per cent in October. In November, the Reserve Bank raised the OCR to that level, noting that the recovery was gathering momentum and economic slack being taken up rapidly. With a view to counteracting inflationary pressures, the Bank continued to increase the OCR in several steps until May 2000, when it was set at 6.5 per cent. In general, financial markets anticipated these moves. Since then, the OCR has been left unchanged. Although the Bank expects inflation to move up temporarily to the ceiling of the target band, it has pointed out that sharply deteriorating business and consumer confidence and the weakening in economic activity tend to reduce potential inflationary pressures over the medium term. Market rates, which had – in anticipation of further official rate increases – edged up toward 7 per cent in mid-2000, have fallen back by a small amount toward the OCR level since then. One effect of the introduction of the OCR has been a much closer relationship between the 90-day bank bill rate and the cash rate. Previously, the gap between the two rates had been 100 basis points or more, even when there was no strong expectation of a change in the stance of

Figure 9. **Monetary conditions**

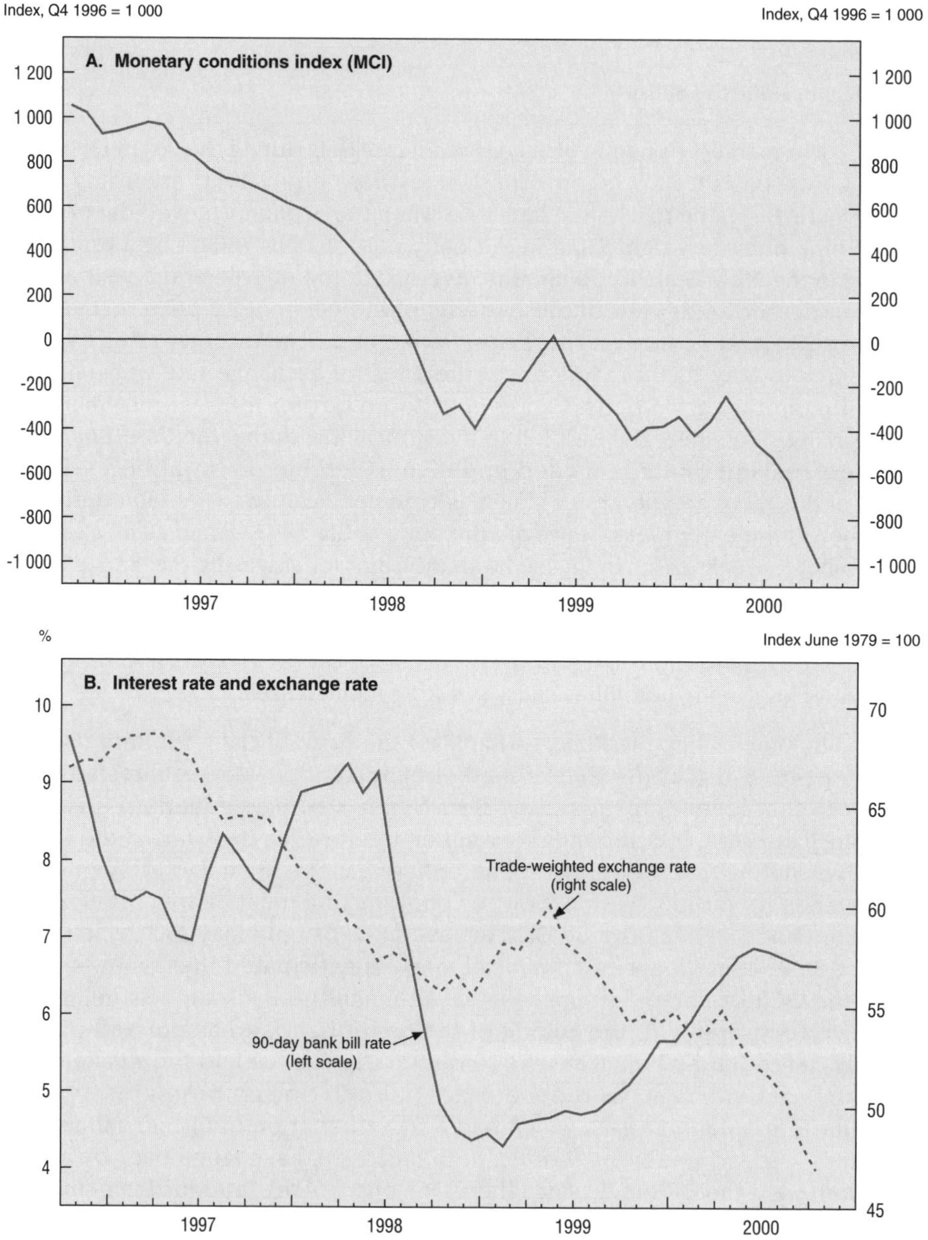
Index, Q4 1996 = 1 000
Index, Q4 1996 = 1 000
A. Monetary conditions index (MCI)
1 200
1 000
800
600
400
200
0
-200
-400
-600
-800
-1 000
1997
1998
1999
2000
%
Index June 1979 = 100
B. Interest rate and exchange rate
10
9
8
7
6
5
4
70
65
60
55
50
45
Trade-weighted exchange rate
(right scale)
90-day bank bill rate
(left scale)
1997
1998
1999
2000

Source: Reserve Bank of New Zealand.

monetary policy. Another effect of the new operating regime has been a much weaker negative correlation between short-term interest rates and the exchange rate than before. That is, short-term interest rates no longer respond automatically to downward pressure on the exchange rate, which had been a salient feature of earlier financial market developments, and the reverse process also appears to have weakened (as it has elsewhere).

The persistent weakness of the New Zealand dollar has surprised most observers (including the Bank), although other commodity-producing countries (like Australia and Canada) have also seen their *exchange rate* appreciate less than could have been expected on the basis of world-market price developments alone. It is true that, with the monetary tightening in the United States, interest differentials have not been as supportive of the New Zealand dollar as usually in the past. However, this has not been unique to New Zealand, and the currency has lost ground not only against the US dollar but also, for instance, against its Australian counterpart, albeit to a limited extent (Figure 10). Country-specific factors therefore may have played a certain role. New Zealand assets have low or no weighting in many of the indices against which many professional investors are assessed. Together with the relatively low liquidity in New Zealand financial markets, this probably implies that some positive interest-rate differential is needed to attract substantial foreign portfolio investment. Moreover, international prices of New Zealand's commodity exports have lagged the recovery evident in the prices of commodities produced by some other countries (such as metals and oil). In addition, global capital markets now appear to be looking primarily at growth prospects and differentiating more strongly between new-technology-based and more traditional economies, assuming that the former promise significantly higher future returns. In addition, the perceived credit risk associated with the high current account deficit and external debt position seems to have affected the willingness of investors to commit further capital to New Zealand. Finally, political developments – uncertainty associated with the general elections and the apparent lack of confidence in the new government's structural policies (see Chapter III) – may also have had a dampening influence on the New Zealand dollar.

Even before the Reserve Bank began to raise short-term interest rates in late-1999, the stimulative effect of the lower exchange rate on aggregate demand was to some extent offset by rising *long-term rates*. Bond yields increased from 5½ per cent to over 7 per cent over the course of 1999, before easing a little this year (Figure 10). Movements in New Zealand long-term interest rates are largely determined by international developments. Nonetheless, over the last decade, there seem to have been significant changes in the risk premium on New Zealand assets, although long-term spreads are also affected by short-term interest-rate differentials. After declining in the first half of the 1990s, the differential between long-term interest rates prevailing in New Zealand and its major trading partner countries has risen again. The major factor behind this apparent swing in the risk

Figure 10. **Interest and exchange rate movements**

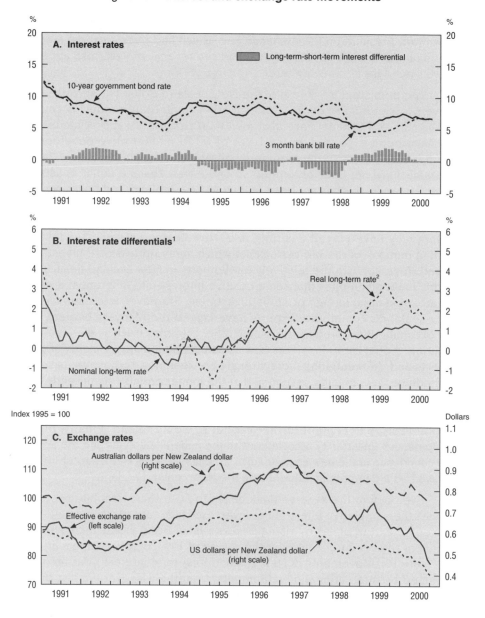

1. *Vis-à-vis* a weighted average of major trading partners: United States, United Kingdom, Japan, Australia, Germany
    and Canada.
2. Relative to consumer prices.
Source: Reserve Bank of New Zealand and OECD.

premium seems to be the development in the external balance, although – as noted above – the political situation and growth prospects may also have influenced overseas interest in investing in New Zealand. With the rise in short-term interest rates from late-1999 and some subsequent easing in long rates, the positive yield gap, which had emerged in late-1998 following a protracted period when the yield curve was inverted, has virtually disappeared. The Bank's assessment is that, following these developments, interest rates are now at levels that probably imply little (interest rate) pressure on aggregate demand in either direction. It is thus the low level of the exchange rate which has kept monetary conditions relatively easy.

Measures of *money and credit* have not featured prominently in monetary policy, as they have not correlated well with inflation following the very substantial changes that have taken place in the financial sector. Nonetheless, the Bank feels that they might usefully supplement other inflation indicators and has therefore made substantial efforts to improve the quality of these statistics. In the recent period, monetary and credit aggregates have broadly moved in line with the business cycle, accelerating through 1999 before slowing more recently (Table 8). This

Table 8. **Money and credit aggregates**

Per cent year-on-year growth rate

	End of month	M1	M3[1]	Private-sector credit[1]	Domestic credit	CPI
1996	March	6.1	11.2	15.2	11.4	2.2
	June	−0.6	14.2	16.3	11.6	2.0
	September	1.9	12.8	13.6	12.2	2.4
	December	−4.5	12.1	11.1	9.5	2.6
1997	March	3.6	8.8	10.7	11.0	1.8
	June	4.4	5.6	8.6	10.1	1.1
	September	7.3	9.1	11.2	10.1	1.0
	December	6.5	7.1	11.2	10.0	0.8
1998	March	0.8	7.7	8.8	10.0	1.3
	June	1.7	6.6	7.6	9.8	1.7
	September	2.6	0.1	6.2	8.5	1.7
	December	10.0	0.2	6.3	8.4	0.4
1999	March	17.4	3.3	7.6	9.1	−0.1
	June	18.8	3.1	9.4	7.0	−0.4
	September	23.0	7.8	9.1	9.1	−0.5
	December	15.5	7.5	9.5	10.4	0.5
2000	March	11.3	2.1	10.4	9.3	1.5
	June	5.4	1.9	8.0	9.3	2.0
	September	1.0	0.7	5.7	6.7	3.0

1. Resident measure.
Source: Reserve Bank of New Zealand, *Financial Statistics*.

swing has been most pronounced for narrow money. Broad money growth also temporarily gathered momentum but has fallen short of credit expansion. This divergence is primarily attributable to rising foreign-currency funding by New Zealand banks to support domestic lending growth. Although credit availability has not been a constraint, lending growth to the business sector has been modest, investment apparently being funded primarily from firms' cash flow. The growth in borrowing demand has come above all from the household sector, reflecting the rebound in the housing market. Most recently, however, the rate of growth in household borrowing has slowed markedly, falling back toward that of disposable income. The fact that credit expansion during the current recovery has remained well below that recorded in the mid-1990s would seem to suggest that inflation pressures have not been building to the extent they did during the previous economic upturn.

The fiscal stance

The strategy

The Fiscal Responsibility Act 1994 (FRA) requires the government to comply with a number of principles in managing public finances. In particular, so as to provide a buffer against future adverse events, operating surpluses must be achieved every year to reduce public debt to "prudent" levels, and budget balance maintained on average thereafter. Fiscal risks facing the government must be carefully managed. At the same time, tax policies have to be reasonably predictable. To prevent long-term departure from these principles, the Act requires detailed and transparent information from the government on how it intends to conform with them, as well as explanations for any temporary departure from them. A policy statement must be produced several months before the budget, containing information on strategic priorities and short- and long-term fiscal objectives. A strategy report released with the budget has to present an assessment of the consistency of projected fiscal developments with these objectives. In addition, the authorities are required to provide a number of economic and fiscal reports at regular intervals, including forecasts for a three-year period (see Box 2 in the 1999 Economic Survey for more details).

The FRA leaves it to the government to define and set fiscal objectives consistent with the Act's principles. The new government's first Budget Policy Statement (BPS), published in March 2000, adjusted a number of its predecessor's fiscal parameters. The previous commitment to reduce public spending to below 30 per cent of GDP in the long run was replaced with an objective to keep public expenditure around current levels of 35 per cent of GDP. This was motivated by the authorities' assessment that the previous goal was unlikely to be achieved or sustained without significant reductions in the provision of government services over the long term. It also reflected the new administration's different view of the appropriate role and size of government. Considering that public debt is already down to prudent levels, the new government decided to aim at keeping gross and net central government debt below 30 per cent and 20 per cent of GDP, respectively, across the economic cycle. The previous administration was committed to bring the respective ratios down to below 25 per cent and 15 per cent, respectively. Given this reassessment of what constitutes prudent debt levels, the objective for the budget balance was modified somewhat in the March 2000 BPS. The long-term fiscal objectives now are to achieve an operating surplus across the economic cycle ensuring that revenues and spending (excluding the funding of the costs associated with the ageing population) are "at least in broad balance", with, in addition, an allowance for pre-funding the costs associated with the ageing population (see Chapter III for more details).

Budgetary outcomes

Since the passage of the FRA, operating surpluses have been recorded at the central government level every year (Figure 11). However, they have decreased considerably since the mid-1990s when they peaked at over 3½ per cent of GDP. Although cyclical influences (as manifest in the temporary emergence of an output gap in 1998-99) have played a role, this reflects above all discretionary measures. While income-tax cuts in 1996 and 1998 led to a marked fall in revenues relative to GDP, a number of new spending initiatives implied that virtually no further progress was made during the second half of the 1990s in lowering the expenditure-to-GDP ratio toward the long-term objective set by the previous government.

The May 1998 Budget was presented before it was clear that the economy had entered recession. It projected the operating surplus to bottom out at 1¼ per cent of GDP in the fiscal year 1998/99 (ending in June) before rising again due to a stabilisation of the revenue-to-GDP after the tax cuts and a resumption of the earlier decline in the expenditure ratio. Following a marked deterioration in government finances associated with the cyclical downturn, the December 1998 Economic and Fiscal Update projected a small deficit, despite expenditure cuts aimed at offsetting some of the working of fiscal stabilisers. In the event, the outcome for 1998/99 was an operating surplus of 1¾ per cent of GDP. However, this better-than-expected outturn largely reflected one-off factors, in particular privatisation proceeds (in excess of the book value of the asset). Asset sales in the electricity sector alone raised revenues by about 1½ per cent of GDP. Excluding these one-off items, the operating surplus for 1998/99 was marginal.

The May 1999 Budget projected a (temporary) move into slight deficit in the fiscal year 1999/2000 (Table 9). Apart from the deterioration in the underlying fiscal position, this reflected a change in accounting practice (that is, bringing on budget the unfunded liabilities of the accident insurance scheme) that lowered

Figure 11. **Budgetary developments**[1]
Per cent of GDP

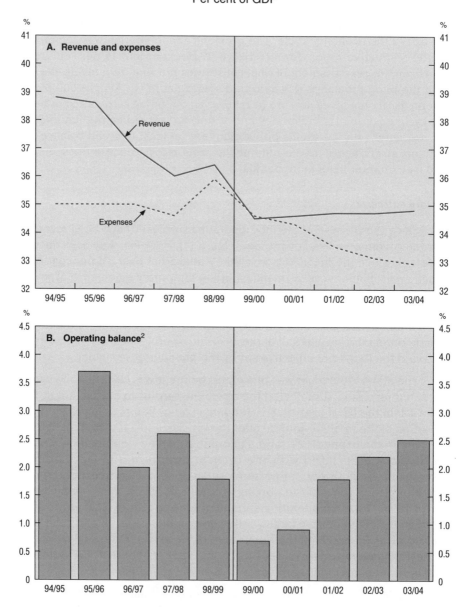

1. Central government. Accrual basis.
2. Includes net balance of State-owned enterprises and crown entities.
Source: New Zealand Treasury, June 2000 Budget.

Table 9.   **1999/2000 Budget: projection and outcome**

NZ$ million

Operating balance (BEFU, May 1999, initial projection)	**(36)**
Forecasting changes	
Revenue forecasting changes	(50)
Expense forecasting improvements	100
Total forecasting changes	**50**
Operating balance (PREFU, October 1999)	**14**
Policy changes	
Removal of previous government's tax cuts	70
Introduction of higher marginal tax rate of 39 per cent	46
Removal of previous government's fiscal provisions	10
New government's fiscal provisions	(150)
Total policy changes	**(24)**
Forecasting changes	
Tax revenue forecasting improvements	321
Improvements to other revenue	80
Other	9
Total forecasting changes	**410**
Operating balance (BPS, March 2000)	**400**
Policy changes	
Change to government's provision allocations	(270)
Forecasting changes	
Tax revenue forecasting improvements	68
Benefit forecasting improvements	45
Treaty settlement forecast revisions	124
Finance cost changes	(46)
Valuation changes (GSF and ACC liabilities)	510
Police (INCIS writedown) and defence (inventory accounting policy change)	(155)
Other	87
Total forecasting changes	**633**
Operating balance (BEFU, June 2000)	**763**
Operating balance (September 2000)	**1 449**

1. Negative figures in brackets. BEFU: Budget Economic and Fiscal Update. PREFU: Pre-election Economic and Fiscal Update. BPS: Budget Policy Statement. GSF: Government Superannuation Fund. ACC: Accident Insurance Corporation. INCIS: Integrated National Crime Investigation System.

Source: New Zealand Treasury.

the operating balance by about ½ percentage point of GDP. Subsequent to the 1999 Budget, the authorities announced a small income tax cut. Nonetheless, more evidence of a strengthening economy, boosting tax revenue and reducing benefit spending, then allowed the Treasury to project a slight budget surplus for 1999/2000 in its October 1999 Pre-Election Economic and Fiscal Update.

After the November 1999 general elections, the new government made a number of important policy changes. Provisions for new initiatives were increased, but this was broadly offset by the removal of tax cuts announced by the previous administration and an increase in the marginal tax rate on high incomes (above NZ$ 60 000) from 33 to 39 per cent (Table 9). With revenues coming in much stronger than expected, the March 2000 BPS raised the forecast for the budget surplus to just under ½ per cent of GDP. Subsequent changes to the phasing of the government's provision allocation to accommodate new policy initiatives in 1999/2000 have been outweighed by a favourable revaluation of the liabilities of the accident insurance scheme (ACC) and government employee pension fund (GSF) equivalent to about ½ percentage point of GDP. As a result, an operating surplus for 1999/2000 of around ¾ per cent of GDP was projected in the June 2000 Budget. According to the financial statements released in mid-September, the surplus finally turned out to have been almost 1½ per cent of GDP. The authorities have pointed out, however, that this further improvement reflects to a large extent timing issues and favourable valuation movements.

In summary, a budget deficit has again been avoided, but the underlying surplus – excluding revaluation effects – has remained relatively small. The new government's initiatives added little to the limited further fiscal easing implied by the previous government's fiscal plans, as additional spending has been to a large extent compensated for by tax increases. In a structural sense – that is excluding one-off factors and adjusted for cyclical influences – the government finances appears to be in broad balance, or possibly a slight surplus position. This compares, however, with an estimated structural surplus in excess of 2 per cent of GDP in the mid-1990s.

Fiscal plans

The new government's first Budget was presented in June 2000. For the fiscal year 2000/01, it projected an operating surplus of just below 1 per cent of GDP, a little higher than foreshadowed by the previous administration. The divergence largely reflects forecasting changes (mainly related to economic developments), with the above-mentioned tax measures expected to continue to finance new policy initiatives. Additional funds were provided primarily for social security and welfare (notably pensions and housing), education (especially schools and student loans), and health care. Other targeted objectives were industrial and regional development, as well as reducing inequality for ethnic minorities. Despite these initiatives, public expenditure was projected to decline relative to GDP. Combined with a rise in the tax ratio, this would imply a slight tightening in the fiscal stance, reversing the trend prevailing in recent years.

The government's medium-term projections for the operating balance in the last Budget were broadly in line with those of the previous administration. The operating surplus was expected to rise gradually to reach 2½ per cent of GDP by 2003/04. According to the March 2000 BPS, the reasons for maintaining this fiscal track are threefold. Building surpluses would allow the government to start pre-funding the future fiscal costs associated with population ageing (possibly from 2001/02). Strengthening the fiscal position during the economic upswing would also take some pressure off monetary policy, and hence interest-rate and exchange-rate settings, thereby helping sustain the expansion. Finally, it should help maintain confidence in the economic policy framework and guard against possible adverse effects associated with New Zealand's large current account defi-cit and high levels of external liabilities. Reflecting the new administration's differ-ent view of the appropriate role and, therefore, size of government, the restoration of the operating surplus is to be achieved, however, with higher levels of both revenue and expenditure. In the absence of a significant rise in the tax burden, the expenditure-to-GDP ratio is officially projected to decline, however, falling significantly below the (upward revised) long-term objective in the next few years (Figure 11). While such an outcome would make it more likely that the objective is actually met on average over time, there are substantial upside risks to the expenditure projections.

The government has set itself a fiscal provision (the amount of money available for new, or the extension of existing, initiatives) of NZ$ 5.9 billion (cumu-latively 2 per cent of GDP at the end of the provision period) over its three-year electoral term. So far, over NZ$ 3½ billion of this provision has already been com-mitted. This reflects the fact that the government aimed to introduce many of its policy intentions in the first year of its term. Still, it means that the amount of money left for new policy measures over the next two years is very limited, given that the fiscal provision is also supposed to provide for cost and volume increases in already existing programmes (such as teachers' pay or police funding). More-over, to meet the NZ$ 5.9 billion cap, government spending increases will have to slow sharply, with little room for volume growth in the period ahead. It is also worth noting that expenditure pressures that may arise from changes in economic conditions are not covered by the fiscal provision. Welfare benefits, for instance, may increase more than projected due to higher inflation and/or slower growth than assumed.

Debt developments

Public debt-to-GDP ratios have fallen considerably in the 1990s and are now relatively low in both historical and international terms. Although the debt data for New Zealand shown in Figure 12 are not on the general government basis applied in most other OECD countries, they are roughly comparable since local government indebtedness, which is not included, is small in relation to GDP. With shrinking budget surpluses, progress in debt reduction has slowed. However,

Figure 12. **Government debt**
Per cent of GDP

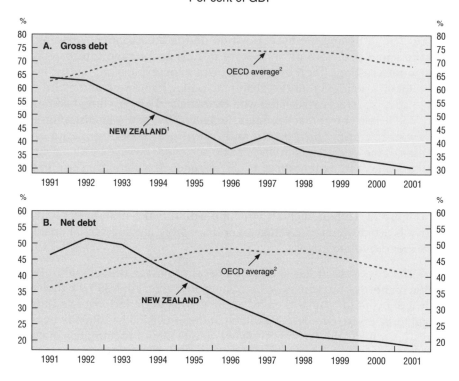

1. Central government. Fiscal years starting in July. Projections from June 2000 Budget.
2. General government. Calendar years.
Source: New Zealand Treasury and OECD estimates.

although the general trend in net debt tends to match developments in the operating balance, this is not the case in every year. While movements in net debt reflect cash flows, the operating balance is an accrual measure that includes non-cash items such as retained surpluses of state-owned enterprises while excluding net capital investment in physical assets.

In 2000/01, gross and net public debt are projected to decrease to 32½ per cent and just over 20 per cent of GDP, respectively. As in the year before, cash flows from operating and investing activities are not expected to generate sufficient funds to reduce debt in absolute terms. The continued fall in debt ratios thus reflects the rise in nominal GDP. From 2001/02, rising operating surpluses are then expected to translate into positive net cash flows. However, the government intends to use these primarily to build up assets to pre-fund future pension expenses, rather than to retire existing debt. As a result, the decline in debt ratios is expected to remain gradual but more than sufficient to meet the government's (upward revised) long-term objectives of 30 and 20 per cent of GDP, respectively, for gross and net debt.

Assessment and challenges

Pragmatic macroeconomic policies have made a valuable contribution to New Zealand's smooth recovery from the 1998 recession. While raising interest rates to fend off inflationary pressures, the authorities have allowed overall monetary conditions to stay relatively easy, taking into account the low level of the New Zealand dollar. Budgetary policies have been slightly stimulative, but the new government has broadly maintained its predecessor's prudent approach to fiscal management. Nonetheless, a decline in domestic and international confidence has clouded prospects for sustained non-inflationary growth and created a more difficult and challenging environment for macroeconomic decision-making.

Experience gained with the inflation targeting framework prompted the Reserve Bank to extend its policy horizon. This extension was warranted by changes to the inflation process, including greater anchoring of inflation expectations and a more competitive marketplace, as well as by the reduced pass-through of exchange rate changes into local prices, which weakened what was a relatively fast-acting channel of the policy transmission mechanism. With an extended policy horizon, there is increased potential for short-term deviations of inflation from the centre of the target (partly accommodated by a wider target band), but in the circumstances less need for offsetting policy actions. Thus, while still aiming to keep inflation within the target range over the medium-term horizon, somewhat more stability in interest rates and to a lesser extent also output and the exchange rate is likely (a concern for which has now been expressed in the Policy Targets Agreement). This change in the policy horizon and the accompanying modifications to the targeting arrangements, which have been recommended in previous *Economic Surveys*, have had positive effects on macroeconomic stability in recent years. However, there are limits to how flexible policies can be without compromising the credibility of the framework and raising inflation expectations, especially in the current environment of weak consumer, business and investor confidence.

These limits are likely to be tested in the period ahead. In keeping with its medium-term approach, the Reserve Bank may be able to "look through" the upcoming inflation spike associated with energy price increases and exchange-rate depreciation. This would be appropriate, provided it does not lead to an upward move in inflation expectations and more generalised inflation pressure. So far, there are few signs of second-round effects. Wage increases, in particular, have remained subdued outside the public sector. However, any generalised pay rises in the latter could spill over into the private sector, and there are considerable uncertainties concerning the impact of changes in industrial-relations legislation (see Chapter III) on bargaining behaviour and hence wage developments. Monetary decision-making is additionally complicated by uncertainties surrounding recent swings in confidence, which seem to have affected both private domestic demand and the exchange rate. Given the boost to exports from the low exchange rate, domestic and international confidence effects may offset each other, requiring no change in monetary policy settings. However, if downward pressure on the exchange rate persists, inflation may remain higher for longer. Businesses, which may not have raised prices in the expectation that the currency weakness would be temporary, may begin to pass through import price increases more fully. The risk of second-round effects would also be much higher than in the case of a mere oil-related spike in inflation. This highlights the importance for monetary policy to react swiftly to any signs of a sustained build-up in inflationary pressures, the more so since such policy action would impact on the economy only with a considerable lag.

While it cannot substitute for judgement in policy making, the operating framework that is now in place should ensure that any required changes to monetary policy are implemented in an effective way. Since the introduction of an official interest rate last year, the system is more comparable to that in most other countries and thus better understood by financial markets. Setting an Official Cash Rate has proved a more effective means of signalling policy intentions than public comments about prevailing monetary conditions. It has given the Reserve Bank control over the overnight interest rate and a considerable influence over other short-term interest rates as well. The volatility in short-term interest rates that existed under the previous regime has diminished substantially (Figure 9, panel B). This has mainly resulted from the breakdown in the strong negative relationship between exchange-rate and short-term interest rate movements, which in turn was a consequence of the previous system's focus on overall monetary conditions. At the same time, short-term exchange-rate volatility has not changed significantly.

The amplitude of New Zealand's exchange rate cycle over the 1990s has become a matter of concern. As noted, an amendment in the latest Policy Target Agreement sought by the new government requires the Reserve Bank to seek to avoid unnecessary instability in the exchange rate (as well as interest rates and output). However, while the Bank's evolving approach should reduce variability in the real exchange rate, there would seem to be limited capacity for monetary policy to restrain exchange-rate swings. Apart from external shocks, these are likely to be influenced by fiscal and microeconomic policies in the future.

A possible currency union with Australia has become subject of public debate given New Zealand's somewhat disappointing economic performance.

Potential advantages of such a union include reduced transaction costs, a stimulus to trade and, less certainly, somewhat lower interest rates. Moreover, the Australian dollar has shown less volatility than its New Zealand counterpart. However, a currency union would also have a number of drawbacks. As the needs of the Australian economy would dominate (GDP is six times that of New Zealand), the magnitude of the business cycle and variability of inflation in New Zealand would probably rise. With no independent monetary policy, New Zealand would have to use fiscal policy more actively and strive to enhance flexibility through further structural reform (though the latter should be pursued in any case). It is worth noting that, while the debate in New Zealand focuses on a currency union, some leading Australian politicians have agreed only to New Zealand eventually adopting their currency. Arguably, however, the effects of "dollarisation" and currency union are similar, both implying New Zealand relinquishing any effective control over monetary policy. In any case, entering a currency union cannot be a substitute for domestic policies that address underlying weaknesses in economic performance, such as relatively poor productivity growth.

One outcome of the official monetary policy review under way may be a change in the governance structure of the Reserve Bank, with responsibility for monetary policy shifting away from the Governor to a committee. It has been argued that relying on the experience of a number of experts would lead to better decision-making, and that a committee structure would tend to reduce the risk that the Governor's credibility will be undermined. However, apart from potential conflicts of interest in a small country like New Zealand, moving in that direction might weaken accountability and transparency, the strengthening of which has been a major concern underlying past public sector reform.

As noted, fiscal policy is likely to affect the exchange rate. More generally, it matters for monetary policy since, given the size of the government sector, it has an important impact on aggregate demand, and hence inflation pressures. In this respect, it is nevertheless worth highlighting that it is above all the change in the fiscal balance that matters for demand management, although its level, and the debt position, are relevant in assessing the vulnerability of the economy to shocks and in considering sustainability and growth prospects over the medium term. The New Zealand framework, as defined by the Fiscal Responsibility Act, implies that fiscal policies are geared toward longer-term goals, and in particular "prudent" government debt levels. This is helpful for monetary policy as it provides a degree of stability and predictability in an environment where monetary policy must be forward-looking. Nonetheless, there is a fair amount of flexibility in the framework. In the March 2000 BPS, the new government underlined that its approach is to let the automatic stabilisers operate where prudent. Moreover, as noted, its fiscal plans are designed so as to take some pressure off monetary policy, thereby moderating movements in interest rates and the exchange rate.

Thus, the course of fiscal policy looks appropriate from a demand-management perspective, although the higher levels of both expenditure and revenue that underlie a broadly unchanged track for the budget balance may have some adverse implications for microeconomic efficiency. While the fiscal stance has been modestly stimulative, a move into deficit has been avoided, and budget projections imply a gradual rebuilding of both actual and structural budget surpluses. However, as noted, there are important risks to this outlook. Apart from the possible detrimental impact of worse-than-expected economic conditions on government finances, the front-loading of expenditure plans is a matter of concern, as it will require a sharp slowdown in government expenditure in the period ahead in the face of strong spending pressures in areas like health and education. The majority of the government's fiscal provision for the three-year election period has already been allocated, leaving a very tight constraint on spending for the rest of its electoral term. At the very least, fiscal plans imply the need for a greater measure of success in reducing spending relative to GDP than has been seen in recent years. The government's intention to pre-fund future pension costs might serve to enhance spending discipline, although its benefits should be weighed against those of tax reductions. Moreover, depending on the final details of, and agreement to, the proposed scheme, it may require a strengthening in the fiscal position beyond current plans. Hence, improving financial management with a view to ensuring better control over public expenditure is vital. These issues are also addressed in the following chapter which reviews structural policies in general.

III. Progress in structural reform

Since 1984, the New Zealand authorities have pursued a broadly-based structural reform agenda that has seen widescale privatisation of state assets; new forms of governance in the public sector; extensive liberalisation of trade, product and financial markets; revamped labour-market legislation and fundamental changes to the conduct of fiscal and monetary policies. Identifying the positive benefits that have arisen from the reform process has, however, proved difficult. On the one hand, New Zealand weathered the tumultuous shocks of the late 1990s (Asia crisis and two droughts) relatively well compared with past experience, avoiding large budget deficits and a run-up in inflation, while resuming output and employment growth quickly. Moreover, New Zealand's relative standard of living has ceased its downward trend. On the other, New Zealand's per capita GDP has yet to make up any ground with respect to other OECD countries, reflecting, in large part, its relatively poor productivity performance. There is also a perception that the reform process has tapered off, and there are concerns that several recent policy actions, particularly in the labour market, may not be sufficient, nor in the right direction, to spur faster productivity growth. Against this background, the chapter begins with an overview of longer-term productivity performance before turning to a discussion of recent developments in labour, product and financial markets, followed by public-sector reforms. It concludes with recommendations for further action.

Productivity performance in New Zealand

Structural performance has improved, but signals are mixed

The comprehensive economic reforms have seen potential output improve appreciably in the 1990s compared with the 1980s. Indeed, growth in potential output is estimated to have been an average of 2.3 per cent per year in the last decade (Table 10) *versus* only 1.4 per cent per year in the 1980s. This is slightly above the OECD average, although well below that observed in New Zealand's closest neighbour, Australia, where economic performance has been better. The employment rate was also greater than the OECD benchmark on average over the decade, and while the structural rate of unemployment rose slightly, it remained below those of most G7 countries. The most disappointing development

Table 10. **Indicators of structural performance in selected OECD countries**

	New Zealand	United States	Japan	Germany	France	Italy	United Kingdom	Canada	Australia	Ireland	Netherlands	Norway	OECD
Annual average													
Potential output growth													
1980-89	1.4	3.0	3.9	2.0	2.3	2.5	2.1	2.8	3.3	3.2	2.0	2.3	2.8
1990-99	2.3	3.1	2.0	3.1	1.8	1.8	2.3	2.6	3.5	6.8	2.8	2.1	1.8
1996-99	2.3	3.5	1.4	1.7	2.0	2.0	2.4	3.1	4.3	8.1	3.2	2.3	1.8
Structural unemployment rate[1]													
1980-89	4.5	6.8	2.4	6.7	8.0	7.8	9.0	9.2	7.4	14.7	7.1	2.8	..
1990-99	6.7	5.6	3.0	7.8	10.1	9.5	8.1	9.0	8.7	12.0	5.8	4.6	..
1996-99	5.9	5.5	3.5	8.0	10.4	10.1	7.6	8.6	8.2	8.8	5.0	4.3	..
Labour productivity growth													
1980-89	2.1	1.5	2.7	1.6	2.1	2.2	2.2	1.2	1.2	3.8	1.4	1.6	2.1
1990-99	0.5	1.8	0.9	0.0	1.3	1.6	1.8	1.3	2.3	..	0.6	2.2	1.7
1996-99	1.6	2.4	-0.1	1.7	1.5	0.7	1.2	1.5	2.8	..	0.4	0.5	1.6
Employment rate[2]													
1980-89	70.2	68.8	67.1	62.8	60.8	52.6	68.2	66.7	64.4	50.3	53.8	74.1	64.0
1990-99	68.3	72.4	69.3	65.0	59.3	52.1	70.3	68.1	66.4	54.3	64.4	74.2	64.8
1996-99	70.3	73.5	69.5	64.4	59.3	52.0	70.9	68.6	67.1	58.2	68.1	77.2	65.1
Share of real GDP													
Business investment													
1980-89	10.0	..	14.8	11.7	10.7	11.1	9.5	9.3	14.9	11.6	11.9	..	..
1990-99	12.1	..	17.5	12.8	11.4	11.7	11.7	10.8	14.7	11.0	12.8	..	..
1996-99	14.0	..	17.3	12.5	11.2	12.1	12.9	12.1	15.9	12.0	13.3	..	..
Machinery and equipment investment													
1980-89	4.6	..	..	7.6	8.5	9.6	8.0	..	6.3	8.0	6.2	..	..
1990-99	6.8	..	..	8.9	10.0	10.3	8.9	8.7	7.3	7.8	6.9	..	..
1996-99	8.3	..	..	8.8	10.4	10.9	10.0	9.8	8.7	8.5	7.4	..	..
Openness to trade[3]													
1980-89	47.7	..	18.4	46.1	32.3	34.0	45.0	41.4	26.0	88.3	88.6	..	..
1990-99	62.6	..	22.7	50.7	43.1	47.7	57.5	63.4	36.3	137.7	108.5	..	..
1996-99	68.1	..	25.0	55.3	48.2	53.0	64.2	73.4	40.4	165.1	117.4	..	..
Agriculture[4]													
1980-89	6.3	..	..	1.5	3.3	3.3	..	2.8	3.4	..	2.8	2.7	..
1990-99	7.2	..	..	1.2	3.0	3.1	..	2.6	3.2	..	3.1	2.3	..
1996-99	7.3	..	..	1.3	3.1	3.1	..	2.5	3.2	..	3.0	2.2	..

1. The structural rate of unemployment is defined as the NAWRU, or non-accelerating-wage rate of unemployment.
2. Total employment as a percentage of the working-age population (aged 15-64).
3. The ratio of exports plus imports to GDP.
4. 1983-89.

Source: Statistics New Zealand and OECD.

Table 11.   **GDP per capita and labour productivity**
Average annual growth

	Growth of GDP per capita			Growth of GDP per person employed		
	1980-90	1990-99	1999	1980-90	1990-99	1999
United States	2.3	2.1	3.2	1.4	1.8	2.6
Japan	3.4	1.0	0.0	2.7	0.9	1.0
Germany	2.0	−0.3	1.5	1.7	−0.6	0.5
France	1.8	1.1	2.5	2.1	1.3	0.9
Italy	2.2	1.2	1.4	2.1	1.6	0.2
United Kingdom	2.5	1.7	1.7	2.0	1.8	0.4
Canada	1.6	1.4	3.7	1.1	1.3	1.7
Australia	1.7	2.4	3.1	1.1	2.3	2.1
Austria	2.1	1.4	2.0	2.1	1.4	0.7
Belgium	1.9	1.6	2.3	1.9	1.6	1.7
Denmark	1.9	1.8	1.3	1.0	2.0	0.8
Finland	2.7	1.3	3.2	2.4	..	..
Iceland	1.6	1.5	3.3	1.0	1.4	1.7
Ireland	3.3	5.9	8.7	3.9	..	..
Korea	7.6	4.7	9.7	5.9	..	..
Mexico	−0.3	1.1	1.6	..	..	..
Netherlands	1.6	2.1	3.0	1.3	0.6	0.6
New Zealand	**1.7**	**1.0**	**3.4**	**2.2**	**0.5**	**2.4**
Norway	2.0	2.9	0.6	1.8	2.2	0.4
Portugal	2.9	..	..	1.5	..	..
Spain	2.6	2.1	3.6	2.3	1.5	−0.9
Sweden	1.8	1.0	3.7	1.5	2.5	1.5
Switzerland	1.5	−0.1	1.2	0.2	0.4	1.0
Turkey	2.8	1.3	−6.5	3.5	..	..

Source: OECD.

has been lacklustre labour productivity performance: annual increases were only 0.5 per cent on average in the 1990s, although there were encouraging signs of a pick-up in the latter part of the decade and into 2000 (Tables 2 – in Chapter I – and 10). Given these developments, it is not surprising that per capita GDP growth was also relatively weak (Table 11).[2] And, the level remains low relative to the OECD average and other small open economies such as Ireland (Figure 13) New Zealand's relative geographical isolation, however, poses challenges that other small OECD countries do not face (see Box 1). It has tackled them in part via more open markets, and the degree of openness is high relative to larger OECD countries, but low compared with other small countries (Table 10). Successive governments had also unilaterally reduced tariffs. While the authorities continue to forge ahead on new bilateral trade agreements, they have backed away from unilateral tariff reductions (see below).

Figure 13.   **GDP per head in selected OECD countries**
At current purchasing power parities, OECD = 100[1]

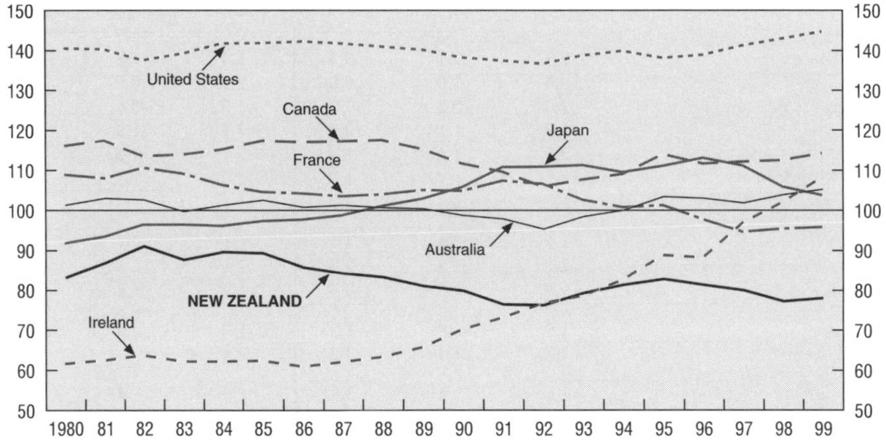

1.   25 countries.
Source: OECD.

Box 1.   **Economic geography and agglomeration**

Because New Zealand is relatively isolated geographically, there has been considerable interest within the country on how this may affect economic performance. As the Treasury notes (Treasury, 1999):

"Draw a circle with a radius of 2 200 kilometres centred on Wellington and you capture within it 3.8 million New Zealanders and rather a lot of seagulls. Draw a similar circle centred on Helsinki and you capture a population of over 300 million from 39 countries."

Traditionally, New Zealand has sought to overcome its isolation by maintaining relatively open markets by international standards and creating a regulatory framework that is conducive to foreign investment. In part, there was a belief that it had to do even more than other countries in these and other areas to remain competitive. Recent research has focussed on the benefits that may arise from agglomeration (Box, 1999). This includes factors such as: lower transport costs; the ability to reap economies of scale and scope; informational externalities, including knowledge spillovers; and greater access to a wide variety of goods and services. Forces towards agglomeration are thought to be relatively weak in New Zealand, and this may impinge negatively on economic performance. New technology may help to overcome some of these barriers by reducing "distance" (through, for example, electronic commerce), but to close the gap in living standards with other OECD countries implies that an even more ambitious reform agenda has to be carried out.

Total factor productivity growth picked up

Amidst these contrasting signals came a pick-up in total factor productivity (TFP) growth, which rose at an average annual rate of 1.5 per cent between 1993 and 1998 versus only 0.9 per cent over the previous 15 years (Table 12).[3] Moreover, work done by Diewert and Lawrence (1999)[4] suggests that there may have been a structural break in 1993, with TFP on a permanently higher growth track since that point, although this finding must be interpreted with caution. This better performance in the latter part of the decade helped to boost the level of TFP cumulatively by about 22 per cent since 1978 (Figure 14).

Table 12.   **Productivity growth**

	1978-84	1985-92	1993-98	1978-92	1978-98
Total factor productivity[1]	1.0	0.7	1.5	0.9	1.0
Labour productivity	2.6	1.8	0.5	2.2	1.6
Capital productivity[1]	−0.6	−0.2	2.2	−0.3	0.4
Capital-labour ratio[1]	3.2	2.0	−1.7	. .	1.2

1. Based on net capital stock.
Source: Diewert and Lawrence (1999).

Figure 14.   **Productivity developments**

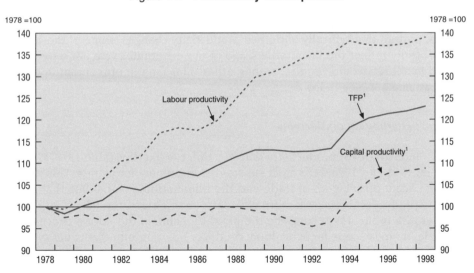

1.   Net capital stock.
Source: New Zealand Treasury official database and OECD.

Until the early 1990s, labour productivity growth dominated aggregate productivity gains, but it slowed thereafter while the pace of capital productivity increases picked up. The increase from 1993 has to be seen in light of its extremely poor performance prior to that period. The reforms to product and financial markets that began in 1984 forced firms to become more competitive or shut down, resulting in some scrapping of capital. At the same time, financial market liberalisation boosted foreign direct investment (and access to technical know-how), which was also spurred by the privatisation programme and the significant change in policy direction (monetary and fiscal) that bolstered investor confidence. Nevertheless, the impact of these changes on the capital stock would take some time to manifest themselves in better productivity outcomes as firms re-engineered themselves to take on the challenges of a more open economy.

A number of factors underlie the slowdown in labour productivity

Capital deepening slowed in the 1990s, contributing to lower labour productivity growth. A number of factors played a role. For example, the Employment Contracts Act of 1991 made it less costly to hire low-skilled labour. At the same time a tightening of unemployment benefits helped to lower the reservation wage, encouraging the low-skilled to offer their services more readily. The initial impact was probably to lower overall labour productivity growth because it would take time for on-the-job training to be reflected in better performance and for capital investment to catch up to enhanced labour supply.[5] By the end of the decade, there was an encouraging rise in labour productivity growth, signalling that some of these benefits may have begun to come through. Nevertheless, given the procyclical pattern that typically underlies productivity changes, some of these gains undoubtedly reflect the favourable stage of the economic cycle. Moreover, sustained increases would require, among other things, an improvement in educational attainment (see below).

Sectoral patterns vary considerably

Industry-level productivity patterns differ markedly (Table 13). TFP gains between 1978 and 1998 were most substantial in primary industries. This reflects the significant opening up of trade and the elimination of subsidies that forced primary producers to become more efficient. Nevertheless, the fall-off in productivity growth in the 1990s suggests the need to maintain the reform process. For example, there is scope for agricultural producer board reform that could enhance the innovation process in that sector (see below). This is important for aggregate productivity performance, since the share of agriculture in output in New Zealand is high relative to other OECD countries (Table 10). Moreover, New Zealand has faced a downward trend in its terms of trade (see Figure 7 in Chapter I), reflecting

Table 13. **Productivity growth by sector**[1]

Annual average rate

	Total factor productivity				Labour productivity				Capital productivity				Capital-labour ratio			
	1978-84	1985-92	1993-98	1978-98	1978-84	1985-92	1993-98	1978-98	1978-84	1985-92	1993-98	1978-98	1978-84	1985-92	1993-98	1978-98
Agriculture	4.1	3.9	3.5	3.9	4.3	3.9	3.2	3.8	3.9	4.0	4.2	4.0	0.2	0.0	-1.1	-0.3
Fishing	12.0	2.7	-4.2	3.6	16.2	4.1	-2.8	5.8	5.4	-1.0	-7.9	-0.9	7.6	6.1	4.5	6.2
Forestry	15.1	11.8	2.6	10.2	24.6	14.7	3.2	14.3	4.8	4.4	0.8	3.5	10.6	10.5	3.4	8.5
Mining	5.9	4.3	-0.5	3.5	6.5	3.6	-2.0	3.0	4.4	6.0	2.7	4.7	1.3	-2.1	-5.5	-2.0
Primary	**4.9**	**4.7**	**3.2**	**4.3**	**5.2**	**4.8**	**3.0**	**4.4**	**4.2**	**4.4**	**3.7**	**4.2**	**0.6**	**0.5**	**-0.8**	**0.2**
Electricity	2.6	3.9	5.2	3.9	2.5	4.3	6.1	4.2	3.0	3.1	3.2	3.1	-0.4	0.9	3.2	1.1
Construction	2.8	0.0	0.0	0.9	3.7	0.2	-0.3	1.2	0.7	-0.6	0.6	0.2	2.9	0.9	-0.9	1.0
Transport	3.6	4.7	3.4	4.0	4.5	5.4	3.8	4.7	1.5	3.1	2.5	2.5	2.5	1.3	-2.1	0.8
Communications	7.5	9.0	6.1	7.7	9.3	10.6	7.4	9.3	3.9	5.4	2.7	4.1	2.7	2.2	1.5	2.2
Infrastructure	**4.0**	**4.1**	**3.5**	**3.9**	**5.0**	**4.5**	**3.4**	**4.4**	**1.7**	**3.0**	**3.6**	**2.8**	**2.9**	**1.5**	**-0.1**	**1.5**
Food	1.7	1.0	1.4	1.3	2.8	1.8	2.0	2.2	-0.7	-1.0	0.1	-0.6	3.7	2.8	1.9	2.8
Textiles	0.4	0.0	1.0	0.4	0.7	1.0	2.4	1.3	-0.2	-2.3	-2.5	-1.7	1.0	3.6	4.8	3.0
Wood	2.0	-0.1	0.1	0.6	2.9	0.7	0.2	1.3	0.0	-2.0	0.1	-0.8	3.2	2.6	0.0	2.1
Paper	2.0	1.8	0.8	1.6	2.4	2.7	1.3	2.2	1.1	-0.4	-0.6	0.1	1.2	3.1	1.9	2.2
Chemicals	-1.3	1.8	1.6	0.7	3.7	3.2	1.2	2.8	-10.0	-2.6	3.1	-3.6	21.0	3.8	-1.0	7.5
Non-metallic minerals	3.9	2.5	3.5	3.2	5.4	3.8	3.7	4.3	0.8	-0.7	2.9	0.8	4.9	4.6	0.7	3.6
Basic metals	-1.5	2.5	4.5	1.7	1.5	3.2	3.9	2.8	-7.3	0.2	5.9	-0.8	12.4	2.1	-2.0	4.1
Machinery	1.7	-0.3	-0.5	0.3	2.8	0.4	-1.0	0.8	-0.4	-2.1	0.4	-0.9	3.5	2.6	-1.6	1.7
Other manufacturing	3.8	2.9	1.5	2.8	3.7	4.0	2.1	3.4	4.4	0.5	-0.3	1.5	-0.6	3.5	2.3	1.8
Manufacturing	**1.1**	**1.0**	**1.2**	**1.1**	**2.8**	**1.9**	**1.4**	**2.1**	**-3.3**	**-1.4**	**0.8**	**-1.1**	**5.8**	**3.2**	**0.6**	**3.3**
Trade	-0.9	-0.3	0.2	-0.4	-0.3	0.1	-0.4	-0.2	-2.4	-1.3	1.7	-0.8	4.2	4.8	5.5	4.8
Financial services	0.3	-1.8	-2.9	-1.4	0.7	-1.5	-2.7	-1.1	-0.7	-2.7	-3.3	-2.2	1.5	1.2	0.5	1.1
Community services	0.6	-0.3	0.8	0.3	0.5	-0.2	0.9	0.3	0.7	-0.5	0.6	0.2	-0.2	0.3	0.2	0.1
Services	**0.1**	**-0.7**	**-0.9**	**-0.5**	**0.8**	**-0.1**	**-0.9**	**0.0**	**-1.4**	**-2.0**	**-0.8**	**-1.5**	**2.5**	**1.9**	**-0.2**	**1.5**

1. Trend rate. Calculated using a Hoddrick-Prescott filter with a smoothing factor of 100.
Source: Diewert and Lawrence (1999) and OECD.

the relative weakness in agricultural commodity prices. To combat the negative impact on living standards requires producers to become even more efficient.

TFP performance was next strongest in the "infrastructure" industries, particularly communications. These sectors saw relatively robust labour and capital productivity gains, despite moderate increases in the capital/labour ratio. This suggests that corporatisation and privatisation led to better investment decisions and boosted the efficiency with which capital was used. To bolster the innovation process in the electricity and communications sectors, the government has undertaken an examination of their respective regulatory frameworks (see below).

Developments in manufacturing industries have been mixed. Five of the nine sub-sectors within it have boosted their TFP growth since 1993, largely a result of better labour productivity performance and continued capital deepening. Two that did not, machinery and other manufacturing, saw TFP growth fall back slightly. Overall, machinery and equipment investment as a share of GDP has remained relatively low compared with other OECD countries, although there were encouraging signs of a pickup in the latter part of the 1990s[6] (Table 10).

The most meagre productivity gains – in terms of TFP, labour and capital – have come in the service sector. While measurement problems abound, poor productivity growth undoubtedly reflects the labour-intensive nature of the sector. Trade, however, saw a large rise in its capital-labour ratio, but this only marginally improved overall productivity performance. Financial services witnessed the worst productivity outcomes. Indeed, its total factor productivity slumped, declining at an average annual rate of 2.9 per cent between 1993 and 1998. This may seem surprising, given the widespread reform undertaken in this sector (see below). But it also reflects the well-known difficulties in quantifying many of the positive changes in quality and output.

There is mixed evidence of a new economy

As in other OECD countries, there is avid interest in whether technological advances and restructuring have enhanced trend performance. Once again, indicators provide a mixed message. One commonly studied gauge of the new economy is investment in information and communication technology (ICT). On this front, investment reached almost 9 per cent of (nominal) GDP in 1997, the highest in the OECD area. About half was spent on telecommunications (OECD, 2000a). New Zealand does not have a large computer industry,[7] and imports of ICT equipment have therefore been strong. They reached about 10 per cent of total volume imports in 1999, up about 1 percentage point over the decade. By contrast, exports of ICT amounted to only about 1 per cent of total exports in 1999, consistent with the country's comparative advantage in low-technology industries. Given the small size of the ICT sector, New Zealand will depend on ICT to boost productivity via capital deepening and through spillover effects (from new technology

Figure 15.   **Expenditure on R&D**
Percentage of GDP

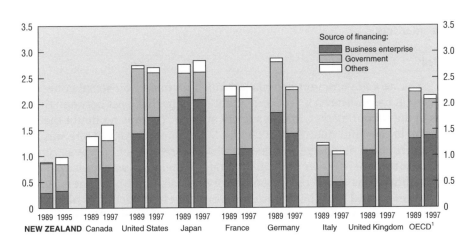

1.   Weighted average, which includes Mexico, Korea, Czech Republic, Hungary and Poland in 1997.
Source: OECD, R&D database.

diffusion). The number of patents, while growing quickly, comes off a low base (OECD, 2000*a*). R&D spending by business remains relatively low by international standards (Figure 15), and the government has implemented a new programme in the hope of encouraging greater private-sector R&D effort. In addition, many firms do not yet appear to be taking up the challenges and potential benefits offered by new technologies, such as electronic commerce (see below).

Structural policy reform should be enhanced

While productivity performance has been disappointing given the scope of reforms undertaken, there are promising signs that this may be turning around. To bolster this trend, it is imperative that the government takes action in a number of areas, including: *enhancing* the incentives to take up work; *boosting* the level of human capital; *adapting* the regulatory framework in product and financial markets in step with changing market conditions; and *evaluating* the quality of government expenditures to ensure that they not only deliver their intended goals, but are directed towards improving growth prospects. Many new policy measures, discussed further below, do not necessarily reflect a coherent approach to improving growth prospects, nor to closing gaps among members of society. The most effective way to better the situation of disadvantaged groups is to ensure a higher standard of living for all New Zealanders. This would also help to close the gap in living standards with other OECD countries, which should also be a primary policy objective.

Labour markets

Overview

The new government has placed much emphasis on social cohesion. In this regard, it has indicated its concern about the gaps that exist between different groups in the labour market, and in society at large. There is no doubt that these gaps exist. In the third quarter of 2000, the Maori unemployment rate was 14 per cent,10 percentage points greater than for Pakeha (people of European descent), despite a substantially lower participation rate. Individuals with no formal educational qualifications and those in poorer regions also had high unemployment rates (Tables 14 and 15). These patterns were largely reflected in participation rates, *i.e.* they are lowest among those with few qualifications, Maori and Pacific Islanders and individuals in relatively poorer regions. To a large extent, however, these gaps have remained relatively stable over the latter part of the 1990s.

Table 14.   **Participation and unemployment rates for selected groups**

Per cent

	Participation rate		Unemployment rate	
	1996 Q3	2000 Q3	1996 Q3	2000 Q3
Male	74.4	73.2	6.1	6.0
Female	58.0	57.6	6.0	5.3
Pakeha	67.5	66.7	4.5	4.2
Maori	60.8	62.8	15.9	14.2
Pacific Islanders	61.5	60.2	14.2	11.3
Other	54.5	54.7	10.4	8.0
Youth: 15-19	57.0	51.2	15.7	15.7
Youth: 20-24	77.2	70.9	8.7	8.7
No qualifications	50.1	48.2	11.2	10.4
School qualifications	63.9	61.9	5.5	5.1
Post-school qualifications	80.3	78.8	3.5	3.6
Overall	**66.0**	**65.1**	**6.1**	**5.7**
Memorandum item:				
Standard deviation[1]	9.3	9.0	4.4	4.0

Note: The data are not seasonally adjusted.
1.   Standard deviation of all of the above categories.
Source: Statistics New Zealand.

Table 15.   **Regional participation and unemployment rates**

Per cent

	Participation rate		Unemployment rate	
	1996 Q3	2000 Q3	1996 Q3	2000 Q3
Northland	62.1	60.3	8.4	8.7
Auckland	68.5	65.3	5.6	5.1
Waikato	66.1	67.1	7.2	6.0
Bay of Plenty	63.7	64.5	7.6	8.1
Gisborne/Hawke's Bay	62.2	62.4	8.7	7.2
Taranaki	61.0	63.7	8.1	6.0
Manawatu/Wanganui	61.6	60.3	6.1	6.5
Wellington	68.8	68.8	5.2	5.0
Tasman, Nelson, Marlborough, West Coast	65.9	65.0	5.9	4.6
Canterbury	65.2	65.9	5.5	5.5
Otago	64.1	63.8	4.3	5.3
Southland	64.9	63.2	5.6	4.9
Overall	66.0	65.1	6.1	5.7
Memorandum item:				
Standard deviation[1]	2.6	2.5	1.4	1.3

Note: The data are not seasonally adjusted.
1.   Standard deviation of all of the above categories.
Source: Statistics New Zealand.

One way that successive governments have combated the impact of unemployment on family incomes has been via the benefit system. But this has been costly. In 1998, benefit payments amounted to about 5 per cent of GDP. Furthermore, over one quarter of the working-age population receives some form of government benefit (Table 16). Moreover, relative to the number of employed – who foot the bill for the system – the share is close to 46 per cent. At this lofty level, trying to expand benefits would be costly and could have significant distortionary effects on resource allocation. Some trends are also disturbing, for example, the rising share of invalids benefit recipients.

A widening in income differentials may have also helped stimulate the government's objective to close gaps. Individual income inequality, as measured by the Gini coefficient, increased in the 1980s and, to a lesser extent, in the 1990s (Table 17). An important underlying factor was an increasing return to education and skill. For example, O'Dea (2000) notes that about 30 per cent of the rise in inequality in weekly full-time earnings between 1984 and 1997 was accounted for by changes in the distribution of workers' formal qualifications and age, and returns to these attributes.[8] Nevertheless, there is some evidence that between 1991 and 1996 the private returns to men with a bachelor's degree stabilised and those for women fell (Maani, 1999). While the reasons behind this are unclear, it may be due to a greater supply of educated workers.

Table 16.   **Developments in income support**

Per cent

	Share of working-age population		
	1991	1996	2000[1]
Unemployment benefit[2]	6.0	4.8	5.3
Training	0.3	0.4	0.2
Sickness	0.8	1.2	1.1
Invalids	1.2	1.5	1.9
Domestic purposes	3.8	3.9	3.8
Widows	0.4	0.3	0.3
Orphans	0.1	0.2	0.0
Superannuation	19.8	16.7	14.9
Veterans	0.1	0.2	0.2
Total	**32.5**	**29.3**	**27.7**
Memorandum item:			
Total as a share of employment	56.1	49.1	45.9

1.   Data pertain to March 2000.
2.   From October 1998, the unemployment, training and sickness benefits became part of the Community Wage programme.
Source: Statistics New Zealand and Work and Income New Zealand.

Table 17.   **Gini coefficients for wage and salary earners**[1]

	1982	1986	1991	1996
Men	0.340	0.339	0.408	0.434
Women	0.479	0.459	0.481	0.486
Total	0.427	0.421	0.466	0.479

1.   Population aged 15-64.
Source: O'Dea (2000).

A widely discussed topic in New Zealand is the so-called brain drain. The debate was fuelled by the turnaround in net migration late in the 1990s (Table 18). Moreover, net emigration of those with the highest skills – as proxied by occupation – rose in tandem,[9] representing a loss of human (and financial) capital. The reasons behind these developments are unclear. To some extent, they may simply reflect differing cyclical performance, particular with respect to Australia. Nevertheless, the fall in net migration risks adverse consequences for potential output growth. This may be further aggravated by recent policy measures such as a higher top marginal income tax rate. Undoubtedly, some individuals will return later in their working lives, bringing with them new skills and considerable work experience. But the best way to avoid a brain drain is to ensure that policies are geared towards raising the living standards of New Zealanders.

Table 18. **Net migration by occupation**[1]

	Professionals	Technicians and associated professionals	Legislators, administrators and managers	Skilled[2]	Others[3]	Total	Skilled share
1996	5 410	999	895	7 304	22 528	29 832	24.5
1997	4 394	245	610	5 249	15 699	20 948	25.1
1998	1 608	−949	−405	254	2 453	2 707	9.4
1999	−567	−1 480	−803	−2 850	−7 349	−10 199	27.9
2000	−621	−1 453	−1 123	−3 197	−5 790	−8 987	35.6

1. Data refer to long-term arrivals and departures in New Zealand, March years.
2. Skilled is the sum of the first three columns.
3. Others refer to all other occupation categories.
Source: Statistics New Zealand.

Industrial relations

The new coalition government implemented the first significant change to industrial relations since the *Employment Contracts Act* (ECA) was legislated in 1991. In October 2000, the *Employment Relations Act* (ERA) came into force, following several months of debate and modifications to the original proposition. In general, unions supported the Act, which strengthens their rights, while many employers expressed serious concerns about its potentially negative impact on labour costs. The Act has two objectives: *first*, to build productive employment relationships through the promotion of mutual trust and confidence in all aspects of the employment environment; and *second*, to promote observance of the principles underlying the International Labour Organisation Convention 87 on Freedom of Association and Convention 98 on the Right to Organise and Bargain Collectively.

The Employment Relations Act modifies provisions under the ECA in several significant ways, as outlined in Table 19. A number of areas are particularly noteworthy:

– *Good faith bargaining.* The government considers the requirement to bargain in "good faith" an essential element of the new industrial relations framework and the emphasis on good faith is designed to result in productivity gains. An Interim Code of Good Faith sets out the principles underlying good faith, and a final code is to be developed by April 2001. To assuage fears that confidential information could be released to competitors in multi-enterprise bargaining, the law allows relevant information to be passed to an independent third party for assessment.

– *Grievances and dismissals.* A frequent complaint under the ECA was the relatively onerous procedures firms had to follow to dismiss non-performing staff (OECD, 1998). The ERA proposes to avoid undue litigation by

Table 19.   **Comparison of the Employment Contracts Act
and the Employment Relations Act**

Provision	Employment Contracts Act	Employment Relations Act
Good faith	No provision.	All parties must bargain in good faith. This has two main principles: that neither party can deceive or mislead the other; and that unions and employers meet together to consider respective proposals. It does not imply that a collective agreement must be signed. A Code of Conduct is in process of being drawn up.
Freedom of association	Union membership is voluntary and no undue influence may be placed on an individual to become part of one.	Same. Unions must have at least 15 members.
Bargaining levels	Multi-employer bargains allowed. No strikes in support of them permitted.	Multi-employer bargains allowed and strikes in support of them are permitted.
Representation on collective agreements	Individual employees choose whether they wish to be represented in bargaining, and if so, by whom. Unions have no statutory recognition.	Only certified unions can negotiate collective agreements. Employees can negotiate collectively without a union, but the agreement will be considered an individual agreement. By default all new employees are considered to be part of a firm's collective agreement for the first 30 days of employment. After that, they must choose to remain party to the agreement or negotiate an individual contract. Collective agreements must contain a coverage clause that details the type of work to which the agreement applies.
Individual agreements	The terms of the agreement cannot be inconsistent with any collective agreement in place and individuals may request a written record.	Possible in any workplace. Employers must give the proposed agreement to employees in advance, advise them that they are entitled to seek advice on it and allow time for advice to be sought. Agreements must include a set of mandatory items, including wages/salary, working time arrangements, description of work to be performed and an explanation of how disputes will be resolved.
Fixed-term agreements	Individuals are free to enter into them (see individual agreements).	The employer must have genuine reasons to employ the worker under such a contract. The employer must advise the employee at the beginning of the contract when and how the contract will end.

Table 19. **Comparison of the Employment Contracts Act
and the Employment Relations Act** (*cont.*)

Provision	Employment Contracts Act	Employment Relations Act
Contractors	Free to contract under mutually agreed upon terms. Individuals can ask the court to determine whether they are employees.	Individuals will be allowed to ask the Employment Relations Authority to decide whether they are "*de facto*" employees rather than independent contractors. A ruling will not apply to all workers in a similar situation.
Continuity of employment	No provision.	A collective agreement must include a clause stating what will happen to workers if any of the tasks covered under the agreement are scaled back, contracted out, or if the business (or part of it) is sold.
Strikes and lockouts	Strikes and lockouts are lawful in support of negotiations for a collective employment contract. They are not allowed in support of multi-employer agreements nor are they allowed during the term of the collective agreement. There are no restrictions on having the work of striking employees done by others.	Strikes and lockouts can only occur 40 days after the end of a collective agreement. Strikes can take place, however, at any time with respect to health and safety issues. Strikes are lawful in support of multi-employer agreements. Workers not affected by the strike cannot be compelled to perform the work of striking employees (although they can do so voluntarily). Replacement workers cannot be hired, except under special circumstances.
Disputes and grievances	All employment contracts must contain procedures to settle grievances and disputes. Default procedures are provided for under the ECA providing for mediation and access to the Employment Tribunal with right of appeal to the Employment Court.	Mediation services, offered by the Department of Labour are the first step in resolving disputes. If not settled, they can be moved to the Employment Relations Authority for investigation, and potentially, referred back to mediation. The Employment Court will hear cases not resolved by the ERA, but only if good faith has been followed by all parties. Under personal grievance, individuals have 90 days to make a claim unless there are exceptional circumstances. In such a case, the individual has six years to file. Re-instatement is the primary remedy.

Source: Department of Labour, New Zealand.

making mediation a mandatory first step. If there is no resolution, the parties can then turn to the Employment Relations Authority, a new investigative body. If the parties do not agree with its ruling, or if the Authority so decides, grievances and disputes are then turned over to an Employment Court. It can redirect the matter back to mediation, to the Authority or make a final judgement (which could ultimately be appealed by the Court of Appeal on points of law).

– *Multi-employer bargains.* Firms are not allowed to replace striking workers, except in exceptional cases (for health and safety reasons), but could ask employees not on strike to perform some of the duties of striking workers on a voluntary basis. This contrasts with Canadian legislation, which enables striking workers to be replaced, unless it is determined that good faith was breached.

– *Independent contractors.* The government intends that all individuals working in a *de facto* dependent employment relationship receive the benefits that would accrue from such contracts. The law allows anyone to ask the Employment Relations Authority to determine whether they fall into this situation, although some occupations retain exemptions (for example, real estate agents and sharemilkers). Collective action in this area must name all individuals involved and have their consent.

– *Union monopoly.* Unions must have at least 15 members and be registered to bargain on behalf of workers. Collective contracts signed under the ECA will carry on until their expiry date, or at the latest, 31 July 2003. Union members can, however, vote to opt out of a contract covered under the ECA and re-negotiate under the ERA from 1 July 2001, while employees who are not union members will remain covered under their collective contract until it expires. Currently, only 1 per cent of contracts, covering about 6 per cent of employees, are multi-employer based.

The ERA moves the industrial relations framework back towards what is in place in many other OECD countries. Although the overall effect of the new legislation is uncertain, it will probably reduce labour market flexibility relative to what had existed under the ECA, but a return to the highly centralised (and distortionary) system that prevailed prior to the ECA is unlikely. There is no requirement that workers join a union, nor is arbitration compulsory. Structural changes in the economy as well as changed attitudes among all bargaining parties will probably also contribute to keeping union density relatively low. It currently rests at about 20 per cent of the workforce, down from roughly 40 per cent in 1991. The government expects a rise to about 30 per cent, a level found in many other OECD countries (OECD, 1997a). Although the government's intent is to make industrial relations more harmonious, strike activity heretofore has been low in New Zealand.

It will be some time before the actual impact of the ERA becomes clear. Employees and employers will have to become familiar with new processes, and several clauses will probably end up being interpreted by the courts. Nevertheless, the new legislation risks adverse macroeconomic and microeconomic consequences, even if their size is difficult to estimate. On the macroeconomic front, bolstering union rights could lead to pressures for "catch-up" wage increases that are not linked to productivity developments. The government can play an important role here by ensuring that wage settlements with its own workers are in line with their expected productivity gains. In addition, strengthening provisions for multi-employer agreements could worsen aggregate inflation performance if they become widespread, since they usually do not account for the different factors facing individual firms. Such agreements may become more prevalent because: workers can strike in support of them; a possible re-alignment of agreements to a similar date would make it easier to bargain across enterprises; and unions must have at least 15 members. This latter condition rules out most small enterprises from having workplace-based unions. Workers who want to be covered under a collective agreement will have to seek multi-employer agreements.[10] A lower threshold, for example below 10 people, would have allowed many more unions to be enterprise-based.

The ERA risks raising compliance costs, which could be detrimental to job creation, particularly among smaller enterprises. *First*, direct costs to businesses will increase to the extent that union members have to be given time off for training and for meetings,[11] and because union dues have to be collected by firms. This would affect smaller enterprises more adversely. *Second*, the continuity-of-employment clause may limit the ability of firms to adjust staff numbers quickly in the face of sudden adverse shocks. This clause can be beneficial by setting out clear rules that are suited to a firm's specific circumstances. Undoubtedly, however, not all contingencies can be covered without undue expense. Thus, the Employment Relations Authority and/or Employment Court will probably get involved in interpreting these provisions. The government might want to consider, in its review of the minimum code (see below), whether advance notice should be given to the public employment service when mass redundancies are likely on the grounds that they usually entail large social costs. *Third*, several notice requirements are placed on employers in the use of fixed-term agreements and for personal grievances that could constitute grounds for dispute. How the Authority and the Employment Court interpret them will be an important factor affecting a firm's decision to hire. *Fourth*, in a similar manner, the grievance and dismissals process could become more protracted, with disputes rotating among the various bodies, raising compliance costs.

Although it is difficult to link an industrial relations framework to economic developments, the government is nevertheless encouraged to monitor the impact of the ERA, given its objective that it lead to more productive working relationships. This should include gathering data on: strikes and lockouts, their duration and the reasons for them; and mediation of grievances and Employment Relations Authority decisions, including the time taken for their resolution, the process followed and remedy required.

Superannuation

The New Zealand Superannuation Fund (NZS) is financed out of general tax revenues and run on a pay-as-you-go basis. Benefit payments are a fixed proportion of average wages, and the new government has increased them from 60 to 65 per cent for married couples, which will raise the costs of Superannuation by about NZ$ 680 million over the current government's term in office. The scheme is relatively generous by international standards (although less so than it was in the 1980s when it replaced almost 90 per cent of wages) and could act as a deterrent to private savings.

In the face of an expected sharp increase in the old-age dependency ratio (from 0.18 retired people per worker now to a high of 0.43 later in the century) and associated costs to Superannuation (Figure 16), the government plans to partially fund the scheme, or, in its terminology, create a smoothed pay-as-you-go system

Figure 16. **Projected developments in expenditures on superannuation, health care and education**

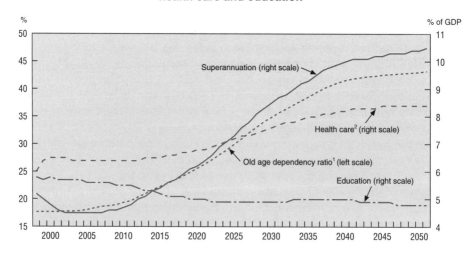

1. Calculated as those 65 and over divided by the working-age population (15-64).
2. These projections only include the public share of health-care expenditures.
Source: Ministry of Health (1999).

to make retirement income policies more sustainable. The authorities would like to see the fund commence operation on 1 July 2001, and the key proposed elements are:

- The government's contributions would be limited to NZ$ 600 million, NZ$ 1.2 billion and NZ$ 1.8 billion between 2001/02 and 2003/04. After this three-year period, the contribution should be sufficient to fund NZS over a 40-year rolling time frame.[12] The government could deviate from the required contribution, but would have to fully explain the reasons why and how it would get back on track. The government expects that contributions would reach about NZ$ 2 billion a year in excess of its pay-as-you-go obligations, beginning in 2004/05, falling to zero by sometime between 2025 and 2029 when fund assets begin to be drawn upon to meet NZS expenditures. The fund's assets are projected to cumulate to a peak of about 50 per cent of GDP at that point, before gradually declining towards zero by sometimewell beyond 2100.

- The government envisages that legislation would require that the fund not be drawn upon until after 2020 to help ring-fence it from current spending pressures.

- An independent crown entity board – the Guardians of New Zealand Superannuation – would manage the fund portfolio on a "prudent commercial basis to ensure that there are strong long-term returns". Board members would be appointed to renewable terms (probably three years in length), based on their qualifications to run such a fund. The board would decide upon the investment strategy, including the broad asset classes that the fund could invest in and in what proportions. It would also establish the fund management structure, including contracting with professional fund managers for the day-to-day operations. The government would have a limited capacity to make directives to the board on its investment strategy. The board would prepare a statement of intent (covering all aspects of operations including the investment strategy) and produce annual (and perhaps quarterly) statements that track how it is faring against the strategy. The fund would be subject to normal taxes.

- The board would not be responsible for determining the contribution rate nor policy parameters for NZS, which would remain solely under the government's responsibility.

There is no general economic analysis that permits a clear-cut judgement as to the relative benefits of pre-funding versus debt pay-down, although compared with a pay-as-you-go system, evidence suggests that pre-funding would raise national savings[13] (Engen and Gale, 1998). The government prefers the creation of an asset-based fund to a more rapid debt paydown (see Chapter II), because it feels that once net debt reaches low levels, there would be less public support to continue the process. It also feels that partial pre-funding would place money aside for the looming retirement bill, protected from current spending demands, which is important, given the fiscal pressures the government will face in the future from population ageing. This is certainly true, but it could have the perverse effect of increasing pressure to make the system more generous – or not to make it less so – as the public sees funds build up solely for retirement. Partial pre-funding could also reduce the incentives for individuals to boost their own (private) savings (see Chapter IV). Debt pay-down is a concrete way to ensure the government is able to meet future financing pressures, while avoiding pressures to spend budgetary surpluses. In addition, it would help to lower the risk premium on government borrowing (although if markets perceive the partial pre-funding to have a similar impact, it too might result in a lower premium).

Another option the government could consider in lieu of partial pre-funding is the scope for further tax cuts with an aim to boost the productive capacity of the economy, and thereby increase the ease with which future pensions can be financed.[14] Indeed, further pressures for corporate tax reductions are likely to arise, since many OECD countries, including Australia, plan moves in this area. In any event, the government should consider carefully how it will achieve the announced partial pre-funding. For example, having higher marginal tax rates on income than otherwise would be more distortionary than raising or maintaining the current level of consumption taxes.

Partial pre-funding would require the authorities to address a number of interwoven governance and operational issues. As noted above, foremost among them would be to decide how much of fund assets to allocate between bonds and equities (or cash and property) and domestic versus foreign content in order to maximise returns. To the extent domestic equities are the chosen vehicle, the board could quickly become a significant shareholder in many firms, given the relatively small size of the domestic share market (market capitalisation of the New Zealand Stock Exchange in June 2000 was only about NZ$ 50 billion). This could lead to rent-seeking activity by firm owners, and greatly expand the responsibilities of board members as shareholders. In this regard, it may be difficult to find well-qualified people to sit on the board that are not in potential conflict-of-interest positions, although the government intends that such conflicts be stated at the outset prior to any appointment. In addition, the government would become a *de facto* owner of a much greater share of the economy, creating risks that mismanagement could have a large negative impact on the economy.

To address some of these issues as proposed, the board should be set up at arm's length from the government and its objectives and investment strategy should be transparent so as to be easily assessed. These moves would counteract any temptation to use the fund to finance government programmes; yet the question remains as to whether it would ultimately prove impossible to ring-fence the funds. Corporate governance problems would be lessened by investing a portion of funds outside the country.[15] It would also allow the fund to potentially capture higher returns, albeit with higher risk. The government could decide that some share (or indeed all) of the funds be invested passively (*e.g.* via index funds) and/ or that it would forsake its voting rights.

The New Zealand authorities are also encouraged to periodically review the Superannuation fund, ensuring that demographic, migration and other key assumptions are subject to rigorous sensitivity analysis. This should also include an assessment of risk arising from any equity investments, and ensuing implications for the contribution rate. In addition, the government should provide an analysis of the savings that could accrue to taxpayers by either lowering the replacement rate, increasing the retirement age or changing the indexation formula (or some combination thereof) of the public pension system. This would allow the public to make an informed decision on whether it would like to maintain the current generosity of the fund and its associated costs.

Unemployment and related benefits

As a whole there have been few changes to benefits (rates and eligibility requirements) since the previous Survey. Replacement rates remain very low by international standards, at 25 per cent of average wages, although they are paid indefinitely. In July 1999, sickness benefit rates and unemployment benefit rates were aligned to remove perverse incentives that had allowed unemployment beneficiaries to claim the higher sickness rate while facing less onerous work-test requirements. Meanwhile, the designated doctor scheme for sickness benefits was discontinued, with the individual's general practitioner now the sole certifier for the benefit (evaluation research indicated that the designated doctor seldom overturned an assessment by the person's own doctor).

The new government has introduced a *Social Security Amendment Bill* that will see three main changes take place in the direction of making it easier to maintain receipt of certain benefits:

- As of November 2000, the work capacity assessment for applicants and beneficiaries with a sickness, disability or injury ends. From 1 January 2001, the income thresholds for the disability allowance will also be increased.

- Beginning 1 December 2000, Community Work[16] will no longer be mandatory. Voluntary work will become a recognised activity for work-tested beneficiaries.

- From 1 July 2001, the community wage will be replaced with a separate unemployment benefit and sickness benefit. While the former will continue to have a work-test, the latter will not (in practice, the work-test for the sickness benefit has rarely been carried out).

Work disincentives are likely to arise from these changes. For example, the work-test changes for sickness beneficiaries create a risk of people moving from the unemployment to the sickness benefit. Moreover, there is a risk of a move to the relatively more generous invalids benefit, which is not work tested. Indeed, the steady rise in invalids benefit numbers – despite a tightening in eligibility criteria in 1998 – highlights the need to continuously monitor caseloads. The ability of invalidity benefit recipients to perform work should be assessed on a timely basis, perhaps via more intensive case management, since the primary focus has been on initial assessment and timely payments, rather than on determining what forms of work and or/training might be suitable to promote job attachment (Ministry of Social Policy, 1999). The government has announced plans to review work-test obligations for all benefits and their impact on various groups, a welcome step that should be carried out as soon as possible. When doing so, the government should maintain these obligations, while ensuring that the other forms of support, including the tax/benefit system, serve to promote labour-force attachment (see Chapter IV).

Active labour market programmes (ALMPs)

ALMPs can also play an important role in helping jobseekers find work. Although there have been no significant changes to the package of programmes offered to jobseekers, as noted above, participation in Community Work will shortly no longer be mandatory, and jobseekers will be encouraged, where necessary, to participate in voluntary work projects. This appears to contrast with findings that indicated that the programme was found useful by Regional Commissioners in helping jobseekers maintain work attachment and develop work-related skills (Department of Work and Income, 1999).

The current government intends to shift the focus more towards training, while maintaining the importance given to placement into unsubsidised jobs. New Zealand already spends more on labour market training than any other intervention (0.24 per cent of GDP in 1998-99 versus 0.04 per cent for subsidies to regular employment). In practice, therefore, it is not clear how much this shift in emphasis will differ from its predecessor. Jobseekers still receive individual back-to-work plans, which in principle are geared towards their specific needs, face work tests and are required to actively seek employment. As the unemployment rate falls, however, it is likely that the remaining caseload will be in need of more intensive assistance to get them ready for the labour market. Evaluation evidence suggests, however, that on-the-job training is more effective than more formal courses for many jobseekers, and it should be considered the main training avenue, using, if necessary, carefully controlled wage subsidies.

To keep long-term unemployment from becoming entrenched among disadvantaged jobseekers, the authorities have also introduced a Work Track programme, which seeks to place customers at risk of long-term unemployment into a managed job-search environment. This is a strategy that has been used successfully in Australia and the United States. The government also plans to assess how the public employment service (PES) assists clients, and whether there is a need for further flexibility by allowing offices more control over how they meet their region's needs. The PES intends to make greater use of outside contractors to make policy advice contestable and bring in outside expertise to deal with some groups, such as services delivered to the Maori and Pacific Islanders.

Evaluations have been carried out for a number of programmes, but, overall, their scope and rigour need to be enhanced to develop a menu of which programmes work best for client groups, and under what circumstances. As part of the process to improve evaluation, the previous government had established an employment evaluation strategy to be managed through the Centre for Operational Research and Evaluation (CORE). The current government has indicated that it will take the next year to develop evaluation methodologies, and it is urged to stick with this timetable. In particular, data collection should be a priority to monitor jobsearch, outcomes and programme impacts (this process is already underway with quarterly PES monitoring reports that detail trends on jobseekers and those receiving income support).

Income-related rents

Another key government platform is the introduction, from December 2000, of rent-setting in state-owned housing on the basis of household income. Currently, a market-based approach is used where financial assistance is provided by an Accommodation Supplement (AS) benefit.[17] This change will adversely affect labour mobility, probably tying some low-income households to their current residence rather than encouraging them to move to where job prospects are brightest. This results from the higher effective marginal tax rates under the scheme, and an expected excess demand for such housing. People with low income[18] will pay no more than 25 per cent of their net income on rent. Above this threshold, rent will increase by 50 per cent of additional net income until market rents are reached. In practice, this is unlikely ever to occur, given the goal of targeting housing on those with the lowest incomes. Equity issues will arise because no one will be forced out of existing housing to make way for those with lower incomes, which may place pressure on the government to lease more accommodation beyond the current 59 000 units (possibly driving up market rents) or to build more houses (potentially affecting housing prices). The government has indicated that any new housing units would be built in areas where labour demand is strongest. There will need to be greater financial contributions by the government over time, placing an additional burden on the budget (costs are expected to reach NZ$ 100 million per annum by 2003/04).

Other labour market issues

In March 2000, the minimum wage was increased by NZ$ 0.55 to NZ$ 7.55 per hour for those aged 20 and over, and for youths between 16 and 19, by 35 cents to NZ$ 4.55 per hour.[19] The government has also decided to review the minimum wage paid to youths and in principle has already decided to lower the threshold for eligibility for the adult minimum wage to age 18. However, this decision has not yet been put into effect. The review will determine whether youths (either on a training contract or exempt) should receive the adult rate or some fraction thereof. Raising the youth minimum wage clearly risks raising youth unemployment, and the government is urged to maintain the current differential. The government also increased the top marginal tax rate from 33 to 39 per cent on incomes above NZ$ 60 000. This reduces the incentive to upskill and work additional hours, and could contribute to a brain drain of highly skilled workers. Finally, the government is committed to reviewing the minimum code, which provides a floor to employment conditions, including the minimum wage, parental leave, employment protection and holidays. When doing so, it should consider any evidence as to how the current code has affected employment.

Product markets

Accident compensation

Workplace accident insurance had undergone a major change in July 1999 with the abolition of the government monopoly in the area and the introduction of a competitive private insurance market. The Employers' Account was closed, and the government set up a Residual Claims Account to fully fund claims established prior to July 1999 when the Accident Compensation Corporation (ACC) had been run on a pay-as-you-go basis.[20] The government also decided to fund claims from other accounts (other than Non-Earners) on a fully-funded basis. Recent legislation retains the full-funding objective but abolishes the provisions for the competitive market and re-establishes the public monopoly, returning to the ACC responsibility for covering workplace and other accidents. Not only is this a costly move (for example, the transactions costs of both setting up and dismantling private-sector contracts and transferring those in the private sector to the public body the latter estimated to be in the NZ$ 6 million range), but with only one year in operation, few economic grounds exist on which to overturn competition. The new government expressed concern that private insurance firms might have set rates at unsustainably low levels to attract clients, resulting in insufficient funds for rehabilitation measures, but there was little objective evidence that this was in fact the case.

The new structure is similar to that in place prior to competition. A new Employers' Account has been established, covering dependent employees, though it is being kept on a fully-funded basis. The self-employed, who briefly had the choice of a private insurer or the public Self-Employed Earner Account, now have only the latter. The average premium rate is actuarially based and has initially been set at NZ$ 1.11 per NZ$ 100 of insurable earnings, lower than the average of NZ$ 1.16 under competition (and NZ$ 1.47 under the previous monopoly), and varies by risk class (there are 115 risk pools based on the main activities of companies) to which each employer is allocated. The government indicates that 70 per cent of all firms now face lower fees. The system is not experience-rated on a firm's accident record, however, implying some worsening in terms of moral-hazard considerations. The government feels that the broader (than firm-level) categorisation will help reduce accident underreporting by firms and encourage them to focus on rehabilitation. Employers are, however, able to have their premiums adjusted to reflect their safety-management practices. Accredited employers (who have met a series of safety standards and financial requirements) also have the option of managing their own claims, or having an administrator do so in exchange for a premium discount.[21]

The intention to move to actuarially-based full funding for all activities of ACC should help to judge whether current premiums are sustainable over the longer term. Nevertheless, rates should be adjusted to more fully reflect employer accident and safety records, thus avoiding cross-subsidisation. However, it is not clear that the new regulatory framework will be as effective as risk-based premia in lowering overall costs. The government plans further legislation to address issues surrounding injury prevention, eligibility for cover and the nature of entitlements (such as treatment, rehabilitation and compensation). In doing so, it should review measures already undertaken by firms to prevent workplace injuries and disseminate them widely.

The Commerce Act

The government takes a light-handed approach to regulation, as outlined under the *Commerce Act* of 1986. This Act lays out general prohibitions that, to a large extent, apply to all businesses in New Zealand, thus setting a consistent set of standards and avoiding detailed industry-specific regulation where possible. The view is that sector participants, subject to market forces, are in the best position to determine the appropriate form of regulation. Nevertheless, in the face of rapidly evolving market conditions and dissatisfaction with how some sections have been interpreted by the courts, the government proposes the following changes:

– Section 36 is to be amended. It deals with preventing *dominant* firms from using their market power to prevent or eliminate competition. The section would be changed to treat those with a *substantial degree of power in the market*, in effect increasing the number of firms and markets subject to scrutiny. In addition, courts have been inconsistent as to whether the plaintiff must prove intent (that the dominant firm intended to use its market power for anti-competitive purposes; this would be clarified so that intent would be inferred from conduct).

– Section 47 on the threshold for business acquisitions will be changed. The current law prohibits mergers and acquisitions that create or strengthen a dominant position in a market but allows those that are likely to generate public benefits in excess of the anti-competitive detriment. It does not allow the Commerce Commission and courts to scrutinise mergers where significant market power can be obtained through a variety of different product/cost situations nor does it consider mergers that facilitate collusion. The proposed legislation would: restate that, contrary to recent jurisprudence, dominance means substantial market power (similar to Section 36); move the threshold away from single-firm dominance to encompass joint dominance (recognising that oligopolies could lead to a rise in prices); and clarify that substantial market power does not necessarily require a large market share.

– Penalties and remedies will be strengthened with a view to increasing deterrence. Currently, a maximum fine of NZ$ 5 million can be imposed. The proposal is to increase this to NZ$ 10 million, in addition to: strengthening the sanctions facing individuals while giving the courts discretion to prohibit worst offenders from serving as managers or directors in firms for up to five years; allowing the Commerce Commission to issue "cease and desist" orders similar to those used by the Federal Trade Commission in the United States; and changing statutory limitation periods so that they run from when the cause of action was discovered rather than from when it arose.

These proposals clearly represent a welcome strengthening of competition, and insofar as they follow current Australian legislation (Australian Trade Practices Act), investors may be guided in assessing how these changes affect the regulatory landscape. Mergers would continue to be subject to a public benefit test (other countries, such as Canada, have this test too). Allowing them to go through even when dominant positions are created can be important in a small country where economies of scale can be difficult to achieve. Nevertheless, when such decisions are made, the public benefits that are expected to accrue should be clearly presented and monitored. One area that is likely to come under review once the changes are made to the Commerce Act is the practice of common rate-setting in shipping. Currently, shipping lines are exempted from the Commerce Act in their rate-setting, and there are suspicions, particularly by importers, that collusive behaviour is having a detrimental impact on fees.

Electricity sector

The opening up of the electricity sector (see Box 2) has underscored the need to modify regulation of the market in step with the liberalisation. Against this background, the new government launched an inquiry into the suitability of the regulatory framework to guarantee that electricity is delivered in an efficient, reliable and environmentally sustainable manner. A number of concerns have arisen over time, namely that: the development of regulations has been piecemeal and may need to be revamped; Transpower's (the operator of the grid) price-setting lacks transparency, which is potentially troublesome given its monopoly position; distribution companies are effective monopolies in some regions, and this may be one reason why lower generation prices have not translated into lower retail prices (particularly in regions where such companies are held in trust by local authorities); the new profiling system for consumers helps to promote competition

---

Box 2.   Recent developments in the electricity sector

The Electricity Industry Reform Act of 1998 required ownership separation of lines and distribution from generation and retail by 2004. As part of this process:

- The government sold a 40 per cent share of the state-owned enterprise, Contact Energy (which produces 22 per cent of all energy) to US-based Edison Mission Energy and the remainder via a public floatation.

- The remaining generator, ECNZ, was then split into three competing state-owned enterprises (Genesis Power, Meridian Energy and Mighty River Power) on 1 April 1999. Since then, the private sector has been responsible for about 40 per cent of all power generated in New Zealand.

- Electricity companies were required to separate ownership of their line and supply businesses by the end of 2003, with a corporate separation by April 1999. In the event, complete ownership separation was completed by that date. Most companies chose to keep their distribution businesses (line businesses of which 30 exist) and sell their retail arms. Transmission remains under the sole power of the state-owned Transpower.

- To foster competition in the retail sector, a profiling system was set up, which allowed retailers to determine the cost of electricity sold to consumers based on average profiles of consumption, avoiding the need to install a costly use meter. The number of retailers plummeted from 40 to about 11 in May 2000, with about 5 per cent of customers switching retailers. The extent of competition varies by region, since some retailers compete in only one sector of the market (household or industrial). In February 2000, the cheapest retailer charged 12.92 cents per kWh relative to the average price of 14 cents per kWh, providing incentives for consumers to shop around. But slow billing practices and excessive delays in switching may prevent them from doing so on a timely basis.

---

in the retail sector, but other barriers may exist, including excessive delays in switching between providers; and the level of fixed versus variable charges may need some adjustment. A fixed component is necessary to recover sunk costs. Too high a fixed charge, however, lowers the incentives for companies to reduce costs and prices, while placing a relatively larger burden on lower-income households (and smaller companies).

The results of the inquiry were reported in June 2000 and form the basis of the government's "Power Package" announced in October with legislation planned for early 2001. This package outlines a set of guiding principles for the electricity industry to follow, of which the main features are:

- *Governance arrangements*: the current bodies will be replaced by an Electricity Governance Board, comprising a majority of independent members and having an independent chair. It will create rules for wholesale, transmission, distribution and retail that will be binding, and which are expected to be developed quickly.

- *Consumer Complaints Resolution System*: the industry is required to quickly set up an independent ombudsman and a process for the imposition of fines when there are breaches of rules related to consumer issues such as billing and disconnection.

- *Retail*: all retailers will have to offer at least one tariff with a fixed charge of no more than 10 per cent of the bill of the average consumer. The Governance Board will enforce protocols allowing consumers to switch retailers.

- *Wholesale*: services should be contestable wherever possible. Along these lines, the Governance Board is expected to implement a real-time market that will allow power users to adjust their use according to prices, helping to reduce peak demand.

- *Transmission and distribution*: individual line companies and Transpower (grid operator) will be placed under price control if they breach thresholds set out by the Commerce Commission. Price control would be of the form CPI-X. The separation of line companies from generation will also be relaxed slightly, allowing them to own generation of up to 2 per cent of the network's maximum demand (or 5 MW, whichever is greater). They can go beyond this restriction if the source of generation is carried out by a separate arms-length company and is from a new renewable energy source.

Given the underlying principle in New Zealand of a light-handed approach to regulation, allowing the industry to continue to find its own solutions is welcome, while maintaining the threat of direct regulation by the government, should it become necessary. In this regard, the Commerce Commission has announced a probe into electricity-line pricing, which will determine whether price controls should be applied. The authorities plan to carefully monitor the introduction of the new arrangements to ensure that they are carried out in a timely way. This is important since it will establish a more certain investment atmosphere. The government is opposed to further privatisation of the remaining state-owned generators (see below), despite the efficiency gains that could result.

Telecommunications

The tremendous changes[22] taking place in the telecommunications sector also led the government to launch an inquiry into regulation of this sector. Market trends towards convergence in what had been distinct services (fixed wire telephony, broadcasting, cable and wireless) with substantial vertical integration among market players, have raised questions as to whether the current sector-specific regulation is still appropriate. The aim of the review was to ensure that telecommunication services are offered in the most cost-effective, timely and innovative fashion and delivered on a fair and equitable basis.

The review's results were released in September 2000. It proposed light-handed industry-specific regulation to replace the current reliance on general competition law. Some of its major recommendations include: i) the establishment of an Electronic Communications Industry Forum, which would include all registered telecommunications and broadcasting network operators, in order to derive solutions to common industry problems; ii) the creation of an Electronic Communications Commissioner with clearly defined responsibilities and powers to regulate designated services where general competition law and self-regulation are found to be ineffective; and iii) the establishment of a designated list of services, which providers would be required to supply at an efficient price in a timely way.[23] The review also recommends that the entire regulatory framework be reviewed within six years, and regulated services at least every five. It anticipates that changes would lead to an annual net gain of NZ$ 44 million to the New Zealand economy.

The thrust of the recommendations appears to reflect a desire to keep sector-specific regulation to a minimum, based on industry-led decisions, while going to government regulators only when there are clear cases of abuse. This approach should help to keep compliance costs down while encouraging innovation, something that is an essential element underpinning the knowledge-based economy.

Electronic commerce and the Internet

On many fronts, New Zealand's Internet development appears favourable from an international perspective. Internet access costs are lower than the OECD average (suggesting adequate competition in the telecoms market) (Figure 17), while New Zealand ranks among the top 10 in the OECD by number of Internet

Figure 17. **Access costs and Internet usage**

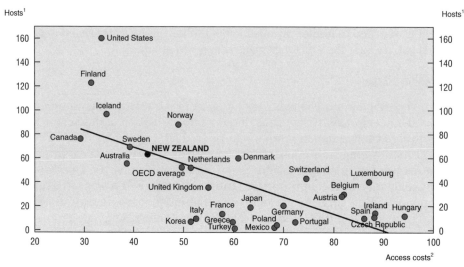

1. Number of Internet hosts per thousand inhabitants, July 1999.
2. Average cost of accessing the Internet for 20 hours per month at off-peak times, 1995-2000, in US$ PPP.
Source: OECD (*www.oecd.org/dsti/sti/it/cm*) and Telcordia Technologies (*wwww.netsizer.com*).

hosts. Furthermore, New Zealand has a large number of secure web servers, considered essential for the development of electronic commerce. In addition, over 40 per cent of households were estimated to have had a computer in early 2000, up about 10 percentage points from 1998.

However, surveys of firms by Ernst and Young (1999) and Deloitte Touche Tohmatsu (2000) on their use of electronic commerce indicate that many do not participate in this activity, nor do many consider an e-business strategy to be important to create or maintain a competitive advantage. This is particularly true for most small- and medium-sized enterprises. Statistics on the value of electronic commerce are scarce. Estimates from International Data Corporation place the value of e-commerce at about US$800 million in 2000 (or about 2 per cent of GDP), and this figure is expected to more than triple by 2004.

As noted above, one potential way to overcome some of the barriers that arise from New Zealand's relative isolation is via greater diffusion of new technology, including electronic commerce. To promote Internet use, the government has proposed a *Model Code for Consumer Protection in Electronic Commerce* to protect consumer interests. It would address such areas as privacy, complaints, exchange policies and security. A proposed *Electronic Transactions Bill* would remove impediments to Internet transactions, setting out the ground rules for electronic trade. Like other OECD countries, it is also examining the tax implications of e-commerce and has stated that the same taxation principles that guide conventional commerce should be applied. The government has also recently been auctioning off second- and third-generation spectrum licences. The process is still under way, but about NZ$ 100 million in bids have been received to date, a figure that rose rapidly once competition began for the third-generation blocks.

Producer board reform

Given the importance of primary industries in New Zealand output, it is encouraging that some small steps forward have been taken to reform producer boards since the 1999 Survey. While productivity growth has been relatively robust in agriculture (see above), and New Zealand is considered a world leader in some industries such as dairy,[24] considerable scope for further gains exist through the introduction of greater competition, while allowing prices to play a more central role in investment and output decisions.[25] Moreover, as monopolists, the boards face little competition that could spur product innovation and cost reductions.

In 1998, the government asked each Board to prepare a plan outlining how it would operate without special statutory backing. Since then, the greatest progress in dismantling the "single-desk structure" has come in the Raspberry sector, where the statutory body was abolished in 1999. Trading now operates under conventional law. Moves in the kiwifruit and apple and pear industries (Box 3) allow some limited competition, but no progress has been made with other major ones, including wool, pork, meat, game and dairy. A private-sector report prepared for the Wool Board by McKinsey (McKinsey and Co., 2000) urges radical changes in this sector. The wool industry has faced a long-term decline in prices and has not achieved the same productivity gains as close substitutes such as synthetic fibres. Moreover, the report notes that wool producers do not have significant market power, despite the traditional argument that a Board can exercise monopoly power against the rest of the world. The report therefore recommends dismantling the Wool Board and the single-desk structure, with part of its duties assumed by new commercial organisations that would market different qualities of wool. Producers could invest in these organisations or set up their own marketing channels, which would help to spur competition.

While welcome, these steps do not go far enough. In particular, the monopoly position of the boards generally remains unchallenged, and the reforms taken to date have resulted in only a small increase in the transparency of price setting. The government is urged to step up the pace of reform. Indeed, greater competition and product innovation from overseas competitors requires corresponding advances in New Zealand. This implies a substantially greater role for price mechanisms to influence supply decisions.

Box 3.   Producer board reform

The *Kiwifruit Industry Restructuring Act*, which came into effect on 1 April 2000, restructured the Kiwifruit Board into Zespri, a limited liability marketing company with tradable shares among growers, operating under a single-desk structure. It is not allowed to discriminate among growers nor diversify its activities.* Kiwifruit New Zealand was set up to enforce regulations.

The *Apple and Pear Industry Restructuring Act* followed a similar path, splitting operations into a marketing company, Enza, with a single-desk structure, and an Apple and Pear Board to enforce regulations. Enza, however, must operate its domestic activities at arm's length. The Board was also required to set up an independent export permits committee to allow growers to export product independently (as long as they do not undermine Enza). About 10 per cent of the 1999/2000 growing season's produce was exported independently.

The *Dairy Industry Restructuring Act*, which was not implemented, provided for deregulation contingent upon the merger of at least 75 per cent of shareholders in co-operative companies which represent at least 75 per cent of shares of the Dairy Board (along with Commerce Commission approval). It would have removed the single desk and seen the Dairy Board merged into a single entity, and, over time, seen the rights to designated quota markets become available on a competitive and neutral basis. The two largest dairy co-operatives have nevertheless agreed to develop a commercial structure to facilitate growth in the sector.

---

*   In addition, it must follow specified information disclosure rules.

Trade policy

The new government has set a clear preference for bilateral and regional agreements and away from unilateral moves. Thus, it has suspended unilateral tariff reductions that had been planned, which would have reduced them to zero by 2006. Instead, they will be maintained at current levels until July 2005. The future path of tariff reduction will be determined by a Tariff Review to be completed by December 2001, although the government still plans to meet its APEC commitments for free trade within that zone by 2010. Tariffs could be lowered in the meantime if the reductions are reciprocal or the result of trade agreements. Since New Zealand has been one of the most vocal OECD countries in espousing the benefits of tariff reduction, pushing its welfare-enhancing merit, the recent policy change is disappointing, though it is hard to criticise a country for adopting a more strategic approach to trade liberalisation when almost all other countries have persisted in such an approach for years. The tariff freeze is consistent with the country's WTO obligations, and roughly 95 per cent of its imports (by value) already enter the country duty free[26] (with tariff revenues only amounting to about NZ$ 186 million or about 0.6 per cent of the value of imports in 1999).

In November 2000, New Zealand and Singapore signed a bilateral free trade agreement (called the Closer Economic Partnership), with an objective to see it enter into force in January 2001. While the static gains are expected to be small in the area of goods – where most are already duty-free – it may be more significant for services (such as professional services). Moreover, New Zealand is seeking strategic gains by developing closer trade linkages with key Asian trading partners. In this regard, it is exploring a similar arrangement with Hong Kong while also examining the possibility of further links between the Closer Economic Relationship (CER) (the New Zealand and Australia accord) and the Asean Free Trade Area. A recent study found that all countries would gain from such a move in terms of productivity, investment, income and welfare (Davis *et al.*, 2000). Both New Zealand and Australia are also engaged in consultations on a possible Pacific Regional Trade Agreement (extending the CER).

As regards trade disputes, New Zealand (with Australia) has one outstanding issue currently residing with a WTO Panel on the tariffs imposed by the United States on US imports of lamb, which it claims is contrary to the United State's obligations under GATT and WTO safeguards. The Panel finding is due in December 2000. New Zealand was also a third party to two outstanding disputes, the first with Australia and the United States, launching a complaint about Korea's measures affecting the import of fish and chilled and frozen beef, and the second with the United States on the European Union's importation of wheat gluten. In each of these cases, WTO Panels ruled in favour of the plaintiffs.

In the area of foreign direct investment (FDI), New Zealand (along with Australia under the CER) agreed to raise the limit on overseas investment screening thresholds for non-land purchases from NZ$ 10 million to NZ$ 50 million in December 1999. The government also announced plans to implement in 2000 the 1998 Overseas Investment Amendment Act that would see investment divided into three types: non-land; farm land and land other than farm land. There are no plans to change the way non-land FDI would be treated, but the sale of farmland to non-residents would require two principles to be met: it must be offered for sale on the open market to New Zealanders; and it must meet a national interest test of "substantial and identifiable benefits" to New Zealand. It will be important that the latter be spelt out in a transparent manner that can be easily interpreted by potential overseas investors. The government has also announced an export credit scheme, which will come into effect in March 2001. It will be targeted on small and medium-sized enterprises and be reviewed after one year to ensure it is meeting the government's goals. While many OECD countries have such programmes, it is unfortunate that New Zealand, which has consistently promoted the value of free trade, feels compelled to consider their introduction in order to be on a level playing field. This action risks the diversion of public funds as a result of a potential rise in rent-seeking behaviour.

Financial support to enterprises: Industry New Zealand

New Zealand has typically shunned any form of industrial policy, preferring instead to make sure that the regulatory framework minimises compliance costs faced by firms, which in itself is conducive to attracting and promoting business development. The new government seeks to create a partnership approach with industry. It has therefore established Industry New Zealand (INZ), with the main task of identifying opportunities for economic and regional development. At the same time, INZ will play a central role in co-ordinating policies that focus on regional development across Ministries. This one-stop-shop approach could help reduce overlap and costs and encourage greater coherence in policy-making and delivery.

The government has allocated NZ$ 331 million over the next four years to fund programmes in this area. Initially, four new programmes have been established, and funding was increased for some existing initiatives (outlined in Box 4). Industry New Zealand has also taken other incentive schemes, most notably the BIZ programme that operates a network of 46 providers of free business management training services. To supplement this work, INZ will create a national database to match investors with investment opportunities.

The latest budget introduced an additional NZ$ 43.6 million to enhance innovation in the economy. Currently, about 0.6 per cent of GDP is allocated to research, and the government would like to see this rise to about 0.8 per cent by 2010, requiring an injection of additional NZ$ 20 million per year. The government has stressed that it is not interested in trying to "pick winners", and there appears to be little appetite by the private sector for such a strategy. The new programmes are relatively small and should not unduly distort the marketplace. Nevertheless, the government should make eligibility conditions for the schemes transparent, along with a mandate to evaluate their effectiveness, each of which should help to reduce rent-seeking behaviour. Evaluation (such as cost-benefit analysis) would also allow the creation of a "what works" list of initiatives that could be diffused across regions, while helping to determine their potential to boost productivity. Overall, INZ oversees a number of economic and regional development programmes and can potentially play an important role in improving their co-ordination and delivery. While there is a risk of funds being wasted, the amount of money targeted towards enterprises is relatively small, and the creation of an appropriate monitoring and evaluation framework would help to minimise this possibility. Moreover, given that there is substantial uncertainty on the impact of such policies, evaluation would help to build up a body of evidence in the area. Given this

---

Box 4. Financial support to enterprises

Enterprise Awards Scheme. This programme offers a minimum of 250 grants of a maximum of NZ$ 10 000 each to provide early-stage financing (seed money) to entrepreneurs and small-business owners.

Regional Partnerships Programme. This scheme is designated to improve regional economies by encouraging partnerships of local government, community and business groups. Up to NZ$ 100 000 will be provided for early planning, with subsequent grants of a similar size to implement the programmes, and up to NZ$ 2 million for major initiatives.

Investment Ready Scheme. This programme provides small businesses with training and information via workshops and seminars on how to raise capital, while helping them leverage up to NZ$ 5 million in capital.

R&D grants. Roughly NZ$ 12 million per annum has been set aside for this new programme (begun 1 September) that will fund up to a third of R&D costs of a particular project. Initially, the government had indicated that it would consider full tax deductibility of R&D investments, but ultimately chose a grants approach, given the possible fiscal costs of tax deductions and the difficulty in verifying eligibility. R&D grants are available to firms during their start-up (or pre-profit) phase, which is considered an advantage by the government because it injects cash quickly.

Technology New Zealand. The government has also announced additional funding of NZ$ 8.5 million (to NZ$ 24.7 million) for this programme that provides matching funding to firms to take up, use and develop new technology. The remaining increase in funds will be allocated to a variety of research institutes such as the *New Economy Research Fund* (which explores new areas of high potential); and the *Marsden Fund* (supports basic research that meets international standards of excellence); and towards research in industry, social policy, health, government and the environment.

---

uncertainty, a positive pay-off to such expenditures cannot be ruled out, but it is unlikely to be large and will, to some extent, be contingent on how well INZ manages the schemes.

Meanwhile, the authorities have also implemented a series of initiatives to help small- and medium-sized enterprises find risk capital. *First*, a New Capital Market has been set up as part of the New Zealand Stock Exchange. It allows investors to seek capital at a lower cost (see below). *Second*, rules have been relaxed on preprospectus publicity, allowing small investors to test the water before committing to a public offer. *Third*, the Securities Commission has made exemptions to venture capital schemes, allowing local authorities and economic development agencies to create a national electronic investment service to registered investors via the Internet.

Financial sector

The financial sector was last reviewed in detail in the 1998 *Economic Survey of New Zealand*. It noted that sweeping reforms from 1984 onwards had helped the financial sector obtain substantial gains: enhanced banking efficiency with lower costs and interest margins; higher service quality and greater product variety; and improvements in bank balance sheets and asset quality. The success of these market-based reforms was reflected in the resilience the sector showed in weathering the Asian crisis, the recession in 1998, and, more recently, the sharp depreciation of the currency.

As a whole, developments in 1999 continued building on trends that had already been observed. Registered banks remained the most important intermediaries in the financial sector with about 70 per cent of total assets. The five largest of the 18 registered banks accounted for 87 per cent of total bank assets. Four are majority owned and controlled by Australian banks. Nevertheless, the market remained competitive as: new businesses entered the mortgage market; retailers investigated the possibility of offering banking services; and niche organisations such as credit unions actively sought to increase market share.[27] As a result, bank interest margins declined to 2.42 per cent in 1999, a fall of 13 basis points from 1998. Asset quality remained high, however, with the Basel capital adequacy ratio for the banking sector at 10.3 per cent. At the same time, underlying profit improved as revenues increased, due to greater loan activity from the economic upswing, and as operating expenses remained flat. Institutions contained costs via rationalisation of branch networks, some centralisation of staff (for example, a move of some back office support to Australian parent banks), and greater use of new technology. Indeed, electronic banking gathered steam in 1999, with all five major retail banks offering such services, whereas one year earlier only one bank had offered them. Nevertheless, as noted above, these developments have not been reflected in better sectoral productivity performance, and part of the reason is undoubtedly measurement difficulties.

Given the dominance of foreign banks, a proposal is currently being considered by the government to create a "People's Bank", as a commercial initiative of New Zealand Post, a state-owned enterprise with branches throughout the country. It is expected that the bank would tailor its activities to be attractive to customers dissatisfied with their current bank such as low-income people who may not have adequate access to financial services. If created, the authorities should ensure that the bank is not used for political purposes (that deposits are not directed towards funding regional programmes) and that it is run on a strictly commercial basis. It should be incorporated as a bank and subject to standard supervisory requirements. If this avenue is not pursued, at a minimum there should be no implicit or explicit government guarantee of deposits, which would create an uneven playing field in the banking sector and potentially lead to moral hazard problems.

In the securities market, the New Capital Market (NCM) of the New Zealand Stock Exchange (NZSE) began operating in March 2000. It aims to improve access to investment capital for small- and medium-sized enterprises, and in particular, those that are high-risk but potentially high-growth. It allows owners to raise between NZ$ 400 000 and NZ$ 600 000 in ordinary share capital up to a total investment of NZ$ I million. Companies are listed on the NZSE, but face less costly listing requirements (via standardised documents and simplified processes) and certain exemptions. For example, an initial public offering on the NCM is exempt from certain Securities Regulations requirements.[28] Currently, three companies are listed on the NCM. In addition, the owners of the New Zealand Stock Exchange are currently examining whether to merge with the Australian Stock Exchange, following the moves offshore of a number of large companies. This would require harmonisation of their standards.

Supervision

An important difference between New Zealand and most other OECD countries in the regulation of financial institutions is its "light-handed" approach, based on strong information disclosure requirements to encourage market discipline. There are a number of different regulators, including the Reserve Bank of New Zealand (RBNZ) which monitors registered banks, the Securities Commission which monitors investment markets and so on.[29] To facilitate co-ordination between regulators, a Financial Regulators Co-ordination Group consisting of representatives from the Reserve Bank, the New Zealand Securities Commission, the Government Actuary and the Registrar of Companies has been established. The blurring of national borders and the entry of new institutions nevertheless create challenges for supervision. Greater co-ordination and integration in supervision between bank and non-bank institutions may be necessary to ensure that similar products are regulated on a consistent basis. In addition, new technology and Internet banking give rise to concerns about consumer protection. With electronic banking law and regulations not fully developed, online customers may be more susceptible to fraud and other criminal activities. While it is difficult to get a sense of how widespread a problem this might be (or potentially could become), regulators will have to monitor new developments closely and assess the adequacy of current regulations.

Banks must publish quarterly statements on a globally consolidated basis. These contain a wide range of information on their financial positions and risk profiles, including their credit ratings where applicable. In principle, the disclosure regime is designed to: encourage banks to monitor and manage their banking risks and gear bank directors to take ultimate responsibility for such risks; and provide depositors and other creditors with high-quality and timely information. Nevertheless, full disclosure does not always imply greater clarity. For example, the use of increasingly sophisticated financial instruments and derivatives suggests retail investors in particular may find it difficult to interpret the risk position of an individual bank on the basis of its balance sheet. In part to overcome this problem the RBNZ plans to introduce a mandatory credit rating requirement for banks. This will provide retail investors with a simple measure of each bank's creditworthiness. The quality and type of information will probably have to continue to evolve to ensure that non-specialists can adequately interpret an institution's financial position.

An important element underlying the supervisory framework is the lack of any deposit insurance (indeed, for any financial institution). The RBNZ feels that the most appropriate response to a failure would be for shareholders and creditors to bear those losses, although it can intervene should a registered bank experience financial distress that poses a significant threat to the financial system. It also realises that a bank failure, (even if all large banks are foreign-owned), could have an adverse impact on the banking system, and the economy.[30] It is therefore exploring different options on how to handle such a potential situation. One proposal would see a failed bank placed under statutory management with a portion of its net assets frozen to re-capitalise the bank (the so-called "haircut" approach). This would, however, be challenging to carry out in practice, because it would require a quick assessment by the RBNZ on the state of an institution's assets and liabilities, and their ownership. This can be difficult because under existing legislation banks can choose to incorporate locally as a subsidiary, or as a branch. In some cases, foreign legislation gives domestic depositors priority in the event of a wind-up (for example, Australia). The RBNZ therefore proposes that banks of system-wide importance, banks with significant retail deposits from countries that do not provide equal protection to creditors in the wind-up,[31] and those from nations where disclosure is not comparable to that in New Zealand, be required to incorporate locally to allow it to lay a claim on domestic assets in the event of a failure.

Proposals currently before the Basel Committee on Banking Supervision on a new capital adequacy framework also pose a challenge to the New Zealand supervisory regime. In many areas, New Zealand follows the core principles on banking supervision closely, for example on capital adequacy. Nevertheless, with its emphasis on a market-based disciplinary approach, the RBNZ has in some cases adopted methods that are different from the Core Principles. For example, the RBNZ does not carry out inspections.[32] If strict compliance with the principles were to be linked to capital risk weights, then New Zealand banks could be required to set aside greater reserves, effectively raising the cost of capital in the country. While the outcome of these international discussions is still underway, New Zealand's approach to supervision should not be dismissed out of hand. It is probably not relevant for larger countries, but it has worked well for New Zealand, which has a highly concentrated market, good corporate governance and accounting standards, a large share of banks owned by investors in countries where regulatory regimes are adequate and parent banks that are well capitalised.

In the securities sector, four initiatives to modify supervision are under-way. *First*, a review of the 1983 Securities Regulations has been launched with a first-stage goal to simplify regulations and reduce repetition. A second stage will then examine whether gaps in legislation have arisen, given the rapid changes seen in the sector in product innovation, convergence, globalisation and informa-tion technology. *Second*, the government is reviewing insider-trading provisions. One area under consideration is whether to make insider-trading a criminal offence. Currently, only civil remedies are possible (up to three times the gain rea-lised or loss avoided). There is a perception that regulatory weaknesses such as these may have led to less enthusiastic participation of domestic and interna-tional investors in the stock market. *Third*, the authorities intend to legislate a Takeovers Code to protect minority shareholders, which would supplant the Take-over Code Regime run by the NZSE since 1994. *Fourth*, there is a programme under way to better co-ordinate the activities of the various agencies with duties relating to the securities market.

Public sector

Health care

An important part of the government's agenda is to radically overhaul the health-care system. This is an area where arguably no OECD country has yet found the most effective system that balances economic and social goals. An underlying motivation was to improve the overall health status of the population and ensure fair access to services, in addition to simplifying the complex system of account-ability. While current expenditures are about what would be expected given income levels (Figure 18), fiscal costs are expected to rise rapidly in the middle of the next decade (see Figure 16 above). In the early 1990s, the government had introduced a model that saw a split between purchasers of health-care services and providers in order to enhance efficiency and contain rising costs. The current government seeks to move away from this arrangement towards a co-operative system (a process already underway in some areas; see below). Thus, the Health Funding Authority (HFA), responsible for the public funding of all healthcare ser-vices, and the Hospital and Health Services (HHS), which ran the public hospitals, will terminate their operations as of 30 November 2000. Their functions will be partially transferred to the Ministry of Health and newly created District Health Boards (DHBs), of which 21 are contemplated, each having a defined district (and therefore population) to whom they are responsible (Box 5).

With the advent of the DHBs, and changes to the structure of the health-care system, accountability lines are changing significantly. For example, the Min-istry of Health will complement its current role in setting health policy with an increased responsibility for monitoring developments. Previously, that task had

Figure 18.   **Health-care expenditures and GDP per capita**
At current PPPs, 1998

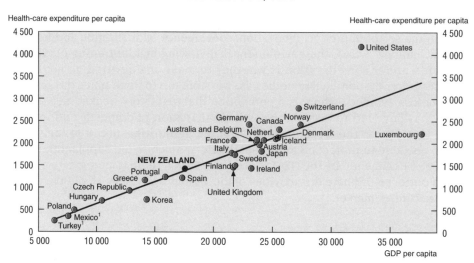

1.   1997.
Source: OECD Health Data 2000.

been shared across a number of organisations, including the Crown Company Monitoring Advisory Unit (CCMAU), the Ministry of Health and the Treasury. The goal is to define more clearly the role for each actor in the system and reduce contractual costs. The new format may improve accountability and therefore delivery. But it risks not having an independent assessment of activities, a role that had existed under the CCMAU. Nor is it clear that transactions costs will fall. Careful implementation of the DHBs, and monitoring of hospitals' financial performance, will be necessary.

Probably the most fundamental change is the shift away from the purchaser/provider split. While this process had already begun – the HFA began to move into a funding role, encouraging collaborative relationships with providers (CCMAU, 1999) – DHBs are allowed to do both as they see fit. The underlying objective is to allow them greater flexibility in managing their funds, while potentially reducing the transactions costs associated with contracting-out. A danger exists, however, that they might favour the use of their own facilities (hospitals) over outside providers who may be able to deliver the service more efficiently. Part of the responsibility of the Advisory Committees (see Box 5) is to ensure that this does not happen, although their advice need not be followed. Another line of accountability is the elected representatives on the board, who in theory should reflect stakeholder interests, although they could also become captive to vested

---

Box 5.   Role and structure of the District Health Boards (DHBs)

Initially, DHBs will reflect the Hospital and Health Services Boards (with some newly appointed members). Each DHB will have a chief executive and a board with seven elected members (via local elections, the first set for October 2001) and up to four members appointed by the Minister. The goal is to ensure that the boards of the DHBs adequately reflect the population of the area (each is expected to have at least two Maori members). DHBs will be charged with the following tasks:

- Improve, promote and protect the health of a geographically defined population, as well as promoting the health, well-being and independence of people with disabilities;
- Reduce disparities in health and independence;
- Establish strategic and operational plans;
- Build relationships with providers;
- Fund various primary health-care and disability-support services;
- Provide a range of health services, including public health services, hospital services and some community services (taken over from the existing Hospital and Health Services).

The DHBs will have three advisory committees to provide advice to their boards:

- A Health Improvement Advisory Committee to provide advice on the mix and range of services that will best meet local health-improvement objectives;
- A Hospital Governance Advisory Committee to advise on the performance of hospitals and related DHB-owned services;
- A Disability Support Advisory Committee to provide advice on issues facing people with disabilities and how they can best be managed by the DHB.

These committees are expected to ensure that when the DHB acts as both purchaser and provider, it takes the most appropriate decisions to meet objectives. To ensure consistency in the availability, access, appropriateness and quality of services across all DHBs, they each have to follow guidelines set out under the New Zealand Health Strategy and New Zealand Disability Strategy. To ensure accountability, DHBs have a strategic plan with a five to ten-year focus, an annual operating plan and monthly and quarterly reports against this annual plan.

---

interests. This is an area, therefore, that needs to be monitored vigilantly, since by default the government is left to deal with cost overruns. Fiscal risks will be managed, in part, by giving DHBs additional financial responsibilities over time in a planned manner, allowing them to become familiar with their tasks before expanding

---

them, while continually monitoring their performance via annual plans. A concern here is that, given the anticipated lags before the DHBs start full operation, there may be less emphasis on evaluation of the impact of policy. Careful planning and evaluation is therefore necessary to assess whether the new arrangements help to contain costs and achieve policy objectives. In addition, in the spirit of co-operation, mechanisms to diffuse promising DHB initiatives should be set up.

One way to contain costs is through greater emphasis on primary care. Reform in this area, as in many other OECD countries, is high on the policy agenda. A key objective is to move towards capitation funding (paying doctors a per-patient fee that varies by age gender, ethnic mix, *etc.*) as opposed to fee-for-service. This would also help to better integrate service delivery. A major constraint, however, is that the government only partly subsidises general practitioner (GP) fees, leaving it with little leverage. Currently, about 15 per cent of GPs receive such a payment. DHBs are also expected to create service arrangements with primary care organisations (that group doctors and other medical professionals together) and encourage people within districts to become a member of one, also with an eye to improving the integration of health-care delivery.

Another government goal is to reduce waiting times for elective services. It has earmarked NZ$ 74 million a year for this effort. The goal is to have surgery take place before patients potentially reach distress or incapacity. New standards include the assessment of people requiring surgery and a commitment to provide it within six months for anyone assessed as meeting a predetermined level of ability to benefit. Resource constraints will to some extent dictate whether these goals are met. But so too will be the accountability arrangements put in place by the DHBs and specialists, and the liaison with GPs.

Education

Fostering better education outcomes is essential to improve the skills base, meet the needs of a knowledge-based economy and raise productivity performance. New Zealand lags most G7 countries in educational attainment (Figure 19). Moreover, the latest Adult Literacy Survey (ALS) indicates that New Zealand fares relatively poorly in literacy compared with many other OECD countries (OECD, 2000 *c*), and some observers allege that there is a skills shortage. Promising signs exist that this situation may improve: for example, entry rates into tertiary education are the highest among the countries surveyed (Figure 20), although enrolment rates appear to have stabilised in the mid-1990s. In addition, the number of hours of continuing education and training by adults is the highest among the 11 countries surveyed in the ALS (Figure 21). These statistics, however, mask the widely differing performance of the Maori and Pacific Islander groups, each of whom are over-represented in lower educational attainment and under-represented in tertiary level enrolments.[33] Given that they are expected to comprise

Figure 19.   **Distribution of the adult population by level of educational attainment**
1998

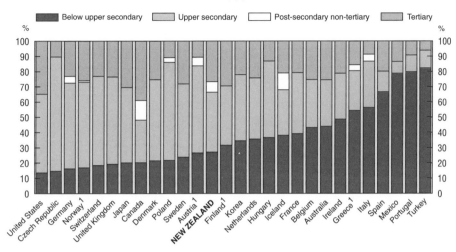

1.   1997.
Source: OECD (2000*c*).

Figure 20.   **Net entry rates for tertiary education**[1]
1998

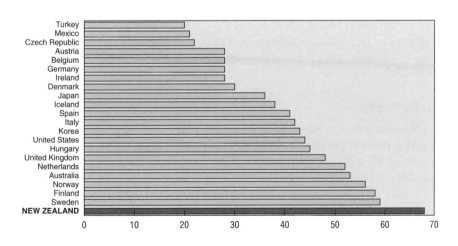

1.   Net entry rates are defined as the proportion of new entrants to tertiary education relative to the total population.
Includes entry rates only into tertiary education institutions that lead to a degree.
Source: OECD (2000*c*).

Figure 21. **Job-related education and training per employee**[1]
1994-1995

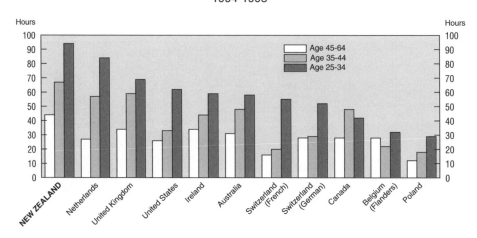

1. Mean number of hours per employee is equal to mean number of hours in job-related continuing education and training per participant multiplied by participation rate divided by 100.
Source: OECD (2000*c*).

a much larger share of the population over time,[34] improving their skill levels takes on increasing importance. More generally, about one quarter of youths aged 16 and 17 are not in education, training or full-time work, and this ratio remained constant in the 1990s. Although the new government plans to boost spending in the education sector substantially (over NZ$ 200 million in new initiatives, including those to close the gaps), the widening income distribution (see above) encourages upskilling.

Recent reforms

The government has also announced a host of changes to the education system. The overall direction is to reduce competition, and choice, and focus on strengthening all state schools with a view to improving outcomes, particularly for Maori and Pacific Islanders.

– *First,* the government has ended the bulk funding initiative that allowed the roughly 30 per cent of schools that had been participating in the programme more flexibility on financing their staffing structures. By July 2001, all must return to central funding. The authorities have injected more funds into education to improve the discretionary resources available to most schools, which they see as more equitable, and have indexed operating grants to inflation. While only in place since 1998, early results from bulk funding were promising, suggesting that schools were using the funds to improve the quality of education (Education Review Office, 2000). The government should study these results to see if any further innovations could be more generally implemented in schools. Along these lines, it has already decided to give schools greater flexibility to recruit and remunerate staff above standard entitlements.

– *Second*, the government has re-introduced school zoning. Parents previously had the right to send their children to any state-funded school, in effect, allowing them to "vote with their feet", with schools competing for the best students and deciding whom to admit. Now, families are given priority access to schools in their local areas, while any remaining places for "out-of-zone" students are allocated on a lottery basis. While the previous system may have led schools in low-income areas to lose students, the process highlighted schools with relatively poor performance records. This could then have enabled the authorities to target more assistance towards them to improve their quality. A periodic assessment of school performance will be necessary to ensure that the government's goal of improving the quality of education at each school is met.

– *Third*, the government has stabilised tertiary education tuition fees for the 2001 academic year at their 2000 level, costing an additional NZ$ 110 million over four financial years. Similar to the increased generosity of the student loan programme (see below), this broadly targeted measure would seem to do little to improve access of individuals who face the greatest barriers.

– *Fourth*, the National Qualifications Framework (NQF), initiated in 1993, has to date focused on vocational qualifications. In 2003, all senior secondary school qualifications will be recorded under the NQF. This should improve the transition to tertiary institutions and facilitate the transfer of credits between qualifications.

– *Fifth*, the government is piloting a Modern Apprenticeship programme, which will be introduced nationwide in 2001. This programme seeks to provide an alternative route into the labour market for youths aged 16 and 17, which, as noted above, have a high drop-out rate from school. Training results in qualifications registered under the NQF. This promising initiative should be carefully monitored and evaluated. The government will also proceed with a review of industry training to consider whether the current system is meeting the needs of industry and employees.

– *Finally*, the government has initiated the creation of an Education Council, which will serve as a professional body for teacher certification and standards setting.

Student loans

A key election platform of the new government was to increase the generosity of the student-loan scheme, which will result, not surprisingly, in higher fiscal costs. Since the beginning of 2000, full-time students (and part-time students earning less than NZ$ 24 596) no longer pay any interest on their government loans while studying. Previously, interest was charged on a daily basis from the start of the loan and compounded annually. Students continue to begin repayments on an (gross) income-contingent basis, with the threshold set at NZ$ 14 768 above which they pay 10 cents on each dollar earned, but now at least 50 per cent of repayments will go to repay principal (effectively eliminating interest payments in some cases). In addition, the amount that can be borrowed for course-related costs was increased from NZ$ 500 to NZ$ 1 000. These changes are estimated to cost NZ$ 400 million over a four-year period, taking money away from areas where it might have been more productively spent. Moreover, it is poorly targeted, benefiting all students regardless of their income situation.

The Office of the Controller and Auditor General (2000*a*) has highlighted a number of risks associated with the scheme. The most evident is the growth of the student loans asset on the government's balance sheet, and the associated credit risk that could negatively affect sovereign bond ratings. In addition, it remarks that evidence is lacking on the socio-economic impact of the scheme, including whether it has improved access to tertiary education and outcomes. Further study is therefore imperative to determine: *i)* the deadweight losses of the scheme (whether students could have financed education themselves); *ii)* whether it has encouraged greater take-up by students from low-income families; *iii)* whether recent changes make it even more favourable to borrow the maximum and leave the country when studying is complete;[35] and finally, *iv)* the interaction of government subsidy rates for tertiary education and loan take-up. The government has indicated that it will review the interest-rate-setting methodology, but it should look urgently at other aspects of the scheme as well.

Expenditure control

As noted in Chapter II, the cornerstone underlying the setting of fiscal policy in New Zealand is the *Fiscal Responsibility Act* (FRA) of 1994, which obliges the government to follow a set of legislative principles for responsible fiscal management – see Box 2 in OECD (1999*a*). New Zealand places strong emphasis on aggregate expenditure control and has put in place a series of reports that allow its progress to be tracked carefully. In addition, the government uses accrual accounting, which attributes revenues and expenditures over the years when they are earned or disbursed. This allows a better indication to Ministers and Parliament of where resources are going and how they are being used.

In carrying out their responsibilities under the FRA, Ministers decide upon aggregate spending, revenue and debt targets, taking into account new policy priorities, which are presented in the Budget Policy Statement. This so-called strategic phase is then followed by a planning and review process for the budget submission of ministries, which, within the overall envelope, make decisions on individual spending proposals. These proposals contain two distinct elements:

- Budget baseline submissions. This sets out the base level of funding over a four-year period. The nominal level of this baseline spending is fixed, forcing departments to make efficiency gains equal to the rate of inflation. There are two exceptions to this rule: welfare benefit spending, where automatic inflation adjustments and update forecasts are tailored into baseline spending, and health and education baselines, which are adjusted for demographic changes.

- Budget initiative submissions. These include new policy proposals and any increase in funding for existing expenditures. The expected costs, benefits and risks for each must be stated. The overall constraint is set by the fiscal provision (which over the next three years is set at NZ$ 5.9 billion; see Chapter II). These are funds set aside for the impact of government policy decisions on top of existing baselines.

Very little flexibility exists to re-allocate spending at the central level once appropriations for departments and programmes have been decided upon.[36] However, government departments have considerable flexibility on how to spend their allotted funds. Indeed, ministers are able to reallocate expenditures (up to 5 per cent) between output classes, and potentially greater amounts with approval of Parliament. Expenditures are tracked against targets over a four-year period and are reported in the Economic and Fiscal Updates. In addition to monitoring and reporting on baseline spending and underlying expense trends, the Updates include separate tracking of expenditures resulting from specific government policy decisions.

The framework has a number of strengths. It sets a cap on expenditures that, in principle must be met, while the top-down approach ensures that funds are allocated in a manner that reflects the government's priorities. In addition, the limited ability to shift funding across appropriations, along with the fixed nominal baseline, encourage Ministers to review programmes in their portfolios and to (re)allocate funds to areas that are considered the most important. Moreover, there has been a shift away from defining detailed input controls, allowing them greater flexibility to manage resources.

Nevertheless, this process is weakened because analysis of expenditures on specific programmes has generally received much less focus. Indeed, there has been no structure to evaluate expenditures consistently at the central level. A re-allocation of funds is therefore seldom based on rigorous evaluation of a programme to determine whether it is meeting its intended goals. Nor is it evaluated as to its ability to improve the productive capacity of the economy. The Audit Office notes that measurable outcomes are not well articulated, nor are they required to be reported (including how they compared with plans).[37] Policy co-ordination and coherence across departments is also weak.

To better assess government spending, the authorities recently announced a *Value for Money Initiative*. Ministers are expected to identify spending within each department for further examination, which may involve both evaluation and benchmarking activities. A comprehensive assessment of the effectiveness of *all* current expenditures, however, will not be carried out, despite the near decade-long span since the last such effort. The 2000 Budget also mandates departments to state how and when all *new* funding proposals will be evaluated. It is important that this not be an *ad hoc* process, but one that becomes entrenched in the policy-making phase to ensure that policies and their expected outcomes are well defined and directed towards areas that will most improve the economy's productive capacity. Critics have noted that a one-year budget cycle does not easily mesh with an evaluation, which usually requires a medium-term focus. However, not only will a mandate to evaluate programmes help to focus them on outcomes, but over time a wealth of evidence would also be built up that could be used to better tailor and target programmes. To address policy coherence, the 1999 Budget process had seen Ministers organised into teams based on the government's strategic priorities. They then decided collectively on the allocation within their separate ministries that would achieve the priorities. This process was not, however, used for the 2000 Budget. The government should consider its re-introduction.

Privatisation

The government has ruled out any further privatisation of state assets during its term of office. While the extent of privatisation has been impressive (since reforms began, over NZ$ 16 billion in assets have been spun-off), there remain several assets that could be sold. For example, while the government completed the privatisation of Contact Energy (see Box 2), this still leaves the Crown with significant holdings in the generation sector. Overall, there are 17 remaining state-owned enterprises with assets of about NZ$ 10 billion in aggregate. Many, such as Television New Zealand, have specific non-commercial objectives. Even where the government does not want to relinquish control of an enterprise, a public floatation of some shares might help to introduce a more market-based approach into its governance.

Environment

The coalition government has a broad agenda on environmental issues, in part stemming from domestic concerns over: the loss of biodiversity; climate change; biotechnology; and cost-effective environmental legislation. The main legislation for the environment is the Resource Management Act (RMA). An RMA Amendment Act is currently being considered by local authorities that would reduce unnecessary delays and costs in the RMA process (the 1998 Economic Survey noted that such costs were estimated to account for as much as 5 per cent of business costs). Indeed, an overriding objective should be to minimise compliance costs, while achieving environmental goals. One way to do so would be to develop a set of best practices for businesses and prospective investors on how to deal with environmental concerns and to ensure that local councils interpret the RMA in a consistent manner.

In the area of climate change, the authorities have announced that they will ratify the Kyoto Protocol by mid-2002. This comes against the backdrop of a greater reliance on fossil fuels over the past decade, which saw gross carbon dioxide emissions from the energy sector increase by 19 per cent between 1990 and 1999. By contrast, methane emissions have trended downwards, with a cumulative decline of about 5 per cent, largely a result of agricultural reforms and smaller herd sizes. The government should ensure that greater use of economic instruments – carbon taxes and emissions permit trading, for example – and the systematic application of the user and polluter pays principles form an integral part of its strategy to meet Kyoto targets. A National Energy Efficiency and Conservation Strategy Act also came into effect in May 2000. The details are to be worked out by April 2001, but it is expected to include guidelines on how to promote energy efficiency, conservation and the use of renewable energy sources, as well as setting targets to be achieved. When considered, the overall compliance costs associated with this Act and the RMA should be examined.

Another challenging area for New Zealand is biodiversity. The government has introduced a new Biodiversity Strategy, setting out national goals to halt the decline in biodiversity, and has committed close to NZ$ 200 million over the next five years to achieve them. Furthermore, it has established a Royal Commission into Genetic Modification to determine how New Zealand should address this issue. On the one hand, the authorities are weighing whether to adopt a "green" approach, favouring organically grown products. On the other, they are worried about whether this would preclude a move towards a more knowledge-based economy that might come from greater use of advanced technologies. This is considered a very important issue, given the importance of agriculture to the economy. Based on a precautionary principle, over the duration of the inquiry (one year to June 2001), a voluntary moratorium on field research and the release of genetically modified organisms has been implemented. In view of the importance of the fishing industry, the government has also taken action to protect some fish species. For example, following the severe depletion of orange roughy stocks, the government once again used a precautionary principle to cut allowable catches under its Quota Management System. It has also announced the development of an "Oceans Policy" to address issues arising from managing the marine environment.

Summary and recommendations for further action

While the positive results that have stemmed from the reform process have not met expectations, the challenge for the government is to continue to refine and reinvigorate the reform process to improve the quality of factor inputs and boost the productive capacity of the economy. Only through greater productivity advances will the relative standard of living of New Zealanders improve, and gaps between some members of society narrow. The government should therefore (Table 20):

Ensure that changes to labour market and social programmes boost work incentives

- The presumption should be that most beneficiaries can work, and case management should be directed towards achieving that goal. In general, this also requires the maintenance of suitable work tests, that active labour market programmes keep abreast of changing market conditions (requiring rigorous evaluation of their impact), while avoiding welfare traps from elevated marginal effective tax rates. In this latter area, the recently introduced income-related rents programme risks hampering labour mobility. Raising the minimum wage could also adversely affect the job prospects of the lower skilled, and large increases should be resisted.

- Wage bargains under the new industrial relations framework should be kept in line with productivity developments (the government could serve a useful signalling role in this regard in its own wage settlements with workers) and the legislation will have to be carefully monitored to ensure that its provisions do not unduly raise compliance costs (and potentially hamper job growth).

- Partial pre-funding of public pensions poses a number of challenges to the government. When deciding whether to finance the fund, the government should consider the relative merits of further tax reduction in lieu of partial pre-funding. If implemented it should determine the least distortionary manner in which funding should occur. The fund would also need to be run, as proposed by the government, at arm's length with clear investment objectives, and careful attention would need to be paid to corporate governance issues.

Bolster product market reforms

- Progress in producer board reform remains slow and needs to be advanced, given the importance of the primary sector. Indeed, the trend decline in New Zealand's terms of trade highlights the need for robust productivity advances in this area.

Table 20. Structural surveillance assessment and recommendations

Issue/Previous recommendation	Action taken/proposed	Assessment	New or follow-up recommendation
A. Labour market and social programmes			
I. Reform unemployment and related benefit systems			
Community Wage programme	The government plans to replace this programme with separate unemployment and sickness benefits, and recipients of the latter will no longer face a work-test.	This could see some shifting from the sickness benefit to the relatively more generous invalids benefit, which is also not work-tested.	Work-tests for all beneficiaries should be bolstered through more intensive case management (see below).
Income-related rent programme	The government will replace the Accommodation Supplement with an income-related rent programme that caps the amount that state-housing tenants spend in this area.	This new scheme will likely raise effective marginal tax rates and diminish labour mobility.	Evaluate the cost and impact of this programme.
Review the current tax/benefit system in order to reduce work incentives	See Chapter IV.		
II. Active labour market programmes (ALMPs)			
Monitor the effectiveness of case management	Some relaxation in the obligation of certain groups of beneficiaries to seek work will soon take effect.	Case management, particularly for those receiving invalidity benefits, has tended to focus on initial assessment and timely payments rather than the appropriate form of work that could be carried out.	Case management should focus on determining appropriate back-to work plans.
Evaluation and assessment of ALMPs	The authorities are studying how to make evaluations more rigorous.	Welcome development, which should be completed quickly.	Increase scope and rigour of evaluations by making a commitment to evaluate part of policy development. Ensure that ALMPs remain suitable to changing labour market conditions.
Training versus "work-first"	The government plans to shift the emphasis of ALMPs towards preparing jobseekers for work through training.	This may be more suitable for those with fewer skills. Evaluation research suggests that on-the-job training has better long-term employment effects than formal training.	Favour the use of on-the-job training (with carefully targeted wage subsidies if required) over formal training.

Table 20. **Structural surveillance assessment and recommendations** (*cont.*)

Issue/Previous recommendation	Action taken/proposed	Assessment	New or follow-up recommendation
Community Work will no longer be compulsory	New proposal.	This is in contrast to findings that employment officers found it useful in promoting work attachment.	Ensure that ALMPs remain used as work tests where relevant.
Greater use of outside contractors to deliver ALMPs	New proposal.	A welcome development that may help improve the delivery of programmes to some groups.	Monitor service delivery.
III. Improve labour force skills and competences			
Reduce early school leaving	Modern Apprenticeship system announced.	This welcome initiative should help to reduce the relatively large share of youths with no formal qualifications.	Carefully track progress of students in this programme and their outcomes.
Implement the National Qualifications Framework (NQF)	NQF under implementation.	This is an encouraging even if tardy development that should help to improve the transparency of degrees.	Fully implement the NQF as quickly as possible.
Monitor closely the various initiatives aimed at raising Maori and Pacific Islander participation in education	Ongoing.	The new government has placed considerable emphasis on improving outcomes for these groups, but relatively little is known about the impact of programmes.	Determine the effectiveness of such programmes.
IV. Wage formation			
Avoid further increases in the minimum wage	The minimum wage was increased for both adults and youths. The government has decided in principle to lower the adult threshold to 18 from 20 and to increase the wage paid to youths undergoing firm-based training.	These increases risk creating unemployment for youths and the lower-skilled.	Resist additional increases in the minimum wage and maintain the adult/youth differential.
Industrial relations	Employment Relations Act replaced the Employment Contracts Act.	It will take time before the new Act's impact becomes clear, but there should not be a return to the centralised and distortionary system of the distant past. Nevertheless, it may have adverse macroeconomic and microeconomic consequences.	Keep wage bargains in line with productivity developments. Ensure that multi-employer contracts consider the individual circumstances facing firms. Carefully monitor strikes and lockouts, their duration and reasons for them. Assess the new dispute resolution procedure to determine whether it is raising compliance costs.

Table 20. **Structural surveillance assessment and recommendations** (*cont.*)

Issue/Previous recommendation	Action taken/proposed	Assessment	New or follow-up recommendation
B. Product markets			
Speed up deregulation of agricultural producer boards	Statutory board abolished in the Raspberry sector. New Acts in the kiwifruit and apple and pear industries.	Slow progress. Pushing forward on deregulation would help to spur innovation in the sectors.	Speed up deregulation.
Trade policy	Ended unilateral tariff reductions and is implementing an export credit scheme.	Unfortunate that New Zealand, which has championed the cause of open markets feels compelled to take these actions.	Consider lowering tariffs where peaks exist (for example, textiles) and carefully monitor the new system of export credits.
Accident Compensation Corporation (ACC)	ACC was renationalised after only a brief period operating under a competitive framework.	Few economic grounds to do so.	Adjust premiums to more fully reflect firm-specific accident records and maintain full funding.
Financial support to enterprises	Creation of Industry New Zealand (INZ) and the announcement of new funding initiatives, including an R&D grant programme.	INZ can play a valuable role in co-ordinating regional policies, delivery of programmes and policy coherence. Even though spending is relatively low, it could lead to rent-seeking behaviour.	The government is urged to carefully target all new initiatives and build a list of which work best.
Regulatory reform	Proposals to modify the Commerce Act as well as enquiries underway into the suitability of regulation in the telecommunications and electricity sectors.	Timely reviews of regulation given the vast changes taking place in some sectors.	New regulations should be implemented quickly to provide a sound environment for investment decisions. The principle of a light-handed approach should be maintained. Where exemptions are given despite the creation of dominant positions, the benefits that are expected to accrue should be presented and monitored.
Internet and electronic commerce	The government proposes a series of initiatives to boost their use.	There appears to be a reluctance by small and medium-sized firms to take advantage of electronic commerce.	Implement the new measures to set the ground rules for electronic commerce.

Table 20.   **Structural surveillance assessment and recommendations** (*cont.*)

Issue/Previous recommendation	Action taken/proposed	Assessment	New or follow-up recommendation
C. Financial sector			
People's Bank	A proposal is before the government to set-up a new bank, as a commercial initiative of the state-owned enterprise New Zealand Post.	There may be temptation to use its assets for regional development purposes. Could lead to moral hazard and competition problems if clients feel that the government will guarantee deposits.	The institution should be incorporated as a bank under the Reserve Bank of New Zealand and subject to standard rules. There should be no explicit or implicit guarantee of deposits.
Information disclosure of banks	New issue.	The type of information that has to be publicly disclosed may need adjustment as assessment of bank balance sheets becomes more difficult.	Continually monitor information disclosure with respect to how it meets the needs of a depositor's ability to assess a bank's risk position.
Ability to seize domestic assets of foreign-owned banks in the case of failure	The Reserve Bank of New Zealand is considering requiring important banks to incorporate locally.	In the case of failure, the central bank may have difficulty seizing assets since some foreign countries give preference to their domestic depositors.	Implement the proposed regulation.
D. Public sector			
I. Health care			
Implementation of District Health Boards (DHBs)	The former system, comprising the Health Funding Authority and Hospital and Health Services, has been terminated.	The government felt that transactions costs were too high and that accountability lines were blurred. It is not clear that these will be any less of a problem under the new arrangements.	Carefully monitor the implementation and operation of the DHBs.
Purchaser/provider split	This has been eliminated.	This shift was a fundamental premise of the old system. The loss of a competitive benchmark may lower incentives to minimise costs.	Evaluate carefully the impact of policies to determine whether they are being delivered in a cost-effective manner. Consider the use of independent evaluators to replace the role filled by the Crown Company Monitoring Advisory Unit.

Table 20. **Structural surveillance assessment and recommendations** (*cont.*)

Issue/Previous recommendation	Action taken/proposed	Assessment	New or follow-up recommendation
Primary care reform	The government is encouraging the set-up of primary care organisations that group together health-care professionals.	This should lead to more integrated service delivery and help to contain costs.	The DHBs should continue to encourage their set-up.
II. Education Student loan programme	Generosity has been increased.	Poorly targeted and costly to the government books. Little is known about the socio-economic impact of this scheme.	Evaluate the impact of the programme to determine whether it is raising tertiary enrolment.
Elimination of bulk funding	This is a move away from market-based mechanisms.	Evaluation of bulk funding found that it led to promising new initiatives in schools to boost the quality of education. Some elements of bulk funding have been retained.	Examine other initiatives and determine whether they should be more widely disseminated. In general, keep track of programmes developed at schools to create a list of those that should be adopted by all schools.
Student zoning	The ability of allowing parents to choose the school that they would like their child to attend has been reduced and school zones re-introduced.	This process helped to highlight schools which needed to improve their quality.	The government should periodically assess school (and student) performance to ensure that its goal of improving the quality of all schools is being met.
III. Government spending Expenditure control	The government has begun a *Value for Money* initiative to evaluate new programmes, and will selectively examine others.	While aggregate expenditures are carefully assessed under a well-defined framework, this is not always the case for individual programmes. More evaluation is necessary to ensure that spending is targeted towards areas that boost the economy's growth potential.	Make evaluation of programmes an integral part of the policy development phase. Ensure that outcomes are well-defined. Widely disseminate good practice.

Table 20. **Structural surveillance assessment and recommendations** (*cont.*)

Issue/Previous recommendation	Action taken/proposed	Assessment	New or follow-up recommendation
Privatisation	The government has halted the privatisation process.	There are over $NZ 10 billion in assets currently being held in state-owned enterprises, many of which could be spun off.	Re-start the privatisation process. In cases where the government does not want to relinquish control, consider a partial floatation of shares to the public.
IV. Pensions			
Partially pre-funding public pensions	The government is proposing to set aside part of the fiscal surplus to pre-fund the public pension plan (Superannuation).	Taking action on this important issue is welcome. Pre-funding raises a host of complicated governance and operational issues. In addition, setting aside funds may provoke demands to increase the already generous Superannuation scheme.	The government should carefully assess the relative merits of further tax reductions relative to pre-funding. If pre-funding goes ahead, the Investment Board should be at arms-length from the government; some portion of the funds should be invested overseas, and investing passively should be considered. The Superannuation scheme should be regularly evaluated, in particular as to the benefits that might arise from reducing its generosity.
V. Environment			
Climate change	The authorities would like to ratify the Kyoto Protocol by 2002.	The increased use of fossil fuels will make this a challenging goal.	Make greater use of economic instruments, such as carbon taxes and emissions permit trading and apply user- and polluter-pays principles more generally.
Resource Management Act	Modifications are currently being considered.	This has been an on-going process since 1998 with no decisions taken.	Implement the changes as quickly as possible, since uncertainty may adversely affect investment. Continue to assess the compliance costs of the RMA.

Table 20. **Structural surveillance assessment and recommendations** (*cont.*)

Issue/Previous recommendation	Action taken/proposed	Assessment	New or follow-up recommendation
Energy conservation	A new National Energy Efficiency and Conservation Strategy has been implemented.	The details have yet to be worked out, but the final legislation will set out targets to be achieved.	Consider how this strategy will affect business compliance costs (and the overall burden placed on firms from this and the RMA).

Source: OECD.

- The reviews of the regulatory framework in electricity and telecommunications sectors appears well timed and appropriate, as do changes to the Commerce Act. Prospective changes should, however, be finalised and implemented quickly to reduce uncertainty in investment decisions. The privatisation process should also be re-started, and even where the government does not want to relinquish control of some holdings, it should consider a partial floatation of shares to the public. The renationalisation of accident compensation insurance set a poor signal on the direction of reforms, and there is unlikely to be any clear efficiency gain to be had with this decision. The intention to fully fund ACC on an actuarial basis should help to judge whether the current low premium rates are sustainable.

- Recently-introduced programmes that direct financial assistance to firms, under the auspices of the newly established Industry New Zealand (INZ), require careful targeting to minimise the risk of rent-seeking behaviour and allow a set of best practices to be developed that could be used to target spending appropriately. INZ can also play a useful role in enhancing policy coherence as regards regional development. If introduced, the proposed People's Bank should be run on strictly commercial principles, without any explicit, or implicit, promise to provide a public guarantee to its deposits, nor to direct its assets towards required development purposes.

- In the area of trade, both the decision to stop unilateral tariff reduction and to consider the introduction of export credits are disappointing, given New Zealand's leadership and commitment towards open and unfettered trading arrangements. Nevertheless, the government should consider lowering tariffs where peaks exist, for example in textiles and clothing, and carefully monitor the new system of export credits.

Adapt the supervisory framework in financial markets

- Given the increasing international and domestic linkages in the financial sector, more co-ordination and integration in supervision of banks and non-bank institutions, as well as with international regulatory bodies, may be necessary.

- The basis of supervision is full disclosure, but this does not always imply greater clarity, particularly given the increasing use of sophisticated financial instruments. The quality and type of information may have to change to ensure that non-specialists can adequately interpret an institution's financial position.

- The central bank's proposal that banks of system-wide importance be required to incorporate locally to allow it to lay a claim on domestic

assets in the event of a failure should be implemented, helping to rein-
force the stability of the domestic banking system.

Improve monitoring and evaluation in the public sector

- Although aggregate expenditure is assessed under a well-defined
  framework, this is not the case for individual initiatives. At present,
  there is no formal mechanism to systematically ensure that government
  programmes are evaluated, and that funds are directed towards areas
  that will most improve the productive capacity of the economy,
  although there are targeted reviews from time to time. Given the number of schemes introduced by the government, many of which imply ongoing spending commitments, there is an urgent need to bolster the
  evaluation process, including cost-benefit analysis where appropriate.
  For example, widespread changes being introduced in the health sector
  will require careful attention be paid to implementation, while the
  move away from the purchaser/provider split lowers contestability and
  therefore requires greater oversight to ensure that health-policy objectives are met in the most cost-effective manner. Reforms in the education sector also require close follow-up, and an analysis of the socio-
  economic impact of the costly student loan programme needs to be carried
  out to ensure that it is meeting its objectives.

IV. The tax system: an appraisal and options for change

Introduction

After radical reform in the 1980s, New Zealand's tax system became one of the most broadly based, neutral and efficient in the OECD (Box 6). Over time, however, various positive features of the system have gradually eroded, and, as in most other OECD countries, it will come under increasing pressure in coming years due to rising spending demands as the population ages and more mobile tax bases. The challenge for New Zealand is how to respond to these developments without undermining the system's still fundamentally healthy state. The starting point is favourable since distortions and inequities are still more limited than in most other OECD countries, even though many of them have improved their tax systems in recent years. The overall tax burden is reasonably low, especially compared with those of European countries, but higher than those of some of its major trading partners in the OECD, including Australia, the United States and Japan (Figure 22). Revenues have also been more volatile than elsewhere, reflecting strong economic cycles as well as the substantial tax changes that have taken place.

The government has announced a review of the entire tax system to be carried out over the next year or so. The first part of the review will take a "top-down approach" to establish which key principles should underlie a future robust tax system. This will be carried out by a group of non-government experts whose recommendations are due by the end of September 2001. Building on these recommendations as well as the wider public debate, the second part of the review will outline specific proposals for tax changes. This chapter addresses many of the issues involved. It first describes some key features of the economic context within which tax policy is formulated, followed by a discussion of major positive characteristics of the tax system as well as its main weaknesses. The final section outlines recommendations for further strengthening equity and efficiency. It is concluded that New Zealand's tax system is basically sound and that there is no urgent need for major systemic reform. However, a range of second-order issues are identified that should be addressed in order to reap the full benefits of what is essentially a well-functioning tax system.

Box 6.   Key elements of tax reform in New Zealand since 1984

The main elements of tax reform were introduced during the second half of the 1980s. The overall direction was to improve the efficiency and equity of the tax system by implementing a broad-based, low-rate system and removing tax preferences (see, for instance, Stephens, 1993). Key policy initiatives included:

- Reduction of the top individual marginal rate from 66 to 33 per cent (increased to 39 per cent in 2000);
- Reduction of the tax rate from 48 to 33 per cent for resident companies and from 53 to 38 per cent for non-resident companies (later aligned at 33 per cent);
- Substitution of a single-rated and broadly based value added tax, the Goods and Service Tax (GST), for diverse wholesale sales taxes (the initial GST rate of 10 per cent was increased to 12.5 per cent in 1989);
- Removal of most tax expenditures by abolishing a wide range of business investment incentives, including export incentives and investment allowances;
- Introduction of a comprehensive fringe benefit tax payable by employers for in-kind compensation provided to employees;
- Introduction of an imputation scheme for corporate dividends to eliminate double taxation of company income distributed to shareholders;
- Introduction of accrual rules which ensure that all returns on "financial arrangements", broadly defined to include most debts and arrangements where there is a deferral of the passing of consideration, are brought into the tax net on a progressive basis over the term of the financial arrangement concerned;
- Removal of tax preferences for income earned and distributed from pension schemes, placing such saving on an equal footing with other forms of saving;
- Introduction of withholding taxes on interest and dividends;
- Introduction of rules aimed at taxing the foreign-source income of New Zealand residents on a current basis (regardless of the foreign entity through which that income is earned and regardless of when the income is distributed).

The background to these radical changes has been discussed in several previous Economic Surveys. Besides a widespread "crisis consciousness" in the public stemming from past policy failures, the reforms were presumably publicly and politically accepted because they were perceived to be fair and administrable, not least because they were deeply rooted, bold and contained a "no exemption" spirit. New Zealand's experience also highlights the importance of sequencing and timing of tax reforms. Taxpayers accepted higher tax burdens from the elimination of investment and savings incentives, broader bases and the introduction of the GST as a trade-off for lower marginal tax rates and more generous allowances to families at the bottom end of the income scale (Toder and Himes, 1992).

Figure 22.   **Total tax revenues in selected OECD countries and regions**[1]
Per cent of GDP

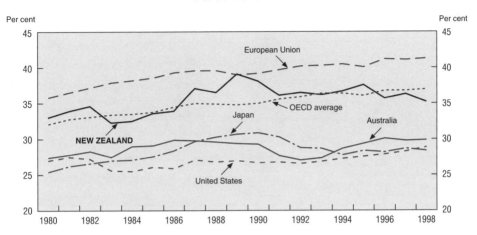

1.   General government total tax revenues, including social security contributions. Note that numbers may not be
     fully comparable across countries and over time due to changes of national accounts from SNA68/ESA79
     to SNA93/ESA95.
     Source: OECD, *Revenue Statistics*, 2000.

The economic context shaping tax policy

International aspects play a key role

Tax policy in New Zealand is grounded within a coherent overall strategy, and changes to various parts of the system are generally scrutinised with a view to how these might affect the efficiency, equity and simplicity of the system as a whole. As in other countries, the tax system reflects a mixture of economic characteristics and political preferences. In particular, the openness of the economy implies a strong focus on international aspects of the tax system – how to promote high economic returns on investment carried out by New Zealand residents and at the same time protect the domestic tax base. Since factors like capital and highly-skilled labour are to a large and increasing extent mobile across borders, tax policy in New Zealand must be carried out with a view to developments elsewhere. One example is the recent decision in Australia to lower its corporate tax rate to 30 per cent by 2001/02, which may reduce New Zealand's future room for manoeuvre in this area.

Household savings are low

New Zealand's rate of national saving is lower than in most other OECD countries, giving rise to large and persistent current account deficits as investment

Figure 23. **Saving rates across OECD countries**
Average 1990-98

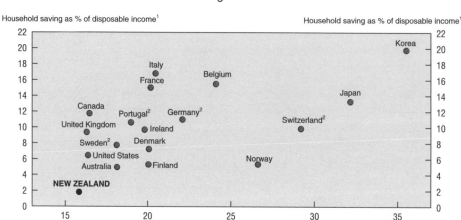

Household saving as % of disposable income[1]

Household saving as % of disposable income[1]

Gross national saving as % of GDP

1. Household saving ratios may not be fully comparable across countries due to differences in definitions (gross versus net saving).
2. 1991-98 for Germany; 1995-98 for Portugal and Spain; 1993-98 for Sweden; 1990-97 for Switzerland.
Source: OECD and OECD *National Accounts.*

Figure 24. **Various measures of household saving**
Per cent of GDP

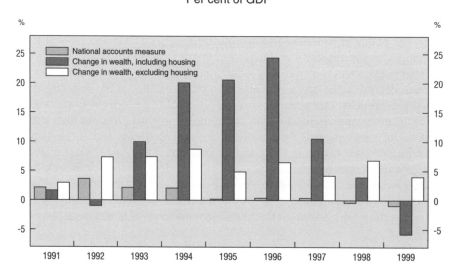

- National accounts measure
- Change in wealth, including housing
- Change in wealth, excluding housing

Source: Treasury estimates from SNA data; WestpacFPG (now Morningstar) household savings indicators.

levels are not correspondingly subdued. In particular, the *household saving rate* is lower than in most other OECD countries (Figure 23), although official national accounts data may give an incomplete picture of both levels and trends in saving insofar as they do not take wealth effects into account (Figure 24).[38]

The question is whether tax policy could and should contribute to raise national saving levels, either through its effects on private savings, or government savings, or both.[39] Empirical evidence as well as theoretical considerations do not suggest that tax policy would be very effective in changing private or household saving levels (Box 7). Increasing government savings through higher taxes, assuming government spending is unchanged and private savings not reduced correspondingly,

---

Box 7. **Empirical and theoretical evidence on the effects of taxation on household saving levels**

The effect on household savings from lower income taxes depends on the elasticity of savings to changes in the after-tax rate of interest.* This effect is ambiguous since income and substitution effects pull in opposite directions unless the household sector is a net debtor. If this elasticity is positive (higher after-tax returns result in higher savings), it follows that, all else being equal, a tax on income would depress household savings more than a tax on consumption, since the latter does not affect the after-tax interest rate. In that case, a change in the tax mix from income to consumption taxes would increase the level of household savings. Most empirical evidence points to small and/or statistically insignificant effects of such a shift in the tax mix – see Choy (2000) for an application to New Zealand.** In a survey of empirical work, Bernheim (1997) thus concludes that "there is little reason to believe that households increase their saving significantly in response to a generic increase in the after-tax return". However, a recent study by Tanzi and Zee (2000) points to more significant positive effects on the level of private savings from lower marginal income taxes when measured across a panel of OECD countries. Overall, however, the theoretical and empirical evidence provides hardly any firm ground for relying on tax policy to affect private savings levels on a significant and permanent basis.

---

*   In addition to, and separate from the interest elasticity of savings, there may also be a short-term impact on saving levels from the income elasticity of consumption: if consumption changes by less than disposable income following changes in taxes, the level (and rate) of saving will also change. However, since the income elasticity of consumption is (close to) unity in the long run, this effect will disappear over time.

** A massive amount of empirical research has also been carried out on the extent to which tax-sheltered retirement savings schemes (such as the IRAs and 401k's in the United States) have raised private and national saving rates. The evidence is rather mixed. It generally points to small or no effects on overall private savings but a significant reshuffling of existing savings into the tax-preferred instruments (see Bernheim, 1999 for a recent survey).

---

is probably a more effective strategy for raising the national saving rate (Leibfritz *et al.*, 1997 and Edwards, 1995), but the costs would be higher deadweight losses and lower economic activity.[40] It follows that tax policy in general should not be considered a very effective instrument for changing saving *levels*. The situation is somewhat different with respect to the *composition* of savings, where international and domestic evidence point to substantial effects from tax changes (see, for instance, Bernheim, 1999 and Arthur Andersen, 1999). Non-neutralities in New Zealand's tax system hence play a significant role in the tendency towards "over-saving" in housing and "undersaving" in productive assets (as discussed below), which to some extent reduces the long-term growth potential of the economy.

Ageing of the population and the funding of public pensions put pressure on expenditure and may affect private savings

Part of the reason for low household savings may relate to the universal access to welfare benefits and services provided by the government (such as education, unemployment insurance and pensions), which would otherwise constitute key motivations for household saving.[41] If the government saves sufficiently for these purposes, there is no need for the private sector to do so, although the balance between public and private savings may have an impact on overall allocative

Figure 25. **Financial assets of institutional investors in OECD countries**
Per cent of GDP, 1996

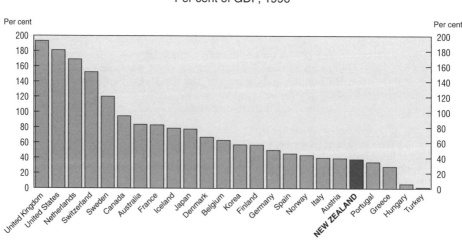

Source: OECD, Institutional Investors, 1998 Statistical Yearbook.

efficiency. The overriding concern is whether the combined government and private savings for future retirement benefits are too low and the returns to national savings are sufficiently high. Private pension savings and other long-term savings are lower than in most other OECD countries (Figure 25), partly as a result of the abolition in 1989 of all tax preferences to such savings (Davies, 1995) as well as the generosity of the public pay-as-you go pension scheme, the New Zealand Superannuation (NZS)[42] – see Chapter III.

The government recently announced its intention to start pre-funding the New Zealand Superannuation (see Budget 2000). If realised, this will imply that the tax-to-GDP ratio and hence government saving over the next 20 to 25 years will be higher than with a balanced budget strategy. Pre-funding is consistent with the traditional tax-smoothing argument: since economic distortions rise more than proportionally with effective tax rates, it would be desirable to stabilise these tax rates over time (Barro, 1979). This argument, however, relies on the presence of sufficiently effective control mechanisms to avoid expenditure creep in the presence of large and sustained fiscal surpluses during periods of accumulation of government assets (Pinfield, 1998). Moreover, the higher tax/GDP ratio will, at least to some extent, suppress economic activity, capital formation and hence future incomes. It may also induce private agents to reduce their own long-term savings due to the greater certainty of the public pensions being sustained at a high level.

Positive features of the tax system[43]

Consumption and property taxes are less distortionary than elsewhere

More than 50 per cent of total revenues are raised from income taxation, which is a higher share than anywhere else in the OECD and much higher than the OECD average of around 35 per cent (Figure 26). This discrepancy is considerably narrowed when taking into account that New Zealand levies only a very limited amount of social security contributions (i.e. the workplace accident insurance premium, ACC). The share of consumption taxes is just above one-third of total revenues, slightly higher than the OECD average. The introduction in 1986 of a broadly based value added tax (the goods and services tax, or GST) has contributed to shifting the tax burden from income to consumption (Panel B). Consumption taxes are also raised more efficiently than elsewhere, since the share of total consumption tax revenue raised through value added taxes is the highest among OECD countries levying such a tax (Figure 27).[44] The share of revenues from taxation of property is in line with those of other countries, and the composition shows a relatively large share of holding taxes compared with transaction taxes (Figure 28).[45] This indicates that property taxation is not acting as a significant barrier to the efficient use of land.

Figure 26. **Tax mix in selected OECD countries**

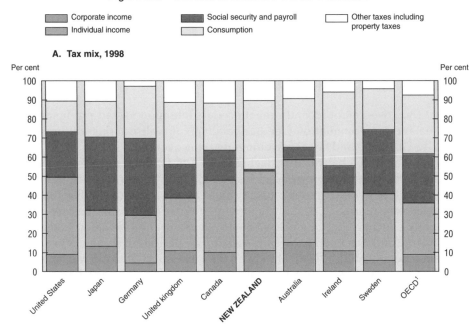

A. Tax mix, 1998

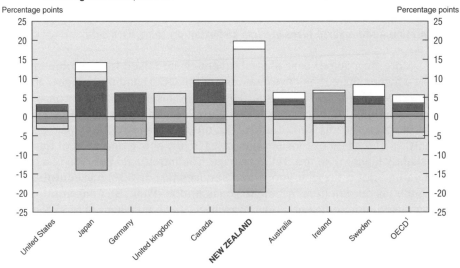

B. Change in tax mix, 1980-98

1.   The OECD average is unweighted and excludes Mexico.
Source: OECD, *Revenue Statistics*, 2000.

Figure 27. **Share of value added tax in total consumption tax revenues in OECD countries**
1998[1]

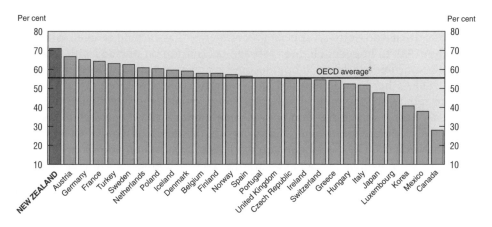

1.   1997 in the case of Greece.
2.   Unweighted average.
Source: OECD, *Revenue Statistics*, 2000.

Figure 28. **Property taxation in OECD countries**
1998[1]

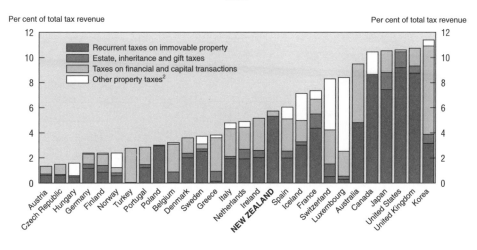

1.   1997 data for Greece.
2.   Includes recurrent taxes on net wealth and some non-recurrent taxes on property (for instance land development permission charges).
Source: OECD, *Revenue Statistics*, 2000.

Marginal tax rates are moderate and bases relatively broad[46]

Taxation of personal income is moderate overall, although the interaction between tax rates and the abatement of tax credits and welfare benefits may create excessively high effective marginal rates for some income groups and family types, as discussed below. A special tax credit, the "low-income rebate", was introduced in 1988 to impose a lighter average tax burden on persons with low wage and salary incomes.[47] Hence, labour income is now taxed at a four-rate progressive scale, while other income is taxed at a different scale with three rates. The low-income rebate has the merit of retaining the original higher taxation of the intra-marginal income of middle- and high-income earners, allowing marginal tax rates to remain moderate for income groups outside the targeted regime. Overall, marginal tax wedges on labour income are moderate for most individuals, as shown by a relatively low average marginal tax wedge, i.e. weighted across the entire distribution of incomes (Figure 29).[48]

The recent hike of the top marginal tax rate on personal income to 39 per cent was officially justified by distributional concerns, including the need for raising revenues for re-instating a higher NZS benefit. The increase in the top marginal rate marked a break with the principle of aligning marginal personal and corporate tax rates. This will imply stronger tax-shifting incentives and larger efficiency

Figure 29. Weighted marginal tax wedges across OECD countries[1]
1998

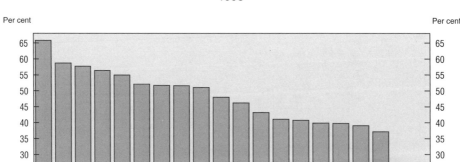

1. The weighted marginal tax rates combine information on marginal effective tax wedges (including social security contributions) for various income groups with the actual income distribution.
Source: OECD, *Taxing wages* 1999 and OECD calculations.

Figure 30. **Highest all-in tax rates in selected OECD countries**[1]
1999

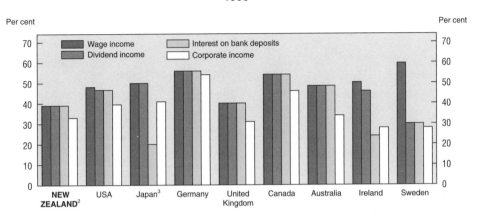

1. The all-in tax rates for wage, dividend and interest income are those applying to individual top-income earners. They include central and sub-central government taxes as well as social security contributions where these are not capped. The all-in tax rates on corporate income include central and sub-central government taxes as well as surcharges.
2. FY 2000/2001.
3. Tax on dividends depends on the size of payment. Tax credits are not included.
Source: OECD Tax Database.

losses. However, only relatively few taxpayers are immediately affected by the higher marginal tax rate and the economy-wide consequences may hence be limited – although the number of potentially affected people, *i.e.* whose marginal tax rates may run into the 39 per cent range if their income increases, could be more substantial.[49] Moreover, it should be noted that no other OECD country has such uniformity of top rates in the personal and corporate income tax system and that the gap created by the tax increase is still smaller than in many other countries (Figure 30). The comprehensive taxation of most kinds of personal income combined with the dividend imputation system ensures that maximum all-in tax rates for individuals are moderate and uniform across most sources of income (excluding capital gains and imputed rental income of owner-occupied housing, as discussed below).

The flat 33 per cent statutory corporate tax rate is in the middle of the range of the rates applied in other OECD countries and is slightly below the unweighted OECD average of 36 per cent. Tax revenue from the corporate tax has been around 4 per cent of GDP in recent years, somewhat higher than the OECD average of 3.3 per cent – a rough indication that the corporate tax base in New Zealand is probably broader than in the average OECD country (Figure 31).[50] Due to the imputation credit system, the corporate tax is merely a withholding levy on the final individual income tax for residents. However, for non-residents, the corporate tax

Figure 31. **Taxation of corporate income in OECD countries**
1998

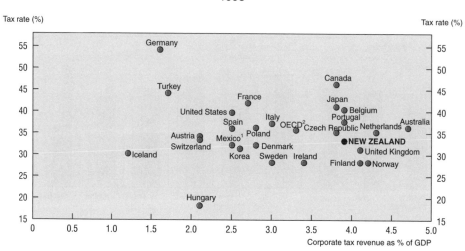

1. Retained earnings.
2. Unweighted average.
Source: OECD, *Revenue Statistics*, 2000; OECD Tax Database.

rate may matter to the extent they are not credited for such underlying tax in their home countries. Rules for loss carry-over and consolidation of losses within holding companies are generally less restrictive than in most other OECD countries (*cf.* Table A2). Although this may have negative consequences for revenues, it allows companies more flexibility for restructuring and lower compliance costs.

Tax preferences to corporations are limited, although general tax relief is provided through the accelerated depreciation scheme ("loading").[51] Concessions are also given to forestry and mining as well as certain kinds of intangible assets, such as intellectual property rights. The limited use of targeted tax incentives implies that investments are generally directed to applications with the highest economic returns (Box 8).[52] In comparison with other OECD countries, marginal effective tax wedges across various investment and financing vehicles are almost uniform, pointing to low overall tax-induced distortions to corporate financing decisions (Table 21).[53] Moes (1999) provides evidence that the neutrality of New Zealand's corporate income tax system increased substantially following the tax reforms of the 1980s and the transition to a low-inflation economy.

New Zealand's value-added tax, the Goods and Services Tax (GST), was introduced in 1986 at a flat standard rate of 10 per cent. The rate was raised to 12.5 per cent in 1989. This is lower than most European VAT-levying countries but higher than Australia (10 per cent) and several Asian countries (including Japan

Box 8.   **Adverse economic effects of targeted tax incentives
to the business sector**

While investors base their investment decisions on expected after-tax returns, the value to the whole economy of an investment is determined by its pre-tax return. If some investments are more lightly taxed than others, differences arise between their pre- and post-tax rankings, resulting in investment patterns that do not generate the highest overall return from a national viewpoint. Lower and more even tax rates across investments (as well as organisational business forms) reduce this distortion. Differences in marginal effective tax rates arise mainly from varying depreciation rules and other tax concessions. Targeted tax incentives for certain sectors or activities are particularly harmful to the economy since they:

- Are difficult to target appropriately. Ideally tax incentives seek to remedy market failures, for instance perceived under-investment in R&D, but to identify such failures requires more information than is normally available. The result is that incentives are often given too widely, which is overly expensive, or too narrowly, whereby they may have little effect.

- Encourage unassisted sectors to waste effort (from the viewpoint of the whole economy) in lobbying for concessions for themselves.

- Lead to increased avoidance and evasion (and costly administrative counter-measures) by attempts to characterise otherwise non-qualifying income or expenditure so that it qualifies for the concession. Therefore, subsidies may flow to unintended activities, persons or companies.

- Subsidise activity that would take place anyway.

- Imply a loss of revenue that is difficult to control.

- Are less transparent than explicit subsidies.

and Korea). By imposing a single uniform rate, the GST avoids the drawbacks of systems with multiple rates. The level of exemptions is also lower than in most other countries, leading to the highest degree of effectiveness of the value-added tax in the OECD (Figure 32).[54] As in other countries, problems of enforcement and equitable treatment are encountered in areas such as imported services, electronic commerce and second-hand goods[55] and may place a constraint on potential future revenues from the GST. Like other OECD countries, New Zealand also imposes a range of excises and duties on various activities and products, in particular petrol, alcohol and tobacco, but these amount to a rather small share of the total tax take. Import duties are larger than in most other OECD countries, around 2½ per cent of total tax revenues compared with an OECD average of 1.4 per cent.

Table 21. **Marginal effective tax wedges in manufacturing in selected OECD countries**[1]

Per cent, 1999

	Sources of financing[2]				Type of assets[3]				Overall	
	Retained earnings	New equity	Debt	Standard deviation	Machinery	Building	Inventories	Standard deviation	Average	Standard deviation
United States	1.67	4.90	1.43	1.58	1.51	2.54	2.02	0.42	1.91	1.20
Japan	2.66	3.88	0.36	1.46	0.97	3.14	2.79	0.95	1.98	1.23
Germany	1.08	2.21	1.21	0.51	0.85	1.40	1.91	0.43	1.24	0.48
United Kingdom	2.74	2.24	1.46	0.53	1.88	2.21	3.09	0.51	2.24	0.53
Canada	4.36	5.42	1.92	1.47	2.66	4.14	5.13	1.02	3.62	1.26
Australia	2.22	0.98	1.96	0.53	1.62	2.16	2.69	0.44	2.01	0.53
Ireland	1.51	3.95	0.66	1.40	1.12	1.44	2.23	0.46	1.45	1.07
New Zealand	0.99	1.33	1.33	0.16	1.17	0.95	1.32	0.15	1.14	0.16
Sweden	1.73	2.17	0.68	0.62	1.14	1.43	1.99	0.35	1.41	0.51
OECD average	1.72	2.59	0.99	0.65	1.17	1.71	2.25	0.44	1.55	0.56

1. These indicators show the degree to which the personal and corporate tax systems scale up (or down) the real pre-tax rate of return that must be earned on an investment, given that the household can earn a 4 per cent real rate of return on a demand deposit. Wealth taxes are excluded. See OECD (1991) for a discussion of this methodology. Calculations are based on an inflation rate equal to the 1998-99 per cent change in the private consumption deflator.
2. Calculated using the following weights: machinery 50 per cent, buildings 28 per cent, inventories 22 per cent.
3. Calculated using the following weights: retained earnings 55 per cent, new equity 10 per cent, debt 35 per cent.
Source: OECD calculations.

Figure 32. **Effectiveness of value added taxes in OECD countries**[1]
1998

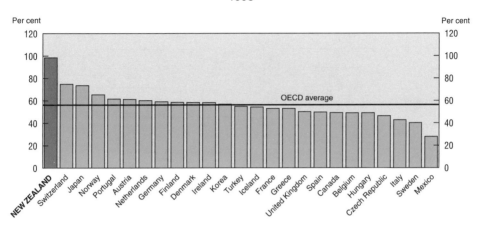

1. Effectiveness of the VAT is measured as the effective VAT rate as a per cent of the standard statutory rate, where the effective rate is VAT revenues divided by the potential VAT base (*i.e.* consumption minus VAT). The effectiveness of the VAT reflects the broadness of the VAT base and the level of compliance.
Source: OECD calculations.

The role of environmental taxes will be considered as part of the tax review. Revenues raised from environmental taxes (in particular, taxes on fuel and road user charges) comprise a share of less than 5 per cent of total tax revenues, which is somewhat below the OECD average. More telling, perhaps, is the fact that the tax on diesel fuel is much lower than that on unleaded gasoline – indeed the lowest in the OECD (Table 22) – indicating that the main consideration behind the fuel tax structure is to gather revenue rather than pursue environmental objectives.[56]

The overall favourable mix of modest tax rates and broad bases implies that the deadweight costs (or excess burden) of taxation in New Zealand is probably at the lower end of the range of OECD countries. Diewert and Lawrence (1994) found that the deadweight costs associated with labour taxation (primarily taxation on the income of wage earners and the self-employed) in New Zealand are around 18 per cent for the marginal dollar of income tax revenue raised and around 14 per cent of the marginal dollar of consumption tax revenue raised.[57] Although these costs are by no means insignificant, they are still moderate compared with estimates of deadweight costs found for other countries, which are typically in the range of 10 to 100 per cent.[58]

Table 22.   **Shares of taxes in total fuel prices in OECD countries**

Per cent, 1999

	Gasoline[1] (premium unleaded)	Diesel[2]	Ratio of diesel/ gasoline tax share
Australia	55[3]	. .	. .
Austria	68	55	81
Belgium	74	56	76
Canada	48[4]	39	81
Czech Republic	63	50	79
Denmark	72	36	50
Finland	74	54	73
France	79	67	85
Germany	74	62	84
Greece	63	57	90
Hungary	67	65	97
Ireland	68	56	82
Italy	73	64	88
Japan	. .	56	. .
Luxembourg	64	54	84
Netherlands	73	58	79
New Zealand	**50**	**1**	**2**
Norway	75	59	79
Poland	63	49	78
Portugal	68	60	88
Spain	67	56	84
Sweden	73	50	68
Switzerland	69	76	110
Turkey	71	64	90
United Kingdom	82	78	95
United States	28	. .	. .
Unweighted average of countries listed above	64	51	70

1. 95 RON.
2. For commercial use.
3. 1995.
4. 1994.
Source: IEA, *Energy Prices and Taxes, first quarter* 2000 and OECD calculations.

Preferential tax treatment of pension savings and fringe benefits is limited

Unlike other OECD countries, New Zealand does not subsidise private pension plans – *e.g.* life insurance and private superannuation schemes – by preferential taxation. Contributions as well as current earnings of pension funds are taxed, while the benefits are tax free, leaving pension savings to be taxed in a way similar to that of all other kinds of savings (the so-called TTE tax treatment).[59] In contrast, most other OECD countries exempt the contributions and earnings of private pension schemes, while taxing benefits. Hence, they apply an EET tax treatment to such schemes (Table 23).[60] As the current earnings of private superannuation funds are taxed at the corporate rate of 33 per cent, individual taxpayers with lower marginal rates are overtaxed (compared with ordinary savings). With the recent hike in the top personal tax rate to 39 per cent, taxpayers in this bracket receive a subsidy.[61]

Table 23. **Tax treatment of private pensions in OECD countries**
1999

	Contributions out of taxed income or exempt	Fund income tax (per cent rate) or exempt	Pensions annuities taxed or exempt	Pension lump sum taxed or exempt
Australia	T	15	T	T/E
Austria	P(C)	E	P(T)	–
Belgium	C	E	T	T
Canada	E	E	T	T
Czech Republic	T	E	T	T
Denmark	E	33.8	T	T
Finland	E	E	T	T
France	E	E	T	E
Germany	T/E	E	T	T/E
Hungary	E	E	E	E
Iceland	E	E	T	T
Ireland	E	E	T	E/T
Italy	E	E	T	T
Japan	E	E	T	T
Korea	T/E	T/E	E	E
Luxembourg	T/E	50	T	T/E
Mexico	E	E	T/E	T/E
Netherlands	E	E	T	T
New Zealand	**T**	**33**	**E**	**E**
Norway	E	E	T	T
Poland	E	E	T	–
Portugal	E/C	E	T	T
Spain	E	E	T	T
Sweden	E	15	T	–
Switzerland	E	E	T	T
Turkey	E	E	E	E
United Kingdom	T/E	E	T	E
United States	E	E	T	T

Note: Key to abbreviations
        C = credit
        E = exempt
        T = taxed
        P = partial
Source: OECD Tax Database.

Employers' contributions to private pension plans are taxed at 33 per cent, which previously prevented this kind of remuneration from receiving tax concessions (and indeed penalised it for low- and middle-income earners). But with the increase in the top personal marginal rate to 39 per cent, high-income earners now receive a tax preference of 6 percentage points on such contributions. There are no restrictions on their amount, but they must stay in the superannuation fund until the employee leaves the job or withdraws the money for reasons of "significant hardship". Otherwise, a 5 per cent withdrawal tax is applied.

New Zealand applies a much more comprehensive taxation of fringe benefits than most other OECD countries. The fringe benefit tax, paid at the corporate level, was previously levied at the highest personal marginal tax rate. This was administratively simple and effectively eliminated tax preferences for benefits in kind over straight pay. The drawback was that employees with marginal tax rates below the top rate were overtaxed. With the recent hike in the top personal rate, the fringe benefit tax rate was adjusted accordingly, implying even more over-taxation of middle- and low-income earners. To remedy this deficiency, employers have recently been given the choice of paying a flat tax on all fringe benefits (corresponding to a 39 per cent marginal tax rate at the level of the individual recipient[62]), or to apply a multi-rate system of the fringe benefit tax.[63] The latter implies that some items are now taxed at the marginal tax rate of the individual recipient, while fringe benefits that are not attributed to individuals, are subject to fringe benefit tax at a flat rate of 49 per cent. Although improving the equity of the fringe benefit tax, compliance costs will also increase, unless the employer chooses the flat-rate option. The scope for avoidance may also have been increased by keeping the pooled-item tax at 49 per cent (*i.e.* effectively 33 per cent at the personal level).

The international tax regime is relatively comprehensive and sophisticated

New Zealand's international tax regime has seen major reforms over the past decade. These have sought to reduce the domestic cost of capital, to limit avoidance and deferral of taxes, and to improve neutrality for residents' between investing at home and abroad, while also observing a practical need for generating revenues from cross-border income flows. These objectives are to some extent mutually incompatible, which requires complex trade-offs to be made. The key principle guiding the international tax regime is that of taxing residents' foreign- and domestically-sourced income as equitably as possible so as to promote an efficient allocation of their investments. The principle of taxing residents on their worldwide income is widely applied in OECD countries.[64]

As most other countries, New Zealand has gradually reduced taxation on the returns from inward investment since the late 1980s. The concern is that such taxes add to the pre-tax return foreigners require for holding New Zealand assets, hence shifting the burden of the tax onto New Zealand residents. This is particularly burdensome for New Zealand, given the rapid accumulation of net foreign liabilities (see Chapter I). Such considerations have led to the introduction of the foreign investor tax-credit scheme and the approved issuer levy, which effectively lower the tax burden on foreign capital (Annex II). A recent step in the same direction was the introduction of the "conduit regime" in 1998. This regime significantly reduces the effective taxation of foreign shareholders on non-domestic income generated by New Zealand companies.[65]

Counteracting the incentives for residents to divert income through low-tax foreign entities necessitates a battery of anti-avoidance and anti-deferral measures. In the New Zealand case, as for most other OECD countries, these include rules for transfer pricing, thin capitalisation, controlled foreign companies (CFCs) and foreign investment funds (FIFs). With respect to the two latter regimes, New Zealand applies somewhat stricter rules than other OECD countries. The CFC regime basically implies that New Zealand residents (parent companies) are taxed on a current basis on their share of income earned by foreign affiliates in order to disallow income to be accumulated offshore at lower tax rates than domestically. The CFC regime is broader than elsewhere, since it includes all kinds of economic activity, whereas most other countries apply CFC-rules only to "passive" investment income and a limited class of "active" business investments.[66] The FIF rules may also, in some circumstances, give rise to higher effective taxation of international portfolio investments (excluding investment in grey-list countries – see below) than of domestic portfolios. This is particularly the case since the taxation of capital gains is more stringent under FIF rules.[67] Furthermore, New Zealand applies the CFC and FIF regimes to many more jurisdictions than most other countries, where the imposition of such rules is generally limited to jurisdictions classified as tax havens.[68] New Zealand has thus chosen to put more weight on equity considerations (between investing domestically and abroad) and less emphasis on competitiveness of domestic firms operating in foreign markets.

After implementing the CFC and FIF rules in the late 1980s, New Zealand chose unilaterally to exempt investment in some countries from these rules, the "grey-list" countries. Countries currently on the grey list are the United States, Japan, Germany, the United Kingdom, Canada, Australia and Norway. They cover around 80 per cent of New Zealand's income from outward foreign direct investment. The intention of the grey list is to eliminate the high compliance costs associated with the FIF and CFC rules for investment in countries where New Zealand residents are thought unlikely to invest for tax reasons. Hence it reflects a trade-off between enforcement of tax payments from offshore entities and equity considerations on the one hand and the practical necessity of trying to limit compliance costs on the other. Predictably, this has given rise to various loopholes, such as financial institutions in grey-list countries being used as conduits through which

New Zealand residents can invest – with tax favouritism preserved – into non-grey-list low-tax jurisdictions. There are look-through rules within the CFC regime to prevent such kinds of avoidance, but these rules do not apply within the FIF regime.

Local governments have a high degree of autonomy subject to balanced budget rules

Local governments raise only around 5 per cent of total government tax revenues against an average of around 13 per cent in other unitary-government OECD countries and more than 30 per cent raised by state and local governments on average in federal OECD countries. More interestingly, however, local autonomy in setting tax rates and bases is greater than in any other OECD country (OECD, 1999c). The main source of tax revenues is the so-called "rates", which are taxes on the holding of real estate. Rates are generally based on a mixture of land (unimproved) values and/or capital (land plus improvements) values, which are determined on three-yearly valuation cycles. Local governments have full discretion to set the rates, subject to a general balanced budget requirement.[69] Other revenue sources include user charges and fees as well as surpluses from local government enterprises. There are no block grants from central to local government, but the central government does contribute funding to certain local government functions, in particular transportation as well as road construction and maintenance.

There are ongoing efforts to improve tax administration

Administrative and compliance costs form part of the economic costs of the tax system in addition to the efficiency losses caused by tax-induced deadweight costs, as discussed above. Evidence – although inherently very uncertain and fragile – points to compliance costs in the order of 2½ per cent of GDP and administrative costs of around ½ per cent of GDP.[70] Compliance costs in particular appear to be relatively significant compared with other countries (Table 24), but as such quantitative estimates are fragile and not readily comparable across countries, they should be interpreted with great caution. Compliance costs in New Zealand are found to be much higher for business tax than for the withholding tax on wages, the fringe benefits tax and the GST. Furthermore, they tend to fall more heavily on small businesses, which are thus put at a disadvantage compared with larger firms – a pattern, which is by no means unusual across OECD countries (Sandford, 1995). Recent initiatives by the authorities to reduce compliance costs and thereby increase compliance include a major rewrite of the tax law to enable taxpayers to understand their obligations more easily and to make the law more accessible; the introduction of a "binding ruling" regime that enables taxpayers to have, as far as possible, certainty as to the future tax treatment of business transactions; new and more efficient dispute resolution procedures; more active involvement of the private sector in designing tax policy through the "Generic Tax Policy Process";[71]

Table 24.   **Estimates of compliance costs in selected OECD countries**[1]

	Year	Compliance costs as a percentage of GDP
United States	1989	0.9
United Kingdom	1986/87	1.0
Canada[2]	1994	0.8
Australia	1990/91	2.1
Netherlands	1989	1.5
New Zealand	**1990/91**	**2.5**
Spain	1990	1.1
Sweden	1990/91	0.7

1. Excluding administrative costs.
2. Excluding corporate income tax.
Source: Sandford (1995).

and introduction of electronic filing for most personal taxpayers so that most salary and wage earners no longer need to file income tax returns.[72] The next step is to consider extending simplification to the self-employed and other non-wage earners, which will be a more difficult task.[73]

Main weaknesses of the tax system

Income tax bases are eroded by the absence of a comprehensive capital gains tax

Perhaps the single most important issue facing the tax system is the capital-revenue boundary. New Zealand does not have an explicit capital gains tax, but makes a distinction between revenue receipts, which are taxable, and capital receipts, which are tax exempt. This means that gains on shares and other assets not held on revenue account are not taxed.[74] Furthermore, various other kinds of income, such as certain one-off payments to employees, are defined as capital and hence not taxed. The capital-revenue boundary is thus being used to transform what is, in substance, ordinary taxable income into the form of a tax-exempt capital receipt. Since the guidelines for what defines capital and revenue, respectively, are not always clear and transparent, the Inland Revenue Department often has to take decisions on a case-by-case basis. This involves resource-demanding ongoing discussion and legal cases with taxpayers to develop the necessary jurisprudence, leading to high compliance costs and taxpayer dissatisfaction, and it inevitably invites attempts to try to shift income into non-taxed forms.

It could be argued that a capital gains tax would enhance both horizontal and vertical equity since capital gains constitute an accretion of income (and hence raise the taxpayer's ability to pay).[75] Moreover, there are a number of adverse consequences of *not* imposing a comprehensive tax on capital gains, especially since New Zealand applies an otherwise comprehensive income tax system: the income tax base is narrowed; the allocation of savings and investment is distorted; tax-shifting behaviour is encouraged, in particular among high-income earners and wealthy individuals; and a non-level playing field is created among different financial instruments. These problems gain particular importance where close substitutes exist on both sides of the capital/revenue boundary. Some of the most notorious examples are the distinction between taxable "active" and non-taxable "passive" financial gains (for income not covered by the accrual regime),[76] as well as various tax-exempt one-off payments to employees.[77]

The main drawback of introducing a comprehensive capital gains tax is the practical problems of taxing accrued rather than realised gains as well as real rather than nominal gains. As a result, capital gains taxes may cause assets to be locked in to sub-optimal uses.[78] Furthermore, a capital gains tax may result in double taxation of retained earnings to the extent these are reflected in capital gains on shares.[79] Despite such concerns, many OECD countries have chosen to impose capital gains taxes on a more or less comprehensive scale and for various reasons, including those listed above.[80] In general, no clear picture emerges when considering the tax treatment of capital gains across OECD countries, except that it generally appears to be lighter than taxation of other kinds of capital income (Table 25).

Base erosion through tax preferences and boundary problems are compounded by the corporate entity structure

Together with the absence of a comprehensive capital gains tax, tax preferences given to certain kinds of investment, such as forestry and the acquisition of intellectual property rights (such as films), constitute vehicles for tax avoidance for (high-income) individuals. These investments are immediately deductible, and, since the stream of income only materialises over a very long time horizon or as untaxed capital gains, taxation can be avoided or deferred. Tax avoidance through such instruments is facilitated by the corporate tax structure, which allows "loss attributing qualifying companies" to allocate deductible losses to their individual shareholders (Box 9). Other avoidance vehicles include trusts, partnerships or setting up personal service companies between the individual taxpayer and his or her employer. These vehicles became more attractive as a result of the increase in the top personal marginal tax rate to 39 per cent, but have since then been weakened by the introduction of an attribution rule. This rule makes sure that income is attributed to the individual who delivers the service, regardless of whether a company structure has been set up in between the individual and the employer (effectively a "look-through" rule).[81] However, some scope for avoidance remains, not least in the area of trusts, where business income, interest and

Table 25. **Taxation of financial gains in OECD countries**
1999; resident taxpayers

	Taxation of financial capital gains (top personal rate of taxation; per cent)[1]
United States	Typical rate: 20. Capital gains are subject to special treatment. The maximum tax rate for capital assets held more than 12 months is 20 per cent.
Japan	Typical rate: 26. For listed companies a central rate of 20 per cent augmented by a local rate of 6 per cent applies. Alternatively, if the sale of the asset is entrusted to a securities company, a separate withholding tax applies. In this case, the central rate of 20 per cent can be applied to 5 per cent of proceeds.
Germany	Typical rate: 0. Capital gains realised through private transactions of resident individuals are generally not subject to income taxation.
France	Typical rate: 26. In most cases, capital gains on securities are taxed at a flat rate of 26 per cent. This comprises the basic rate of 16 per cent plus social surcharges (CSG, CRDS and Social Levy).
Italy	Typical rate: 12.5. Net capital gains on shares and other securities are subject to a flat rate. For gains on non-substantial holdings, the rate is 12.5 per cent.
United Kingdom	Typical rate: 40. Capital gains of an individual are aggregated with income and are taxed at income tax rates. The first £6 800 are tax exempt.
Canada	Typical rate: 54.1. Treated as ordinary income, but only 75 per cent of capital gains net of losses are subject to taxation.
Australia	Typical rate: 48.5. Treated as ordinary income, but only 50 per cent of net nominal capital gains of individuals are taxed.
Austria	Typical rate: 0. In general capital gains are not included in taxable income.
Belgium	Typical rate: 0. Capital gains realised by individuals not engaged in a business activity are in principal not taxable.
Czech Republic	Typical rate: 0. Gains from the disposal of securities held for 6 months are exempt from taxation.
Denmark	Typical rate: 40. Capital gains are taxable as capital income if held less than three years or if they exceed DKr 36 000.
Finland	Typical rate: 28. Income from capital is subject only to a national income tax levied at 28 per cent.
Greece	Typical rate: 0. Gains derived from the sale of securities (other than non-listed companies with limited shares and limited liability companies) are not taxed.
Hungary	Typical rate: 20. Capital gains on securities and on listed derivatives are taxed at a flat rate of 20 per cent. In absence of documentation of acquisition price, 25 per cent of the proceeds are taxed.
Iceland	Typical rate: 10. Gains from the sale of privately owned shares are generally included in taxable investment income and are taxed at a rate of 10 per cent. Gains may be exempt up to a maximum of IKr 349 911 (IKr 699 822 for a couple) provided that the company has been approved by the Internal Revenue Directorate.
Ireland	Typical rate: 20. Capital gains are generally taxed at a flat rate of 20 per cent.
Korea	Typical rate: 0. In general capital gains are not included in taxable income.

Table 25. **Taxation of financial gains in OECD countries** (*cont.*)

1999; resident taxpayers

	Taxation of financial capital gains (top personal rate of taxation; per cent)[1]
Luxembourg	Typical rate: 47. There is no separate capital gains tax. Capital gains are generally included in taxable income.
Mexico	Typical rate: 0. Gains on specified shares or other securities traded through an authorised stock exchange or similarly active market are tax exempt.
Netherlands	Typical rate: 0. In general capital gains are not included in taxable income.
New Zealand	**Typical rate: 0. In general capital gains are not included in taxable income.**
Norway	Typical rate: 28. There is no separate capital gains tax, but capital gains are included in taxable income. With respect to the computation of gains on disposal of shares of a resident company, special rules apply to avoid double taxation of company profits and gains to the shareholder.
Poland	Typical rate: 40. Capital gains are included in the taxable base as part of income from money investments, income from the sale of real estate, or business income.
Spain	Typical rate: 48/20. Treated like ordinary income. For holding periods in excess of 2 years, capital gains are subject to a flat rate of 20 per cent.
Sweden	Typical rate: 30. In general, all capital gains realised by an individual are included in the category income from capital. Income from capital is taxed separately at a flat rate of 30 per cent nationally (no municipal taxes apply).
Switzerland	Typical rate: 0. Capital gains are exempt.
Turkey	Typical rate: 50. Capital gains are generally included in capital income.

1. These rates apply to capital gains that arise from the disposal of securities, excluding speculative (or short holding periods) transactions, disposal of substantial interest holdings, or from gains realised in the course of a regular business activity.
Source: National sources and the European Tax Handbook (1999).

dividends can be channelled to people with low marginal tax rates (for instance children or non-working spouses) as trust beneficiary income.[82]

The variation in tax treatment between different corporate entities implies that the choice of ownership is sometimes based on tax considerations rather than economic objectives such as risk sharing, governance or transaction costs (Arthur Andersen, 1998). The corporate tax system also contains other distortions, which may not be crucial for New Zealand's macroeconomic performance, but nevertheless contribute to less than optimal investment behaviour. One of the more remarkable flaws in the corporate tax law is the current tax treatment of R&D expenditure on capital goods (R&D outlays on wages and salaries are, of course, expensed). Depending on whether these expenditures are classified as being for

---

Box 9. Loss attributing qualifying companies

A loss attributing qualifying company (LAQC) is a closely held company with five or fewer unassociated shareholders, satisfying certain requirements (see Greenheld, 1998). Losses incurred by a LAQC *must* be attributed to shareholders in the year in which the losses are incurred. If shareholders have sufficient income (from other sources) to absorb the loss attribution, it is generally advantageous for a loss-making qualifying company to become a LAQC. However, this is not necessarily the case if shareholders are in a loss position or have marginal tax rates less than 33 per cent. In such cases the benefits forfeited by the company (not being able to carry the loss forward to future periods) may outweigh the benefits gained by the shareholders (a reduction in taxable income that is negative anyway, or obtaining a tax saving of less than 33 per cent). The number of LAQCs almost doubled over the period 1994-98 (from 15 000 to 30 000 companies) and so did the losses passed on to the shareholders (from NZ$ 200 to 400 million, or from 0.2 to 0.4 per cent of GDP).

"scientific research" or "development", the tax treatment of R&D investment can be concessional or penal relative to the treatment of other capital assets. R&D capital expenditures for "scientific research" can generally be written off immediately. This is concessional compared with the costs of creating or acquiring other capital assets (which are generally amortised over the life of the asset). On the other hand, R&D capital expenditure on "development" may not be deductible at all, the so-called "black hole" expenditure. The definitions of which R&D expenditure falls under which category are not at all clear, which adds to the uncertainty of the R&D investment decision (even though most companies are in practice able to manoeuvre their accounts so as to avoid falling into the R&D "black hole").

Personal income tax credits may discourage labour market participation of exposed groups

Unlike other OECD countries there are virtually no deductions in the personal income tax system, but several tax credit schemes are in place to lower effective tax rates for low- to middle-income taxpayers (see Annex I). The annual budgetary costs of these credits amounts to 1½ to 2 per cent of GDP. The credits mostly benefit individuals (and families) in the lower five income deciles, whose actual average tax rates are substantially below the rates that would have applied in the absence of such credits (Figure 33).[83] The abatement of the credits (as well as welfare benefits such as the domestic purpose benefit and the accommodation supplement), while helping to contain revenue losses, also implies potentially

---

Figure 33. **Average implicit tax rates**
1999/2000

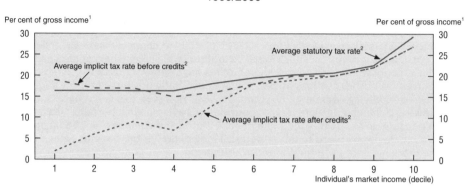

1. Gross income includes market income and gross transfers.
2. The average implicit tax rate is income taxes actually paid (including the ACC premium) by each income decile
   divided by the average gross income of each decile, before and after deduction of tax credits.
   The average statutory rate measures the average tax rate that should be paid by an average taxpayer in each
   decile in the absence of any tax credits, earning wage income only. The main difference between the average
   implicit tax rate before tax credits and the average statutory rate (including the low income rebate) in the lower
   income deciles is due to individuals earning capital income (hence is taxed at a minimum rate of 19.5 per cent).
   Source: Treasury's tax model (based on data from the 1997/98 Household Expenditure Survey inflated to 1999/2000)
   and OECD calculations.

very high marginal effective tax rates (METRs) for persons in the abatement
ranges. High METRS, up to the vicinity of 100 per cent, are to be found mostly for
low-income earners with children, in particular sole parents (Figure 34 and
Box 10). This is not surprising, since most tax preferences – as in many other OECD
countries (OECD, 1997*b*) – are targeted at families with children and since the
domestic purpose benefit is mainly paid to sole parents.[84]

High METRs may have substantial adverse consequences for the labour
supply of disadvantaged groups such as sole parents.[85] However, there is no reason to assume that wider macroeconomic implications are substantial, basically
since these groups are rather small.[86] Moreover, New Zealand does not appear to
have particularly high METRs for most family situations and income ranges compared with other OECD countries (Figure 35). The share of New Zealand taxpayers
facing relatively low marginal tax rates (below 40 per cent) is also large compared
with many other countries, while the share facing very high marginal rates (above
80 per cent) is more or less equal to those of other countries (Figure 36). Even
though such shares may not give the full picture of those affected by high tax
rates, since taxpayers respond to taxation, at least they provide an indication that
overall labour market distortions caused by taxation are not more substantial in
New Zealand than elsewhere – possibly quite the contrary.

Figure 34. **Marginal effective tax rates for various family types**
1999/2000

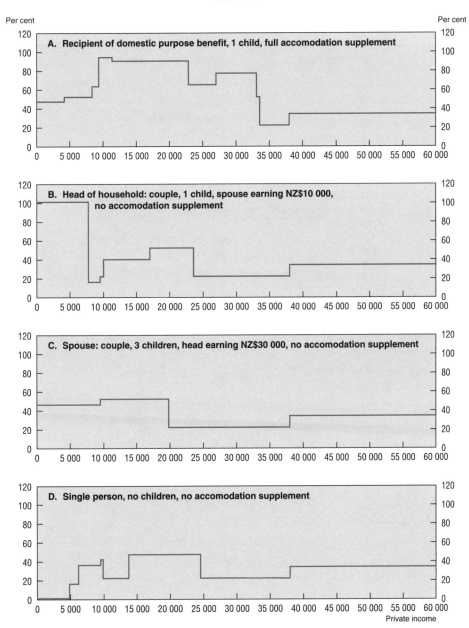

Source: New Zealand Treasury.

Figure 35.   **Marginal tax wedges on labour income in selected OECD countries**[1]

At multiples of average production worker earnings, 1998

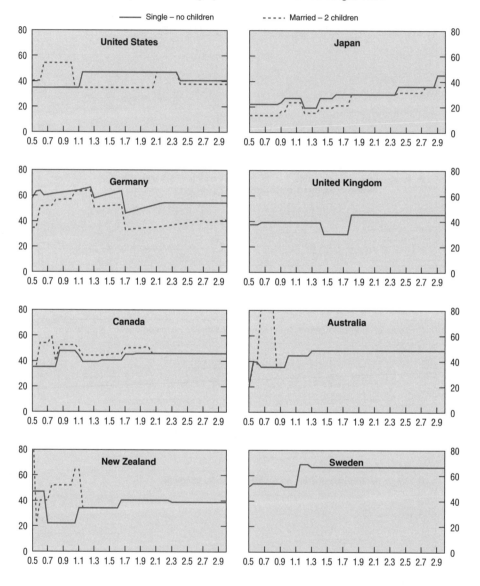

1.   Marginal tax rate, covering employees' and employers' social security contributions and personal income tax, with respect to a change in gross labour costs, by family type and wage level, assuming spouse earns no income. Data for New Zealand are for 1999/2000.
Source: New Zealand Treasury; OECD Tax equations.

Figure 36. **Distribution of marginal effective tax rates
in selected OECD countries**[1]

Early/mid-1990s

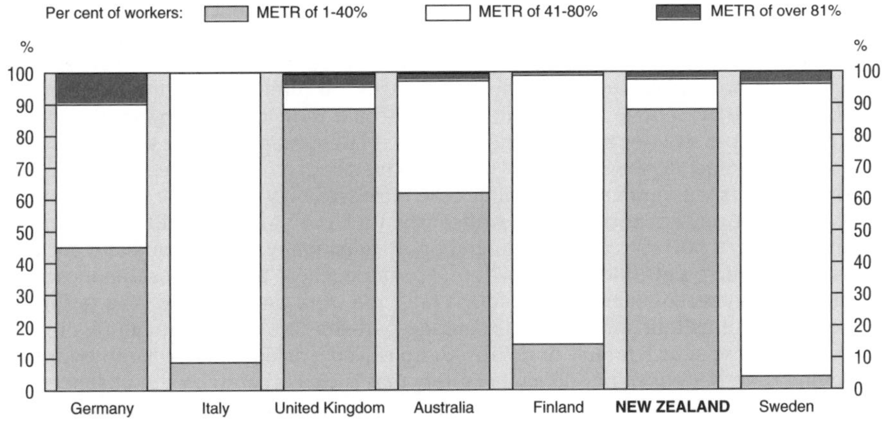

Per cent of workers: METR of 1-40%   METR of 41-80%   METR of over 81%

1. Marginal effective tax rates calculated for employed persons only (because data on the unemployed and non
    employed are not comparable across countries).
Source: OECD (1997).

Allocative efficiency of household savings is hampered by horizontal inequities

Household saving rates in New Zealand are not only lower than in most
OECD countries, the allocation of savings may also be less efficient, at least from a
growth-maximising perspective. Many households hold basically one major asset
(their residence) and one major liability (the associated mortgage). Since the
implied rental value as well as capital gains on the residence are untaxed, and
since the mortgage interest is non-deductible, the optimal saving strategy is to
pay down debt, rather than diversifying the portfolio of assets. By exempting
investment in housing from taxation other than the local property tax, a tax preference is (generally) allowed to such investment compared with financial investments, which are taxed on income and in some cases also on capital gains.[87] The
relative advantage allowed to housing investment depends on the amount of debt
financing: non-deductibility of mortgage interest claws back the tax advantage so
that only investors with fully equity-financed houses receive the full benefit of the
preferential tax treatment. Comparing historical returns to various assets there is a
clear pattern that pre-tax returns to housing investment are significantly lower
than those on equity investment. However, when taking into account the tax
advantages allowed to housing, the *relative* after-tax performance of housing

---

Box 10.   Marginal effective tax rates for individuals

The likelihood of facing high METRs (say, over 50 per cent) for individuals in various family and income situations can be illustrated using the Treasury's tax model and data from household expenditure surveys (Figure 37). Considering both marginal and discretionary income changes,* it turns out that the likelihood of facing a METR above 50 per cent for low-income individuals (earning less than NZ$ 25 000 per year, or two-thirds of an APW) is substantially higher when considering an income increase of NZ$ 10 000 (one-quarter of an APW) rather than NZ$ 1. The reason is that more substantial income increases may take these persons into higher tax brackets and, more significantly, into the various credit abatement ranges, where METRs tend to be high. In particular, many sole parents and social assistance recipients find themselves in a position where their disposable income cannot be increased significantly unless full-time work can be found. The tax and benefit systems thus interact to discourage part-time work.** Although this may encourage the search for full-time jobs, there is also a risk that it may keep people in long-term benefit dependency (an effect that is exacerbated by the absence of time limits for unemployment and domestic purpose benefits). Few persons earning more than NZ$ 25 000 face METRs above 50 per cent (Panel B). For those who do, effective marginal tax rates tend to drop if an additional NZ$ 10 000 is earned rather than only NZ$ 1. This reflects the fact that such a large income increase may place them beyond the abatement range of income-tested assistance.

Most labour market decisions are not "marginal" in the sense of working a few more hours or trying to earn a slightly higher wage but consist of large, discrete changes in status – from not working to working, from working part time to full time, or from changing between jobs with substantial differences in remuneration.

** However, the share of part-time work in New Zealand is no lower than elsewhere in the OECD area. On the contrary, part-time employment is around 23 per cent of total employment against an OECD average of 14 per cent. The female share of part-time employment – around ¾ – is close to the OECD average.

---

against other savings instruments is much more favourable (Table 26).[88] Over the 1990s as a whole, after-tax returns to investment in housing even turned out to match those of investment in equities (Westpac Trust, 2000).

The preferential tax treatment of housing implies that investment is diverted from more productive uses and possibly contributes to a higher cost of equity capital.[89] The share of owner-occupied housing in New Zealand is thus relatively high compared with other countries, as is the share of housing capital in household portfolios (Figure 38).[90] Preferential tax treatment of owner-occupied housing is widespread among OECD countries (Table 27), but it could have more adverse effects in New Zealand than elsewhere, since private pension saving is not subsidised as in other countries. Hence, there is not the same amount of pension

Figure 37. **Marginal effective tax rates: marginal versus large income increases**
2000/2001

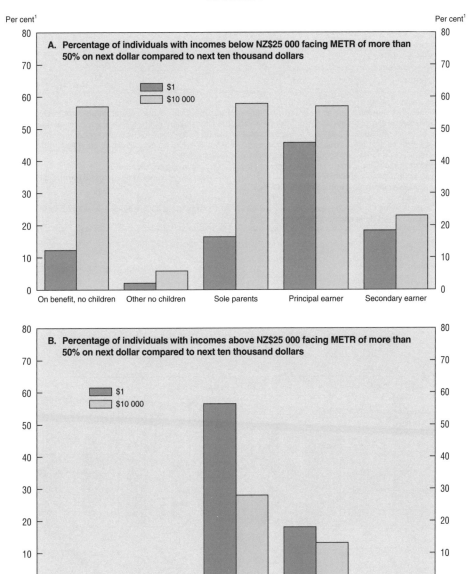

1. Per cent of population in the family category concerned.
Source: New Zealand Treasury, 2000.

Table 26. **Effect of taxation on asset returns**[1]

Asset	Nominal pre-tax return (per cent)	Nominal post-tax return (per cent)	Post-tax return as per cent of pre-tax return
Housing	14.0[2]	13.0[3]	93
Funds held in financial institutions	9.5[4]	6.4	67
Private shareholdings	27.4[5]	18.3	67
Passive investment funds	27.4	18.3	67
Managed funds	27.4	14.3[6]	52

1. Average annual nominal returns (1970-98).
2. Residential housing including an estimate of 2.5 per cent per annum for implicit rental minus maintenance.
3. Although capital gains and imputed rents on owner-occupied housing are not taxed, local government rates are still payable (assumed to be 1 per cent of market values) and no deductions for interest expense or maintenance allowed. This return figure could be lower for rental housing as rental income could be taxable, but deductions would be allowed for interest expenses, maintenance and depreciation.
4. Average six-month deposit rate (1970-98). Interest income taxable at 33 per cent.
5. Average return for the NZSE 40 (and previously Barclays index) for 1970-98, including dividend returns, and grossed up to reflect the effect of tax on company earnings.
6. Fund manager may be able to delay payment of tax until assets are sold.
Source: Joint Working Group – Treasury Officials and ISI (1999), "Saving Rates and Portfolio Allocation in New Zealand", New Zealand Treasury Working Paper No. 1999/9.

Figure 38. **Housing investment in selected OECD countries**

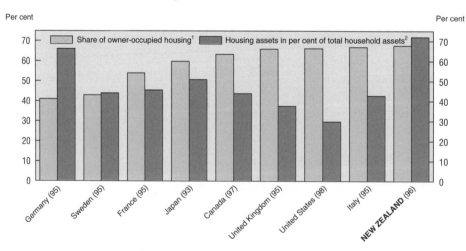

1. Data in brackets is the census year.
2. 1998 figures for all countries. These data are particularly fragile due to difficulties of measurement of household portfolios and may hence not be fully comparable across countries.
Source: National sources and Mylonas et al. (2000).

Table 27. **Tax treatment of owner-occupied housing in OECD countries**
1999

	Acquisition cost payable out of taxed income or deductible	Interest on loan for acquisition payable out of taxed income or deductible	Capital gain taxable or exempt	Imputed rental income taxable or exempt
Australia	T	T	E	E
Austria	PD	PD	E (if owner-occupied for at least 2 years)	E
Belgium	D	D	E	T
Canada	T	T	E	E
Czech Republic	T	D	E (if owner-occupied for at least 2 years)	E
Denmark	T	D	E (if owner-occupied for at least 2 years)	T
Finland	T	D	E (if owner-occupied for at least 2 years)	E
France	T	T	E	E
Germany	T	T	E (if owner-occupied for at least 2 years)	E
Hungary	T	PD	T	E
Iceland	T	T	E (if owner-occupied for at least 2 years)	E
Ireland	T	T	E	E
Italy	T	D	E	E
Japan	T	T	T	E
Korea	T	T	T/E	E
Luxembourg	T	D	T/E	T
Mexico	D	T	E	E
Netherlands	T	D	E	T
New Zealand	**T**	**T**	**E**	**E**
Norway	T	D	E	T
Poland	D	T	T/E	T
Portugal	PC	PC	E	E
Spain	D	PC/C	E	E
Sweden	T	D	T	T
Switzerland	T	D	T/E	T
Turkey	T	T	E	T
United Kingdom	T	PD	E	E
United States	T	D	E	E

Note: D = deductible
E = exempt
T = taxed
C = credit
PC = partial credit
PD = partially deductible
Source: The OECD Tax Database.

assets to be invested in productive capital formation. This is a consequence of the New Zealand tax system being more neutral with respect to pension saving than elsewhere, but still not fully neutral. The high concentration of households' wealth in housing assets may also imply an undesirable macroeconomic exposure to the performance of the housing market. A "first-best" solution to reduce the "oversaving" in housing would be to align the tax treatment of such savings with that of any other savings instrument (imposing neutrality vis-à-vis more productive saving). This would require taxing the imputed rental value, while allowing mortgage interest as well as depreciation and maintenance costs to be deducted.

Further strengthening neutrality and efficiency

New Zealand has come a long way in implementing a truly comprehensive income tax system with broad bases and moderate rates. However, distortions stemming from remaining tax concessions have adverse consequences for equity and efficiency and should be addressed in a more thorough manner in order to reap the full benefits of an otherwise well-functioning tax system. Implementing a comprehensive capital gains tax as well as introducing taxation of the imputed rental value of owner-occupied housing would be instrumental in this respect, in particular by contributing to an improvement in the allocative efficiency of household savings. Introducing tax incentives to other kinds of savings would not be a proper solution to the problem of savings allocation nor would it be effective in raising the level of private or national savings. A summary of recommendations for possible tax changes are given in Box 12 at the end of the chapter.

Broadening the base should be given first priority

Introducing a comprehensive capital gains tax would eliminate or substantially reduce many of the weaknesses of the tax system discussed above, in particular the non-neutralities arising at the capital/revenue boundary. Tax revenues from the capital gains themselves would presumably be marginal, but a much more significant effect would come from limiting tax-shifting possibilities and hence protecting the income tax base. A capital gains tax would also have re-distributional consequences since such gains accrue mostly to high-income and/or wealthy households. Broadening the income tax base by including capital gains would therefore effectively make the tax system more progressive without having to increase marginal tax rates – thereby improving the trade-off between equity and economic efficiency objectives.

The most obvious way of implementing the tax would be simply to include capital gains in the income tax base, but it could also take the form of a separate tax with a single flat rate somewhere in between the statutory rates in the income tax system.[91] Theoretically, the capital gains tax should be levied on an accrual basis, covering real gains arising from all household assets. In practice, however, it could be modified in several ways without limiting the bulk of beneficial effects. Taxation of gains on an accrual basis tends to create significant administrative problems with asset valuation and could have adverse effects on liquidity-constrained individuals and companies. In most countries, therefore, such a tax has been implemented on a realisation basis, and that would be appropriate here as well. In order to mitigate lock-in effects, interest could be charged on the deferred tax payment,[92] although this not a common practice in other OECD countries. The potential double-taxation of retained earnings associated with a capital gains tax on shares could be overcome by taxing only the part of the gain that exceeds the increase in the stock of retained earnings of the company.[93] As the rest of the tax system, the capital gains tax could be on a nominal basis without causing undue distortions, assuming that the current low inflation environment is sustained. A specific issue is whether it should apply to principal residences or not. Only very few OECD countries tax gains on owner-occupied housing, but practices in other countries may not be the best benchmark in this case.[94] If introducing a full-scale capital gains tax is not feasible in the short term, a partial tax – taxing only the gains on listed and unlisted stocks as well as those on commercial real estate – would make a good starting point. If implemented along with a more stringent taxation of various kinds of remuneration of employees currently defined as capital payments, the vast majority of boundary problems would be solved. If this is not feasible either, at a very minimum the rules determining what are (non-taxable) capital transactions and what are (taxable) current revenues should be made clearer, and it should be ensured that close substitutes are given identical tax treatment.

Another important area of base-broadening, which would take the income tax system a significant step forward towards a truly comprehensive base, would be to include imputed rental values of owner-occupied housing in the tax base (with deductibility for mortgage interest, depreciation and repairs). This is already done in several other OECD countries, cf. Table 27 above. Such a step would improve the tax system, although there would be both positive and negative effects. First, since mortgage interest becomes deductible (in order not to discriminate against housing investment), the pay-off from using available funds to reduce the mortgage relative to other investment will decline. The bias towards housing investment implied by the current preferential tax treatment would be reduced, which in all likelihood would lead to an improved allocation of savings and higher overall economic returns to national savings. It is important to stress that such positive effects cannot be achieved solely by allowing tax deductibility of mortgage interest; it requires imputed rent to be taxed as well (Box 11). Second, there would be an increase in the tax base that could potentially be substantial.[95] However, the main purpose of including imputed rent is not to raise more revenues but to improve the allocation of savings, and there could thus be offsetting cuts elsewhere in the tax system in order to make the change revenue neutral.

Box 11.   Tax deduction of mortgage interest should not be separated
from taxing imputed rent

A proposal has been put forward to allow a tax deduction for mortgage interest without taxing imputed rental income (Arthur Andersen, 1999). In order to curb
avoidance and contain revenue losses, deductions should be allowed only
against capital income. The proposal would imply a zero marginal tax rate on all
investment income up to the amount of the mortgage interest, which would
indeed encourage households to hold additional financial assets. However, it is
not obvious that any substantial reallocation of investment would take place.*
The proposal would also imply a significant subsidy to wealthy households with
large investment incomes, without affecting their marginal savings decisions. The
income effects thus created for these groups may even result in a lower overall
household saving rate. Moreover, there would be a substantial risk of initiating a
tax-induced price spiral in the housing market, because many taxpayers would be
encouraged to borrow more and buy larger houses, with adverse macroeconomic
and distributional consequences. Finally, the costs in terms of revenue foregone
could be very substantial. Total interest payments on household mortgages are
estimated at around 5 per cent of GDP, corresponding to a tax value of 1 to
1.5 per cent of GDP (Figure 39). There is also an administrative issue, since mortgage

Figure 39.   **Household debt and interest payments**[1]
Per cent of GDP

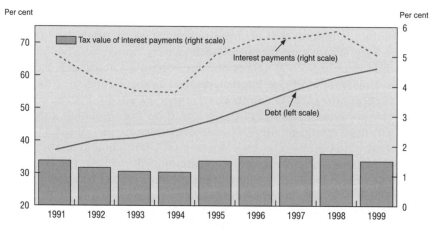

1.   Debt and interest figures include mortgages as well as other household liabilities (roughly around 10 per
cent of the total). The tax value of interest payments is calculated assuming a personal marginal tax rate
of 33 per cent and mortgage interest amounting to 90 per cent of all household interest expenditure.
Source: Thorpe and Ung (2000).

Box 11.   Tax deduction of mortgage interest should not be separated
from taxing imputed rent (*cont.*)

borrowing in New Zealand allows the use of home equity to secure loans for cars
and other consumer items, and banks do not report loans for pure housing separately. In conclusion, the issue of mortgage deductibility should not be seen in
isolation from taxation of imputed rental values.

---

*   The home-owner's acquisition of financial assets would be financed by higher debt,
which, in a world of substantial capital mobility, would imply an offsetting change in the
portfolios of other, possibly foreign, investors, who would simply hold more mortgage
bonds and less equity

But, on the other hand, compliance costs would increase as there would be a need
for regular estimates of market rents for owner-occupied homes as well as depreciation and maintenance costs. Obviously, some trade-offs would have to be made
between accuracy of the assessment and the need to contain compliance costs.[96]
In addition, relative after-tax returns to housing would fall which would lead to a
downward adjustment in housing prices and hence to potentially substantial capital losses for current owners.

In order to protect the tax base and minimise efficiency losses and inequalities, introduction of new tax concessions should generally be avoided. There
is currently an unwritten "code of conduct" that is quite unique internationally,
where demands for tax concessions by various interest groups are almost
absent – partly because there is an almost unanimous public opinion that tax concessions are undesirable, and partly because these groups have come to the conclusion that lobbying for tax concessions does not pay off. If this consensus is
undermined, even by a few limited tax incentives, the road may be paved for
much more lobbying and eventually more substantial base erosion in the future.
The political risk of introducing tax incentives to savings or investment, including
pensions or R&D investment, may thus be much more important than the immediate revenue and efficiency losses.

Streamlining tax credits could reduce complexity and perhaps also marginal effective tax rates

Earned income tax credits may help to encourage welfare benefit recipients to seek work and have indeed proved to be effective in several countries, in
particular in raising labour force participation of disadvantaged groups such as

---

sole parents.[97] One partial response to the dilemma of promoting part-time work without necessarily discouraging full-time work is to recognise that for some groups, such as lone parents, part-time work may be the more realistic option. The idea is that some work effort by these groups is better than none, not least with respect to keeping benefit recipients in touch with the labour market and alleviating poverty.[98] The tax credits and welfare benefits could be adjusted to lower the combined abatement rates for these groups in order to remove the current disincentives for taking on part-time work. A step in this direction was already taken by lowering the abatement rates for sole parents in 1996,[99] but further moves along these lines may be warranted. Such efforts could also re-consider the coverage of the various tax credits and welfare schemes, since these have gradually been extended well beyond the low-income range and into the middle class (thereby substantially exceeding the original objective of alleviating income shortfalls of poor families). The issue is whether the coverage of tax credits could be reduced without conflicting with equity objectives or creating poverty traps. In this context, it should be noted that targeting of the assistance is made easier by the widening of the market income distribution that has taken place over the past 15 years (O'Dea, 2000). In any case, the sheer number of credits and welfare benefit schemes as well as their mutual interactions make the system unduly complex, and there may be some scope for streamlining without compromising distributional objectives.[100]

The fact that most tax credits and welfare benefits are means-tested at the level of family income implies that the incentive for one member of a family to work can be affected by the labour market position of another (the earnings of one spouse reduce the benefits entitlement of the other). Individual entitlements may alleviate this problem, but they do not remove the work disincentives created by the abatement of benefits. It may also prove to be an overly expensive option, either because it overcompensates households with two recipients of welfare benefits and/or since the incentives to misreport family status will increase if such households receive less than the sum of two individual benefits. Overall, however, the experiences gained in Australia from a switch to individual benefit entitlements in 1995 have been positive, in particular by improving the incentive for unemployed couples to take on part-time work or low-paid full-time work (OECD, 1996).

Enhancing the quality of savings and investment is difficult to achieve by tax concessions

The first-best solution to achieve a higher quality of saving and investment would be to broaden the tax base along the lines discussed above. To the extent this is not feasible, limited tax preferences may be applied as second-best ways of improving allocative efficiency. This would not be without costs, however,

since it would in effect alleviate existing distortions by creating new ones. Revenues foregone as well as the political risk of encouraging pressures for new concessions may also be considerable.

Household saving decisions can be influenced by applying tax incentives
to private pension plans. This could strengthen the role of institutional investors
and possibly encourage long-term saving by households.[101] While employer-
sponsored pension plans are already subsidised for top income earners, the government is currently contemplating the introduction of a new tax concession for
long-term pension savings. The idea is to replace the current TTE-regime with a
TET-regime for such savings. This would increase the tax liability for short-term
holdings but reduce it over time as the fund accumulates free of tax. The number
of years required before the TET-regime "breaks even" depends on the rate of
return and the tax rate applying at withdrawal. If, for instance, the rate of return is
10 per cent and the tax rate is 33 per cent, effective taxation will be lower in the
TET-regime if funds are held for more than 14 years (Figure 40). The problem with
the TET-regime is that the tax savings are "back-loaded", and hence the effects on
savings allocation may be limited. It may even be more efficient to switch to an
ETT system instead, as the tax savings are then given up front (in terms of deductibility of contributions).[102] This would also preserve the "no concession" spirit of
private pension plans,[103] although the effective tax rate tends to be lower at retirement age when benefits are withdrawn than when contributions are paid in. A shift
to ETT would, however, also give rise to immediate and potentially significant revenue losses for the government against uncertain future gains.[104] Considering
more generous schemes, such as the EET treatment applied in most OECD countries, would run counter to the efforts carried out in New Zealand over the past
15 years to abolish tax concessions to private pension savings and put the consensus on the undesirability of tax incentives at risk. The conclusion is therefore that
there are no overriding reasons why New Zealand should change its existing taxation of pension savings.

The scope for improving the quality of investment is probably rather limited, given the overall neutrality of the corporate tax system. The most pressing
concern is the tax treatment of R&D capital expenditure. This should be defined
more clearly and the rather arbitrary distinction between scientific research and
development abandoned. Some inspiration could perhaps be gathered from the
accounting treatment of such expenditure, even if the purposes are different. To
be precise, for accounting purposes, research costs are expensed in the period in
which they occur. If development costs relate to a clearly defined, technically feasible product or process that is useful or marketable, the costs are amortised over
the economic lifetime of the asset. If these criteria are not met, the development
costs are written down or written off. Also, the concessions given to forestry, mining and intellectual property rights should be phased out (perhaps using sunset
clauses) or substantially reduced.

Figure 40. **Examples of TTE versus TET taxation**[1]

Present value of total tax payments

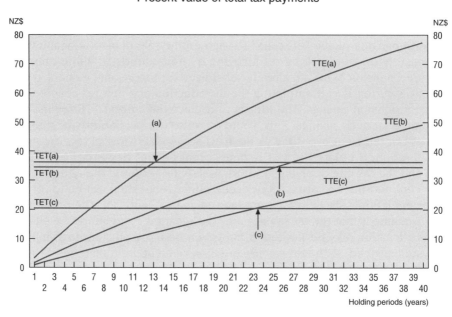

1. The figures shows, for varying holding periods, the present value of tax payments on a 100 dollar deposit in a
    pension plan with TTE and TET taxation, respectively (disregarding tax on the initial contribution which is identical
    under the two regimes). Three different situations are shown : a) tax rate of 33 per cent on both earnings and
    withdrawal, rate of return 10 per cent; b) tax rate of 33 per cent on both earnings and withdrawal, rate of return
    5 per cent; c) tax rate 19.5 per cent on both earnings and withdrawal, rate of return 5 per cent. The points at
    which the TET breaks even compared with TTE are marked a, b and c respectively (these are the points where
    total tax payments on a TTE pension scheme starts exceeding those on a TET pension scheme). The household
    discount factor is assumed to be identical to the rate of return.
    Source: OECD calculations.

The taxation of various corporate entities could be streamlined. Although
steps have already been taken to limit tax avoidance through corporate vehicles
such as trusts, partnerships or personal service companies, there is still some
scope for using such vehicles to reduce taxation of personal investment and
employment income. The ability to use loss-attributing qualifying companies
(LAQCs) for tax planning should be reduced, preferably by removing the underlying cause for using them as avoidance vehicles (absence of capital gains tax, concessions to forestry, etc.). However, the existence of LAQCs is linked with the issue
of how to place new start-up companies on a more equal footing with more mature
firms: since new firms are normally not in a tax-paying position, they are not able
to use write-offs immediately. Even though they may carry over losses, these are

not correctly discounted, and new firms may also face significant liquidity constraints. The LAQCs help to alleviate this disadvantage, but the question is whether it is possible to construct an alternative mechanism that is less vulnerable to tax avoidance, for instance allowing the losses of new firms to be tradable (whereby the new start-ups could immediately cash in the tax value of the loss). In any event, supplementary regulation or restrictions would seem to be needed to prevent abuse and put a brake on revenue losses caused by such arrangements.

A tax system for the future – is a change in the tax mix desirable?

While the basic structure of New Zealand's tax system is sound, it may nonetheless be worthwhile to consider options for more fundamental changes in tax policy in the longer term. This is especially true since the recent increase in the top marginal personal tax rate and the problems of achieving a truly comprehensive income tax base, as well as steps taken in other countries to lower marginal income tax rates, may put the current tax structure under pressure in the future. The upcoming tax review is also expected to investigate such long-term issues. Two options may be of particular interest. One is increasing value-added taxation while lowering income taxes. The other is to move towards a dual income tax system, where the taxation of capital and labour income is separated. The two options are not mutually exclusive, and the first option would also be compatible with the current comprehensive income tax system.

Increasing the value added tax and lowering the income tax would move the tax system in the direction of an expenditure tax. This would reduce the inherent distortions to private savings embodied in all income tax systems as well as allow for lower marginal tax rates on labour income, thereby reducing deadweight costs.[105] Such a change in the tax mix would also reduce the size of the "hidden" economy, although probably not significantly (Giles, 1999). The effects on personal savings from lower income taxes would probably at best be moderate, as discussed above. A change in the tax mix would also result in a one-off increase in the price level and, as most welfare benefits are indexed to consumer prices, part of the increased revenues from a higher GST would presumably go to finance compensating increases in benefit levels, leaving less room for income tax cuts. Higher consumption taxes may have immediate undesirable distributional effects, although the evidence does not seem to vindicate such concerns. Indeed, a study by Creedy (1998) found that the GST in New Zealand generally does not bear on lower-income groups any more than on high-income groups and that distributional effects are moderate overall.[106]

In terms of income taxation, the most obvious alternative to the current comprehensive structure would be to introduce a so-called dual tax system, as applied in the Nordic countries.[107] The basic principle is to separate the taxation of labour and capital income, thereby allowing countries with high marginal tax

---

Box 12. Recommendations for tax changes

New Zealand's tax system compares favourably with those of other OECD countries and is not in urgent need of major reform. However, in order to reap the full benefits of an otherwise well-functioning tax system, New Zealand should consider addressing a number of second-order issues. It should hence:

- Consider implementing a comprehensive capital gains tax, at a minimum with respect to gains on listed and non-listed equities as well as commercial buildings. To make it administerable, the tax could be imposed on realised nominal gains, but possibly with interest charged on deferred tax payments. Such a tax could solve many of the problems faced by the tax current system and would, in all likelihood, not create excessive lock-in effects. The government has recently taken steps to strengthen the taxation of various kinds of employee remuneration currently considered as capital payments, but more efforts may be required in this area to ensure a truly comprehensive taxation of wage and salary income.

- Consider taxing the imputed rental value of owner-occupied housing in order to broaden the income tax base and improve the neutrality of households' savings decisions. If – and only if – such a tax is implemented, mortgage interest should be made deductible, but only against the imputed rental income.

- Not allow new concessions in the corporate tax scheme (for R&D etc.). Various corporate entities should be taxed on a more uniform basis, and loopholes should be closed (e.g. loss attributing qualifying companies and trusts).

- Address some unfinished business in the area of international taxation, in particular how to counteract tax avoidance taking place through the grey-list regime without unduly increasing compliance costs.

- Not apply new tax incentives to private pension savings. The over-taxation of low- and middle-income earners in superannuation and life insurance schemes should be addressed, as should the concessions given to high-income earners through employer contributions to private pension plans.

- Consider streamlining of the tax-credits/welfare-benefit system. Reducing marginal effective tax rates at the lower end of the income scale would help to promote part-time work by disadvantaged groups, but such a step may conflict with the need for targeting in order to contain revenue losses. In this context, a change to individual entitlement of welfare benefits may be considered as a way of improving incentives for labour force participation. A more general issue is to what extent the coverage of tax credits and welfare benefits can be reduced without compromising equity objectives.

- Consider how the tax system should best respond to the increased mobility of tax bases and the future expenditure pressures stemming from an ageing population.

---

rates to maintain a heavy (progressive) tax burden on labour while taxing capital income at a lower uniform rate. The main objective is to reduce barriers to capital formation and avoid capital flight. Such a system is also better suited for avoiding non-neutralities across various kinds of capital income. However, applying different tax schemes to labour and capital income raises tax-shifting incentives, which require complex administrative countermeasures, and reduces vertical equity (see Van den Noord, 2000). In countries with relatively low personal tax rates, it is normally better to combine the taxation of all income into one comprehensive schedule (the Shantz-Haig-Simons principle). With a top marginal tax rate of 39 per cent on personal income, New Zealand is in an intermediate position, making it unclear whether comprehensive taxation of capital or a dual system is preferable. Maintaining a comprehensive tax system in the long term probably requires base broadening in the personal tax system along the lines described above. This would allow tax rates to be sufficiently low to avoid capital flight and excessive emigration of highly skilled labour (see Chapter III above).[108] Otherwise, a dual tax system may be the better option, since it would not impose the same straight-jacket on the top personal rate (on wage income).

Notes

1. A Policy Targets Agreement is required by the Act.

2. Per capita GDP growth is equal to a combination of growth in labour productivity, in the employment/population ratio and in the working-age population.

3. Productivity developments are examined over three periods that are relatively standard in the literature, pertaining to roughly the pre-reform period, 1978-84, restructuring and stagnation, 1985-92 and post reform, 1993-98.

4. Diewert and Lawrence (1999) use two databases to study productivity issues: one is an official database created by the New Zealand authorities, and the other one they created themselves. This section draws primarily on results from the official database. Their paper describes in substantial detail each database and their respective strengths and weaknesses.

5. See Maloney (1998) for a full exposition on the impact of the Employment Contracts Act.

6. In nominal terms, the share of machinery and equipment investment has remained broadly stable over the 1990s. The combination of prices indexed to 1991/92 levels and computer price declines has led to sharp growth rates in real investment. The rates will be much lower when revised national accounts, which incorporate chain-linked indices, are released in the near future.

7. Estimates of the share of ICT in output place it at about 3 per cent of GDP in 1995 (OECD, 2000*b*).

8. Contributing factors to individual income dispersion include shifts in labour force composition, and widening income differentials by occupation, education, industry and age. About half of the household widening resulted from changes in household composition, and changes in the age mix, employment status and qualifications of the population (O'Dea, 2000).

9. However, departures from New Zealand in the skilled category have remained relatively constant at about 50 per cent of all departures over the last nine years.

10. While employees could still bargain collectively, they would each receive an individual agreement in the absence of a union. One reason to prefer a union might be the right to strike in pursuit of a collective agreement.

11. Union members are annually entitled to two paid meetings of up to two hours per year. They must give 14 days notice and make arrangements with the employer to ensure that the business is maintained during the period. Union members can take up to five days paid leave in any one year for training. While employers are expected to collect dues on behalf of the union, this can be altered in a collective agreement or deleted if the parties so decide.

12. In particular, the contribution rate would be re-calculated each year by the Treasury with the horizon for the calculation pushed out one year. The amount would be stated in the annual Budget and would be treated as a capital expenditure.

13. While discussed further in Chapter IV, among other things this assumes that full Ricardian equivalence does not hold.

14. Because New Zealand Superannuation rates are linked to average wages, economic growth will contribute only in a limited manner to meeting higher future pension costs, highlighting the need to also periodically review the parameters of the system.

15. In deciding how much to invest outside the country, the board would have to weigh the positive benefits from the potential for lower capital costs and more liquid capital markets within New Zealand from its domestic investments that would be lost.

16. Community Work offers unemployed jobseekers employment in community-based projects to help them gain work-related skills.

17. The accommodation supplement was introduced in 1993 to assist all low-income households with housing costs. Most AS recipients are also in receipt of other social benefits.

18. Low income is set with respect to the net living-alone and married-couple rates under New Zealand Superannuation.

19. In addition, in mid-1999, exemptions began to be allowed for trainees in all industries where employees undertake substantial amounts of training linked to the National Qualifications Framework. Specifically, exemptions are available when there is a training agreement in place with an employer to undertake at least 60 credits per year (each credit being about 10 hours of training), each registered under the Framework.

20. These claims are funded on the basis of a levy that lasts for 15 years, with the outstanding claims liability recognised on the Crown Financial Statement as at 30 June 1999.

21. Three discounts are available (10, 15 and 20 per cent), depending on a firm's health and safety management practices. In addition, partnerships with the ACC on self-management allow for discounts of between 37 and 43 per cent for short-term partnerships and up to 90 per cent for employers who fully manage their injury and rehabilitation programmes.

22. The telecoms sector was deregulated in 1989, and the monopoly provider (Telecom) was privatised in 1990. At that time, the government introduced the Kiwi Share Obligations, which require Telecom to offer a free-calling option to residential users and to not increase the real price of residential access charges nor reduce service availability. In 2000, it was also required to begin publishing financial statements for its "local loop" business separate from its other telecommunications businesses (including transfer prices between businesses) and to disclose the net economic cost of complying with the Kiwi Share Obligations.

23. Designated services are interconnection to Telecom's fixed-wire network and wholesaling of its retail services. In addition, a set of specified services with a lower level of regulation was also recommended, including interconnection between all networks.

24. This does not mean that there are no problems in dairy production (as outlined in Box 3).

25. For example, the price paid to a producer typically bundles together all costs and profits, thus not recognising differing degrees of innovation, risk, changes in asset prices (most notably land). See Sinclair (1999) for a full exposition of the costs and benefits of producer board deregulation.

26. Some goods remain subject to high tariffs. For example, textiles, clothing and footwear face a 19 per cent tariff.

27. Credit unions may be assisted by a recent decision to allow the deposit ceiling to increase from NZ$ 40 000 to NZ$ 250 000. To take advantage of this increase, credit unions must adopt a trust deed and appoint an independent trustee by 30 April 2001. To date, only 2 of 75 have done so.

28. NCM companies must complete a "key transaction" within 18 months. This can take various forms, including the acquisition of assets or amalgamation with another business, and the size of this transaction must be at least NZ$ 1 million.

29. The Securities Commission oversees securities markets, including the New Zealand Futures and Options Exchange. Other key regulations in the financial sector draw on the Life Insurance Act 1908, the Unit Trusts Act 1960 and the Superannuation Schemes Act 1989. While the Ministry of Commerce administers these Acts, other regulators remain relevant in some areas. For example, non-bank deposit-taking financial institutions, unit trusts and superannuation schemes are subject to monitoring by independent trustee corporations and, in the case of superannuation schemes, by the Government Actuary.

30. The RBNZ would intervene in an insolvent bank only where the situation were to pose a significant threat to the soundness of the financial system. If that is not the case, a failed bank would generally be wound up using the liquidation procedures set out under the Companies Act.

31. While this is disclosed, it may make it more difficult for domestic depositors to assess the risks they face For example, local depositors may fare worse than would have been expected from the financial information presented in the branch bank's disclosure statement.

32. Bank directors are given primary responsibility for ensuring that their systems and controls are adequate, and are required to make regular attestations to this effect. The Reserve Bank also has the power to require a bank to obtain an independent report on its financial and accounting systems and controls where necessary.

33. The brief to the Minister (Ministry of Education, 1999a) prepared for the change in government notes that while Maori made up 19 per cent of all 17-23 year olds in 1996, they accounted for only 10 per cent of tertiary enrolment. In addition, in 1998, over 41 per cent of Maori men had no formal qualifications versus about 15 per cent for non-Maori men (Ministry of Education, 1999b).

34. Currently these groups account for about 20 per cent of the population, and this share is expected to rise to over one-third by 2050.

35. The government is exploring the possibility of reciprocal agreements with Australia and the United Kingdom to collect money owed on student loans by New Zealanders living in those countries.

36. In addition, if an existing allocation is not used in the time frame set out for it (usually one financial year), the authority to spend the money lapses.

37. The Public Finance Act of 1989 defines outcomes in a general manner and requires that appropriations identify the link between outputs and the government's desired outcomes. It does not, however, indicate how outcomes should be defined to allow them to be measured nor how strong the link between outputs and outcomes should be (Office of the Controller and Auditor General, 2000b).

38. For more detailed discussions, see OECD (1998), OECD (1999a), Savage (1997) and Scobie (2000). There are arguments for and against the inclusion of changes in housing wealth in the estimate of household saving rates. In any event, it is possible that part of the decline in household saving rates since 1992 shown by national accounts data may have been a response to the build-up in the capital value of the housing stock during the house price boom from 1993 to 1996 (a wealth effect encouraging higher consumption). There is also a possibility that changes in household saving rates may simply reflect a tendency to offset – at least partly – saving changes in the business and government sectors (Ricardian equivalence). Finally, it should also be noted that the apparent trend decline in the household saving rate, as measured by national accounts data, disappears when adjusted for inflation: measured over the past 30 years, the inflation-adjusted household saving rate seems to have been characterised by a constant mean, but with strong pro-cyclical fluctuations (Scobie, 2000).

39. It could be argued that for an open economy with access to world capital markets, there is no particular reason for economic policy to be concerned with domestic saving levels, since any lack of domestic savings can be covered by inflows of foreign savings. However, to the extent that foreign borrowings are not invested at a sufficient return and/or the level of foreign debt places a risk premium on such borrowings, the need for higher domestic savings is greater.

40. The alternative, keeping taxes unchanged and reducing government expenditure, may imply (but not necessarily) a smaller efficiency loss than raising taxes with unchanged expenditure.

41. This is not the whole story, however: several other countries with universal access to welfare benefits and public services at similar or even more generous levels than New Zealand also have higher household saving rates as well as current account surpluses (such as Denmark, Norway, Finland and the Netherlands).

42. The life insurance, superannuation and managed funds industry has captured the largest share of growth in household financial assets since the removal of capital market controls in the early 1980s (see Chapter III above). However, the share of these assets in total household financial assets has been rather stable since the abolition of tax incentives in the late 1980s (Thorpe and Ung, 2000).

43. Key statutory features of New Zealand's tax system are outlined in Annex I.

44. Other consumption taxes, such as excises or tariffs, are typically found to be more distortionary than value added taxes (see, for instance, Guerin, 1999).

45. However, income tax data do not allow capital gains taxes paid on housing to be singled out from other revenues. Nonetheless, since most gains are untaxed, the share of capital gains tax revenue is presumably marginal.

46. Annex Tables A1-A3 compare main statutory features of personal and corporate income taxation as well as the VAT systems for selected OECD countries.

47. It also reduced the marginal tax rate for very low-income earners, i.e. those with an annual income below NZ$ 9 500.

48. The marginal tax wedges for different income groups are based on the OECD's tax equations for production workers, which also include social security contributions. A few limitations of these data should be borne in mind. First, take-up rates for deductions and exemptions as well as fringe benefits are not included in the tax equations. Second, large groups of taxpayers, such as the self-employed, retirees and transfer recipients, do not pay social security contributions in many countries.

49. Tax data for 2000/01 show that around 7 per cent of personal tax payers had taxable incomes above NZ$ 60 000, where the 39 per cent rate kicks in. Some 4 per cent had incomes in the range NZ$ 50 000 to 60 000, 11 per cent in the range NZ$ 40 000 to 60 000 and 23 per cent in the range NZ$ 30 000 to 60 000.

50. This is indicative only since no account is taken for differences across countries in the composition of GDP nor of taxation of income not included in GDP.

51. The depreciation loading allows depreciation rates to be set at 120 per cent of estimated economic depreciation. However, this implies only a modest divergence between taxable income and "true" economic income (Arthur Andersen, 1998).

52. This indicates that New Zealand's relatively weak productivity performance over the past couple of decades is presumably not caused by features of the corporate tax system.

53. The smaller the variance in tax wedges across financing and investment instruments, the smaller is the overall distortion. The marginal effective tax wedge reflects the pre-tax rate of return an investment has to earn in order to provide an individual investor with the same after-tax return as a bank deposit earning a pre-tax 4 per cent real rate of interest. The estimates shown in Table 21 are based on the King-Fullerton methodology (see OECD, 1991). The results should be interpreted with caution, since they may not adequately reflect the effects of taxation on incentives when making investment and financing decisions. The marginal investor, for instance, may not be a fully complying individual (as assumed here) but rather a *de facto* tax-exempt entity. Other simplifying assumptions include perfect competition, a rudimentary treatment of financial structures and the intermediation process, the absence of uncertainty, perfect loss offsetting and capital irreversibility. For a discussion of these assumptions and data measurement issues, see OECD (2000*d*).

54. The effectiveness of the value added tax is measured as the effective rate (defined as value added tax revenues divided by consumption) as a per cent of the statutory rate. High effectiveness indicates that the base is broad and/or that compliance is high.

55. See, for instance, Inland Revenue Department (1999*a* and 1999*b*).

56. It should be noted, however, that truck owners have to pay road user charges for the cost of trucking in terms of road wear (depending on distance driven and the weight of the vehicle).

57. These costs are additional to the collection costs.

58. See Diewert and Lawrence (1994) and Leibfritz *et al.* (1997). In particular, the former study refers to estimates of deadweight costs in Australia ranging from 23 to 65 per cent and 17 to 56 per cent in the United States. Scully (1996) found that a tax/GDP ratio of around 20 per cent would be optimal for New Zealand in a growth-maximising framework. The study, however, contained severe methodological weaknesses and has largely been dismissed by most tax experts as well as the government (see, for instance, Inland Revenue Department, 1999*c*).

59. The first T stands for tax on contributions, the second T for tax on earnings of the funds and the last E states that benefits are exempt from tax.

60. A more detailed discussion of the various kinds of tax treatment applied to pension saving in OECD countries and their economic effects is given in, for instance, Dilnot (1992), Arthur Andersen (1999) and Dalsgaard and Kawagoe (2000). Besides New Zealand, a few other countries (Australia, the Czech Republic, Denmark, Luxembourg and Sweden) deviate from the general EET treatment of pension saving, although these countries still subsidise private pension saving to some extent. For instance, the pension tax

regime in Australia imposes taxes at all three stages (contributions; earnings; and benefits), but at relatively low effective rates. It hence offers some subsidisation of pension saving, but there is a significant reduction in the net value of benefits received compared with an EET treatment (Atkinson, Creedy and Knox, 1999).

61. The previous government attempted to solve the problem of inequitable taxation of the earnings of superannuation funds but did not succeed in passing a proposal through parliament.

62. The flat fringe-benefit tax rate corresponding to 39 per cent at the individual level is 64 per cent. This can be seen as follows: the fringe benefit is tax free at the level of the employee, hence the employee is indifferent between receiving a taxable wage of NZ$ 1 and a tax-free fringe benefit worth NZ$ $(1 - t^i)$, where t^i is the individual's tax rate. The cost to the company of providing the fringe benefit is thus $(1 - t^i)$, which is deductible. In order to ensure that the same total amount of tax is being paid on the fringe benefit as on a corresponding ordinary wage, the company has to pay a tax rate of $t^f * (1 - t^i) = t^i$ on the fringe benefit, hence $t^f = t^i/(1 - t^i)$. If t^i is 39 per cent, then $t^f = 0.39/(1-0.39) = 64$ per cent. Since the fringe benefit tax payment is tax deductible at the company level, the total combined tax paid by the company and the employee will be exactly the same whether remuneration takes the form of a fringe benefit or ordinary salary.

63. The new rules for the multi-rate fringe benefit tax were introduced in the March 2000 tax bill. The rules apply as follows: certain benefits (motor vehicles other than pooled vehicles, low interest loans and other benefits with a taxable value exceeding NZ$ 1 000 a year) must be attributed to the individual employee receiving them and taxed at the employee's marginal tax rate. Fringe benefits not attributed to an individual employee as well as pooled fringe benefits (such as pooled motor vehicles) will be subject to fringe benefit tax of 49 per cent.

64. New Zealand, as most other countries, does not apply a pure residence-based taxation as prescribed in the traditional theory of optimal taxation (see for instance Diamond and Mirrlees, 1971 and Feldstein and Hartman, 1979). The theory suggests that a small open economy should tax the return to capital export (net of underlying foreign taxes) at the same rate as domestic capital (in order to avoid any distortion in the allocation of capital invested at home and abroad), and capital imports should not be taxed at all. This result is valid only in the absence of untaxed economic rents on inward foreign direct investment. Depending on the elasticity of supply of inward investment, the optimal tax rate on imported capital may be higher than zero (Hines, 1997). Moreover, the government may in practice be constrained in setting the effective tax rate on capital exports equal to that on domestic capital.

65. See Harris (1998) for a critical evaluation of the conduit regime. He concludes that it is more complex than those of, for instance, Australia and the United Kingdom. He also concludes that it is patched onto, rather than incorporated in the corporate tax framework, and that the mechanism adopted is inequitable and inefficient because New Zealand companies engaged in the same offshore activities are not treated in the same manner. It should also be noted that in order to make the conduit regime entirely coherent, the 15 per cent non-resident withholding tax would ideally have to be abolished (thereby fully exempting non-residents from tax on income earned overseas).

66. Most countries are willing to forego current domestic tax on undistributed earnings of foreign affiliates of domestic firms if these represent "active" foreign incomes (that is, the domestic corporation is operating in the foreign market for non-tax business reasons). By deferring any additional home-country tax on such earnings, this policy helps

place foreign affiliates of domestic firms on a more level playing field with firms subject to the same host country tax burden. New Zealand's strict application of the CFC rules can be viewed as a way to move the tax system closer to the residence principle (Devereux, 1996).

67. While domestic gains are mostly untaxed – and if taxed, then on a realisation basis – capital gains are always taxed under FIF rules and often even on an accrual basis.

68. New Zealand applies the CFC and FIF regimes to all jurisdictions, except eight countries defined as "grey-list" countries (see below).

69. Local authorities are required by law to set operating revenues at a level sufficient to cover operating expenses in any financial year (with a few relatively narrow exceptions to run deficits). There is no regular, formal role for central government in reviewing or approving the budgets of local authorities and also no obligation on central government to assist those local authorities which experience financial difficulty. For example, the Local Government Amendment Act (No. 3) of 1996 states explicitly that local authority loans are not guaranteed by central government. However, in rare cases the central government has provided limited financial assistance to local authorities.

70. See Sandford and Hasseldine (1992). The study was carried out for the income year 1991. No more recent estimates for overall compliance costs are available.

71. The Generic Tax Policy Process was introduced in 1995 as a mechanism to give affected parties a formal voice in the formulation of tax policy changes. The process ensures that extensive consultations between the government and private-sector parties take place from the early stages in the policy process. The purpose is not to give the private sector a veto over policy initiatives, but to enable the government (and its officials) to tap the technical knowledge of the business community, to factor in compliance and administrative effects of policy changes as well as other concerns expressed by the private sector, and to communicate the rationale of policy changes.

72. Until 1999, salary and wage earners were required to file a tax return if their main sources of income were wages and salaries, interest or dividends. As part of a move toward tax simplification, a threshold has been introduced (currently NZ$ 38 000) under which filing is voluntary unless the taxpayer has Family Support, Child Support or Student Loan obligations. From the 1999/2000 income year most of the 1.2 million wage and salary earners no longer had to file tax returns.

73. This category comprises the self-employed, shareholder employees, partners and any person who has significant other income that has no tax withheld, such as rental income. Such persons are required to pay provisional taxes, provided their final tax liabilities exceed a minimum threshold (currently NZ$ 2 500). Of the 800 000 taxpayers in this group, 200 000 pay provisional tax, while the rest have relatively small amounts of income.

74. Various measures exist that levy taxes on some capital gains, notably the accruals regime, which taxes gains on some financial arrangements in a comprehensive way (cf. Annex I). However, despite these measures, most capital gains remain untaxed.

75. Vertical equity refers to taxation according to ability to pay. Horizontal equity is achieved when individuals with the same economic capacity (measured, for example, by income) are taxed to the same degree.

76. Whether capital gains are classified as "active" or "passive" is determined by applying rather ad hoc methods, such as the so-called "trader/non-trader" test, to establish if there is an intention to earn from capital appreciation or not.

77. The government announced in its 2000 Budget various measures to tighten the taxation of such one-off payments. However, as long as the distinction exists between revenue and capital, there will be an incentive for employers and employees to find new ways of re-labelling remuneration as non-taxable forms.

78. Lock-in effects are defined as the holding of appreciated assets in order to defer tax on gains already accrued. This leads investors to accept a lower before-tax rate of return than they would require for new investment without such accrued gains, resulting in a distorted allocation of resources and an inefficient portfolio selection.

79. Assuming that retained profits are in fact deferred dividends that are reflected in the share values, the associated capital gains are already taxed at the company level.

80. Some countries, including Japan and Korea, have attempted to use capital gains tax as an anti-speculative device, but only with limited success. Some countries also find that increases in private asset prices, such as land, caused by externalities from public development projects, should be taxed to capture some of the rent accruing to private owners (Dalsgaard, 2000).

81. The rule will apply only if certain criteria are met, most notably that at least 80 per cent of the income of the intermediary company is derived from the services of a single person or a single group of related persons. This is akin to the look-through rule applied in Australia.

82. For instance, in 1998 a total of NZ\$ 27 million of income stemming from business activities was distributed to children under the age of six. This figure excludes interest and dividend income distributed by trusts. The government is currently considering introducing legislation to tax trust distributions to minors at 33 per cent rather than the minor's marginal tax rate, which would in many cases be 19.5 per cent.

83. The median taxable income in the fifth decile is as low as NZ\$ 14 400 per annum, only around one-third of the earnings of an average production worker.

84. Tax in New Zealand is levied on individual income, whereas welfare benefits and family assistance are targeted with reference to family income. The main objective for these instruments is to supply income support to low-income families. The various tax credits combine with the statutory tax rates and income-tested welfare benefits to yield a complex set of marginal effective tax rates (METRs). The fact that gross welfare benefits are taxable income and the abatement regime is on net rates further complicates the calculation of METRs.

85. It should be stressed, however, that some of the credits causing the high METRs (the family tax credit, the child tax credit, the parental tax credit and the transitional tax allowance) are earned income tax credits, specifically designed to shift the balance between income in and out of work and thus to encourage labour force participation.

86. In particular, there are only around 150 000 sole parents out of a total working-age population of around 3 million individuals. The vast majority of the potential workforce is subject to moderate METRs of 50 per cent or less (Treasury, 2000). Unfortunately, there is not much empirical evidence available for New Zealand on structural labour market parameters such as the elasticity of labour supply and demand with respect to taxation.

87. The exception to the general tax concession given to home-owners is where losses are incurred: since home-owners are not taxed, they cannot offset imputed losses (deficits in imputed rents less interest and maintenance) against other or future income, whereas commercial investment can use such losses to offset other income or carry them forward.

88. See, for instance, Westpac Trust (2000), Joint Working Group, Treasury Officials and ISI (1999) and Arthur Andersen (1999). These conclusions obviously depend on the time period over which the returns are considered and what implied rental values are assumed for housing. Moreover, they should be taken with some caution, since differences in risk between various investments were not considered.

89. This claim is valid only to the extent some market segmentation exists across countries, as shown by Feldstein and Horioka (1980), for instance.

90. There may be other – and more significant – explanations than taxation for the relatively high share of housing in total household assets, including the relatively low average disposable incomes of New Zealand households (Joint Working Group, Treasury Officials and ISI, 1999).

91. The latter option would retain most of the beneficial effects and at the same time mitigate the "bunching-problem": a capital gain that has accumulated over several years will be taxed in one specific year and hence may be taxed at a marginal tax rate that is "too high" in a progressive tax system.

92. In practice, this can be done *ex post* by distributing the observed capital gain linearly over the holding period. This would significantly mitigate lock-in effects, although not entirely eliminate them.

93. Such a system, the so-called opening value adjustment method, is applied in Norway for instance (Van den Noord, 2000).

94. If such gains are included in taxable income, the issue arises of how to correct for improvements and whether to tax gains on land only (since buildings ultimately depreciate to zero without maintenance). Furthermore, taxing capital gains on residences may have adverse implications for inter-regional mobility in the labour market.

95. According to Statistics New Zealand, imputed rent and other rents in 1997 were equal to around 12 per cent of GDP. From this should be deducted mortgage interest payments of approximately 5 per cent of GDP as well as (unknown) maintenance and depreciation. It is probably not unrealistic to assume that the net increase in the income tax base would be of the order of 5 per cent of GDP, resulting in additional tax revenues of 1 to 1.5 per cent of GDP.

96. One option could be to use the assessments carried out for the local property tax every third year.

97. For a discussion of the effects of earned income tax credits (EITCs), see for instance OECD (1997b), Hotz and Scholz (2000) and Dilnot and McCrae (2000). A basic finding is that EITCs are most likely to work in countries where benefits are low relative to average earnings and the market earnings distribution is wide. Meyer and Rosenbaum (1999), for instance, find that for the United States the EITC has had substantial positive effects on single mothers' labour supply decisions (both in terms of labour market participation and hours worked).

98. As Stephens, Frater and Waldegrave (1999) note: "The 1996 Census showed that only 36 per cent of sole parents were in either full-time or part-time employment, and as the sole parent benefit is below the 60 per cent poverty line, it is interesting to speculate whether it is the Accomodation Supplement plus part-time earnings which are the mechanisms how sole parent families escape poverty".

99. The abatement rate of the domestic purpose, widows and invalids benefits was reduced from 70 to 30 per cent over the range of NZ$ 80-180 of weekly non-benefit income.

100. An extreme solution to simplifying the tax/benefit system has been proposed by the Investment Savings and Insurance Association of New Zealand Inc. (ISI). It suggests replacing all the current tax credits and welfare benefits by a guaranteed minimum income to each individual, leaving only some strictly targeted benefits for persons in extreme need, such as invalids requiring high-cost care. Abandoning the principle of targeting would make the tax/benefit system much simpler and pave the way for a substantial lowering of marginal effective tax rates at low- to middle income ranges. But it would also be much more costly. For example, in order to generate the same net revenue from personal taxes (personal income tax minus total expenditure on social welfare), a flat tax rate of 37 per cent would have to apply to *all* market income just to finance a guaranteed minimum income of NZ$ 7 500. This is substantially lower than the net income currently received by many beneficiaries and superannuitants, in particular those belonging to single-adult households. See ISI, 1999.

101. Arguments that governments should subsidise long-term savings are based mainly on moral hazard considerations: given the existence of public pension schemes, individuals may not save "enough" for their retirement, which would increase future demands on the government. This argument is valid mostly in countries where public pensions are means tested, and the future savings for the government would in any case have to be weighed against the revenue loss created by the tax concession.

102. This basically assumes that households are myopic. Several studies have found that this is indeed the case, *i.e.* that upfront incentives are more likely to be successful than an equivalent-value downstream initiative (Arthur Andersen, 1999). This implies that ETT is probably better than TTE for encouraging long-term savings.

103. ETT and TTE are similar if the effective tax rate at the point of contribution equals that upon withdrawal.

104. However, it could be argued that such a time profile for revenues could be more appropriate in order to match the expenditure pressure arising over the next decades due to the ageing of the population.

105. As mentioned above, Diewert and Lawrence (1994) found that, at the margin, the deadweight loss of the GST was smaller than that of the personal income tax. Note that the reduction in distortions to savings would not necessarily entail higher saving levels (as income and substitution effects may work in opposite directions, as discussed above).

106. These findings basically confirm previous research by the Treasury, see Lewis (1995). The Treasury found the GST to be regressive at both ends of the income distribution but roughly proportional for 80 per cent of households. If distributional concerns should arise despite such findings, it would be wrong to address them by introducing multiple GST rates or tax exemptions. Such steps would undermine the neutrality of the system and increase compliance costs, whereas distributional effects would at best be marginal. Indeed, the Creedy study finds that the increase in progressivity that could be achieved through exemptions of food and domestic fuel and power would be negligible.

107. For a survey of tax systems in the Nordic countries, see Sørensen (1998).

108. It could be argued that the need to reduce tax rates on capital income is less apparent in New Zealand than elsewhere given its strict taxation of foreign source income.

Bibliography

Arthur Andersen Corporate Finance (1999),
   Taxation and Saving in New Zealand, Report prepared for the Superannuation 2000 Task-
   force by Peter Goss and Alex Duncan, Wellington.

Arthur Andersen (1998),
   An International Perspective: Examining How Other Countries Approach Business Taxation, Report
   commissioned by the Commonwealth of Australia.

Atkinson, Margaret E., John Creedy and David M. Knox (1999),
   "Some Implications of Changing the Tax Basis for Pension Funds", Fiscal Studies,
   Vol. 20, No. 2.

Barro, Robert J. (1979),
   "On the Determination of Public Debt", Journal of Political Economy 87 Part 1, October.

Bernheim, B. Douglas (1999),
   "Taxation and Saving", National Bureau of Economic Research Working Paper No. 7061,
   March.

Bernheim, B. Douglas (1997),
   "Rethinking Saving Incentives", in Auerbach, Alan J. (ed.), *Fiscal Policy: Lessons from Economic
   Research*, MIT Press, Cambridge.

Box, S. (1999),
   "Economic Geography – Key Concepts", Treasury Working Paper 00/12, New Zealand.

CCMAU (1999),
   Briefing to the Incoming Minister of Health on Monitoring of and Advising on Hospital and Health Services,
   Crown Company Monitoring Advisory Unit, November.

Choy, Wai Kin (2000),
   "Determinants of New Zealand National and Household Saving Rates: A Co-integration
   Approach", New Zealand Treasury Working Paper (forthcoming).

Creedy, John (1998),
   "The Welfare Effect on Different Income Groups of Indirect Tax Changes and Inflation in
   New Zealand", The Economic Record, Vol. 74, No. 227, December.

Dalsgaard, Thomas and Masaaki Kawagoe (2000),
   "The Tax System in Japan: A Need for Comprehensive Reform", OECD Economics
   Department Working Paper No. 231.

Dalsgaard, Thomas (2000),
   "The Tax System in Korea: More Fairness and Less Complexity Required", OECD
   Economics Department Working Paper (forthcoming).

Davies, E.P. (1995),
Pension Funds, Retirement Income Security, and Capital Markets: An International Perspective, Oxford: Clarendon Press.

Davis, L., W. McKibbin and A. Stoeckel, (2000),
Economic benefits from an AFTA-CER free trade area, Year 2000 study, Centre for International Economics, Canberra and Sydney, June.

Deloitte Touche Tohmatsu (2000),
Deloitte e-Business Survey: Insights and Issues facing New Zealand Business, Deoloitte Touche Tohmatsu.

Department of Work and Income (1999),
Ministerial Briefing Paper, December, New Zealand.

Devereux, Michael P. (1996),
"The New Zealand International tax Regime", Report commissioned by four New Zealand companies (BIL, Carter Holt, Harvey, Fletcher Challenge and Lion Nathan).

Diamond, Peter and J. Mirrlees (1971),
"Optimal Taxation and Public Production, I: Production Efficiency and II: Tax Rules", American Economic Review, No. 61.

Diewert, W. Erwin and Denis A. Lawrence (1994),
The Marginal Costs of Taxation in New Zealand, Report prepared for the New Zealand Business Roundtable by Swan Consultants (Canberra) Pty Ltd.

Diewert, E. and D. Lawrenece (1999),
"Measuring New Zealand's Productivity", Treasury Working Paper 99/5, New Zealand.

Dilnot, Andrew and Julian McCrae (2000),
"The Family Credit System and the Working Families Tax Credit in the United Kingdom", OECD Economic Studies No. 31, 2000/II.

Dilnot, Andrew (1992),
"Taxation and Private Pensions: Costs and Consequences", in OECD, *Private Pensions and Public Policy*, Social Policy Studies No. 9, Paris.

Education Review Office (1999),
Good Practice in Managing the Fully Funded Option, October.

Edwards, Sebastian (1995),
"Why Are Saving Rates So Different Across Countries?: An International Comparative Analysis", National Bureau of Economic Research Working Paper No. 5097, April.

Engen, E.M. and W.G. Gale (1998),
"Effects of Social Security Reform on Private and National Saving", Federal Reserve Bank of Boston.

Ernst and Young (1999),
eCommerce in New Zealand: First Annual Study Results, April.

Feldstein, Martin and D. Hartman (1979),
"The Optimal Taxation of Foreign Source Income", Quarterly Journal of Economics No. 93.

Feldstein, Martin and Charles Horioka (1980),
"Domestic Saving and International Capital Flows", Economic Journal, No. 90.

Giles, David E.A. (1999),
"Modelling the Hidden Economy and the Tax-Gap in New Zealand", Empirical Economics, No. 24.

Guerin, Kevin (1999),
    "Indirect Taxes in New Zealand", mimeo, New Zealand Treasury.

Greenheld, Jon (1998),
    "The Tax Environment in New Zealand", in Keith Hooper *et al.* (eds), *Tax Policy and Principles: A New Zealand Perspective*, Wellington.

Harris, Peter A. (1998),
    "An International Comparison of Flow-Through Regimes: How Does New Zealand's New Regime Rate? ", International Bureau of Fiscal Documentation Bulletin, March.

Hines, James R. (1997),
    "Analysis of 'The New Zealand International Tax Regime'", Mimeo, New Zealand Treasury.

Hotz, V. Joseph and John Karl Scholz (2000),
    "Not Perfect, But Still Pretty Good: The EITC and Other Policies to Support the US Low-Wage Labour Market", OECD Economic Studies No. 31, 2000/II.

Inland Revenue Department (1999*a*),
    GST – A *Review*, Wellington.

Inland Revenue Department (1999*b*),
    Supplementary Briefing Papers, Volume 1: Tax Policy, Wellington.

Inland Revenue Department (1999*c*),
    Supplementary Briefing Papers, Volume 2: Report on Research Commissioned by Inland Revenue, Wellington.

ISI – The Investment Savings and Insurance Association of New Zealand Inc. (1999),
    Towards An Ideal Taxation Regime – A *Discussion Document*, Wellington.

Joint Working Group – Treasury Officials and ISI (1999),
    "Saving Rates and Portfolio Allocation in New Zealand", New Zealand Treasury Working Paper No. 1999/9.

Leibfritz, Willi, John Thornton and Alexandra Bibbee (1997),
    "Taxation and Economic Performance", OECD Economic Department Working Papers No. 176.

Lewis, Geoffrey (1995),
    "An Analysis of the Distributional Impact of Cutting the Rate of GST", mimeo, New Zealand Treasury.

Maani, S.A. (1999),
    "Private and Public Returns to Investments in Secondary and Higher Education in New Zealand Over Time: 1981-1996 ", Treasury Working Paper 99/2, New Zealand.

Maloney, T. (1998),
    Five Years After: The New Zealand Labour Market and the Employment Contracts Act, Institute of Policy Studies, Victoria University of Wellington, New Zealand.

McKinsey&Co (2000),
    Report to New Zealand Woolgrowers on Improving Profitability, Summary of Recommendations, McKinsey&Company, June.

Meyer, Bruce D. and Dan T. Rosenbaum (1999),
    "Welfare, the Earned Income Tax Credit, and the Labour Supply of Single Mothers", National Bureau of Economic Research Working Paper No. 7363, September.

Ministry of Education (1999*a*),
    Briefing for the Incoming Minister of Education, November, New Zealand.

Ministry of Education (1999b),
    Annual Report on Maori Education 98/99 and Direction for 2000, New Zealand.

Ministry of Health (1999),
    "Population Ageing and Health Spending: 50-Year Projections", Occasional Paper No. 2,
    December.

Ministry of Social Policy (1999),
    Post Election Briefing Papers 1999, New Zealand.

Moes, Alowin (1999),
    "Effective Tax Rates on Capital in New Zealand – Changes 1972-1988", New Zealand
    Treasury Working Paper 1999/12.

Mylonas, Paul, Sebastian Schich and Gert Wehinger (2000),
    "A Changing Financial Environment and the Implications for Monetary Policy", OECD
    Economic Department Working Papers No. 243.

O'Dea, Des (2000),
    "The Changes in New Zealand's Income Distribution", New Zealand Treasury Working
    Paper No. 00/13.

OECD (1991),
    Taxing Profits in a Global Economy, Paris.

OECD (1996),
    Economic Survey of Australia 1997, Paris.

OECD (1997a),
    Employment Outlook, OECD, Paris.

OECD (1997b),
    "Making Work Pay: Taxation, Benefits, Employment and Unemployment", *The* OECD *Jobs
    Strategy*, Paris

OECD (1998),
    Economic Survey of New Zealand, OECD, Paris.

OECD (1999a),
    Economic Survey of New Zealand, OECD, Paris

OECD (1999b),
    Employment Outlook, OECD, Paris

OECD (1999c),
    Tax policy studies No. 1, OECD, Paris

OECD (2000a),
    OECD *Science, Technology and Industry Scoreboard* 1999: *Benchmarking Knowledge-Based Economies*,
    OECD, Paris.

OECD (2000b),
    Economic Outlook, June, OECD, Paris.

OECD (2000c),
    Education at a Glance, OECD, Paris.

OECD (2000d),
    Tax policy studies No. 2, OECD, Paris

Office of the Controller and Auditor General, (2000a),
    Student Loan Scheme – Publicly Available Accountability Information, June.

Office of the Controller and Auditor General, (2000*b*),
Evaluation: Its purpose and Use, New Zealand.

Pinfield, Chris (1998),
"Tax Smoothing and Expenditure Creep", New Zealand Treasury Working Paper No. 1998/9.

Sandford, Cedric, ed. (1995),
Tax Compliance Costs: Measurement and Policy, Fiscal Publications in association with the Institute for Fiscal Studies, Bath.

Sandford, Cedric and John Hasseldine (1992),
The Compliance Costs of Business Taxes in New Zealand, The Institute of Policy Studies, Wellington.

Savage, John (1997),
"New Zealand Household Savings: An International Comparison", Report for WestPac and FPG Research, Wellington, April.

Scobie, Grant (2000),
"Saving in New Zealand", mimeo, New Zealand Treasury.

Stephens, R, P. Frater and C. Waldegrave (2000),
"Below the Line: An Analysis of Income Poverty in New Zealand, 1984-98", mimeo Ministry of Social Policy.

Scully, Gerald W (1996),
"Taxation and Economic Growth in New Zealand", Pacific Economic Review, No. 1:2.

Sinclair, G. (1999),
"Costs and Benefits of Producer Board Deregulation", Treasury Working Paper 99/4, New Zealand.

Soerensen, Peter Birch (1998),
Tax Policy in the Nordic Countries, Macmillan, London.

Stephens, Robert (1993),
"Radical Tax Reform in New Zealand", Fiscal Studies, Vol. 14, No. 3.

Tanzi, Vito and Howell H. Zee (2000),
"Taxation and the Household Saving Rate: Evidence from OECD Countries", BNL Quarterly Review, No. 212, March.

Thorp, Clive and Bun Ung (2000),
"Trends in Household Assets and Liabilities since 1978", Reserve Bank of New Zealand: Bulletin Vol. 63, No. 2, July.

Toder, Eric and Susan Himes (1992),
"Tax Reform in New Zealand", Tax Policy Forum: Tax Notes International, August.

Treasury (1999),
"Towards Higher Living Standards for New Zealanders: Briefing to the Incoming Government 1999", The Treasury.

Treasury (2000),
"The New Zealand Tax and Benefit Systems 2000/2001", mimeo, New Zealand Treasury.

Van den Noord, Paul (2000),
"The Tax System in Norway: Past Reforms and Future Challenges", OECD Economics Department Working Paper No. 244.

Westpac Trust (2000),
"Have New Zealand Households Been Adversely Affected by Investing Such High Proportions of Their Surplus Savings in Housing Assets?", Feature viewpoint, Westpac Trust.

Annex I

The tax system in 2000

I.   Personal income tax[1]

Tax unit: *the individual*

Tax base: besides labour income, the statutory personal tax system applies separately to investment income (interest income, dividends and certain kinds of capital gains). The statutory rates for investment income combine with the Low Income Rebate (LIR) to produce the effective tax scale for labour income (including self-employed, welfare benefits, recipients of New Zealand Superannuation and veterans' pension income). The LIR is applied to labour income only but abated on all income. Domestic withholding taxes apply to wage and salary income, dividends and interest income. Self-employed, shareholder employees, partners and any person who has significant other income that has not had tax withheld (such as rental income) are categorised as "other persons" (*i.e.* having income apart from wages and salaries). These taxpayers have to file an income tax return but are otherwise taxed at the same rate as wage and salary earners.

Tax rates:

National	Local	Highest all-in marginal rates
Statutory rates:	New Zealand has no state or local income tax.	Residents:
NZ$ 0-38 000: 19.5 per cent NZ$ 38 000-60 000: 33 per cent Above NZ$ 60 000: 39 per cent		Wage income: 39 per cent Self-employment income: 39 per cent Dividends: 39 per cent Interest: 39 per cent
Effective rates on labour income (statutory rates adjusted for LIR):		
NZ$ 0-9 500: 15 per cent NZ$ 9 500-38 000: 21 per cent NZ$ 38 000-60 000: 33 per cent Above NZ$ 60 000: 39 per cent		

Withholding taxes:

Residents: dividends at 33 per cent; interest income at 19.5/33/39 per cent (the choice of rate is optional for the taxpayers – but if no Inland Revenue Number is provided the default rate is 39 per cent). The PAYE is a withholding tax on salary and benefit income.

Non-residents withholding tax (NRWT) of 15, 15 and 30 per cent is levied on interest, royalty payments and dividends, respectively, but these rates are generally reduced to 10, 10 and 15 per cent under New Zealand's double taxation agreements. Relief from double taxation on dividend distribution is provided through New Zealand's Foreign Investor Tax Credit (FITC) regime, which extends New Zealand's imputation system to non-resident shareholders of New Zealand companies. Non-resident withholding tax on interest and royalty payments is deductible to the company to ensure that no double taxation arises. For certain registered securities, resident borrowers are subject to an approved issuer levy (AIL) of 2 per cent. There is no obligation to deduct the non-resident withholding tax from interest paid to offshore investors for these securities.

Foreign dividend withholding payments (DWP): when companies, unit trusts (including Group Investment Funds, category A income) and superannuation funds derive dividend income from overseas, they are required to deduct a dividend withholding payment on behalf of their shareholders. The withholding rate is currently 33 per cent. A credit for the foreign dividend withholding payment is deducted from the shareholder's liability once the dividend is passed on. This is similar to the way imputation credits can be passed on to shareholders.

The taxation of dividends, interest and royalties can be summarised as follows:

From/to	Companies		Individual investors	
	NZ resident	Non-resident	NZ resident	Non-resident
Dividends				
NZ resident company	Imputation credit available	NRWT; FITC available	Imputation credit available	NRWT; FITC available
Non-resident company	DWP with underlying foreign tax credit if ownership > 10 per cent	–	Credit for withholding taxes paid	–
Interest				
NZ resident company	Resident withholding tax to extent not imputed	NRWT/AIL Deduction may be subject to thin capitalisation rules	Resident withholding tax to extent not imputed	NRWT/AIL Deduction may be subject to thin capitalisation rules
Non-resident company	Credit for withholding taxes paid	–	Credit for withholding taxes paid	–
Royalties				
NZ resident company	Taxed as part of income	NRWT	Taxed as part of income	NRWT
Non-resident company	Credit for withholding taxes paid	–	Credit for withholding taxes paid	–

Tax credits and allowances:

The *Low Income Rebate* applies where income is below NZ$ 38 000 (*cf.* rate schedule above).

The *Transitional Tax Allowance* is available to persons who work for more than 20 hours per week and the person and his/her spouse do not receive family assistance. The rebate is NZ$ 728, reduced by 20 cents on each dollar earned over NZ$ 6 240 – thus the rebate is exhausted at NZ$ 9 880. Children are not entitled to the Transitional Tax Allowance.

The *Family Support Tax Credit* allows a tax credit for low- and middle-income families with dependant children according to the following schedule: for the eldest child aged 0-15: NZ$ 2 444 per annum; aged 16-18: NZ$ 3 120 per annum. For each other child: aged 0-12: NZ$ 1 664 per annum; aged 13-15: NZ$ 2 080 per annum; aged 16-18: NZ$ 3 120 per annum. It is reduced by 18 cents for each dollar of gross family income between NZ$ 20 000 and 27 000 per annum, and by 30 cents for each dollar of gross family income above NZ$ 27 000 per annum. The Family Support Tax Credit can be paid in addition to income-tested benefits.

The *Family Plus Tax Credit* (merging the former Independent Family Tax Credit, or IFTC, and the Guaranteed Minimum Family Income, or GMFI, and also adding a new element, the Parental Tax Credit) is assistance for working families with children, *i.e.* it is generally not available to those receiving welfare assistance. It consists of three separate components:

- The *Family Tax Credit* (formerly GMFI) is available to sole parents who work at least 20 hours a week and to couples who work at least 30 hours a week in total. It provides a guaranteed income level net of tax below which a family's income cannot fall. If a family's net-of-tax income drops below the guaranteed level (currently NZ$ 15 080 per annum), the government tops up the difference. The Family Tax Credit is payable to a family receiving payments from the workplace accidence insurance, ACC.

- The *Child Tax Credit* (formerly IFTC) is a top-up of the Family Support Tax Credit, but for working families only. It allows a tax credit of NZ$ 780 per dependent child per annum provided that the family does not receive welfare benefits, and has not been on accident compensation for a period of greater than three months. The full amount of the credit is available to eligible families with taxable incomes up to NZ$ 20 000 per annum. It is reduced by 18 cents for each dollar of family income between NZ$ 20 000 and 27 000 per annum, and by 30 cents for each dollar of family income above NZ$ 27 000 per annum.

- The *Parental Tax Credit* (in effect from October 1999) provides a payment of NZ$ 1 200 after the birth of each child for families who also qualify for the Child Tax Credit. The same abatement criteria apply.

The abatement is applied first to the Family Support Tax Credit, second to the Child Tax Credit and last to the Parental Tax Credit.

Children: no credit to parents. A child below 15 years of age, or under 18 and attending an educational institution, may claim the child rebate against their own earnings. The rebate is calculated as 15 per cent of gross earnings from employment, up to a maximum allowance of NZ$ 156 on NZ$ 1 040 of income. Interest and dividends are excluded from the calculation of this rebate.

Non-standard allowances: none.

The main welfare benefits are and their abatement rates are:

- The community wage (unemployment benefit) – abatement rate of 70 per cent for non-benefit income above NZ$ 80 per week.

– Invalids, widows and domestic purpose benefits – abatement rates of 30 per cent for non-benefit income above NZ$ 80 and below NZ$ 180 per week, thereafter 70 per cent (the income test on the domestic purpose benefit is sometimes applied on an annual, rather than weekly, basis, which provides greater scope for income smoothing). For full-time work-tested domestic purpose benefit recipients (i.e. if youngest child is aged above 14), the abatement rate is 70 per cent on income above NZ$ 80 per week.

– The accommodation supplement – for welfare benefit recipients the abatement rate is 25 per cent for non-benefit income up to NZ$ 80 per week. For those who do not receive welfare benefits, the abatement rate is 25 per cent when weekly income exceeds the rate of the gross invalidity benefit plus NZ$ 17.92 (e.g. NZ$ 239.92 per week for a single person with no children). For a couple, the gross rate of invalidity benefit is calculated on the basis that the entire net rate is paid to one taxpayer.

– The most common transfer payment, the New Zealand Superannuation (the public pension), no longer affects marginal effective tax rates after the elimination of the NZS-surcharge in 1998/99.

Other notable features of the personal income tax system

Income taxed at preferential or discriminatory terms:

New Zealand does not have an explicit capital gains tax. This means that certain items of economic income are exempt from tax. The main examples are gains on shares, housing, commercial real estate and other assets (excluding financial arrangements) not held on revenue account. There are taxes in place that have the same effect as a capital gains tax for certain areas:

a) The accruals regime taxes all gains from some financial arrangements – with the notable exceptions of equity, life insurance, etc. – as being held on revenue account (but does not necessarily treat them for deductibility purposes).

b) There are rules that buttress the "business" and "income from ventures" tests. These rules are more extensive for land. Some gains that would ordinarily be regarded as capital are caught by these rules as taxable income.

Employers' contributions to private superannuation schemes, irrespective of the marginal personal tax rate of the employee, are taxed at the corporate rate of 33 per cent. There are no restrictions on employers' contributions to superannuation funds as a way of remunerating employees, but in order to curb tax avoidance, the contributions must stay in the superannuation fund until the employee leaves the job or withdraws the money for reasons of "significant hardship". Otherwise, a 5 per cent fund withdrawal tax will apply.

Income accumulating in life insurance and private superannuation funds is taxed at 33 per cent, irrespective of the marginal tax rate of the investor. Thereby a subsidy is given to individuals with a marginal tax rate of over 33 per cent, while a penalty is imposed on individuals with lower marginal tax rates.

A comprehensive multi-rate fringe benefit tax is levied at the employer level. New rules for the fringe benefit tax were introduced by the March 2000 tax bill. Employers will have the choice of paying a flat 64 per cent tax on all benefits (corresponding to a 39 per cent marginal tax rate at the level of the individual recipient), or to apply a multi-rate system. The rules applying to the latter are as follows: certain benefits (motor vehicles other than pooled vehicles, low-interest loans, other benefits with a taxable value of NZ$ 1 000 a year or more and miscellaneous fringe benefits with a taxable value of NZ$ 2 000 per year or more) must be attributed to the individual employee receiving them and taxed at the employee's marginal tax rates (*i.e.* 27, 49 and 64 per cent, respectively, corresponding to individual marginal rates of 21, 33 and 39 per cent, respectively). The value of the attributed benefits will be included in the calculation to determine the fringe benefit tax payable on these benefits. Fringe benefits not attributed to an individual employee as well as pooled fringe benefits (such as pooled motor vehicles) will be subject to fringe benefit tax at 49 per cent. Some small fringe benefits are untaxed.

Taxation of pension saving : life insurance schemes and private savings plans (superannuation) are taxed as TTE, *i.e.* contributions are made from after-tax income, the current earnings of the funds are taxed at a flat rate of 33 per cent and the payments are untaxed.

Taxation of trusts: the current tax system allows business income, interest and dividends to be channelled from trusts to people with low marginal tax rates (for instance, children or non-working spouses) as trust beneficiary income. The government is currently considering introducing legislation to tax trust distributions to minors at 33 per cent rather than the minor's marginal tax rate, which would in many cases be 19.5 per cent.

II. Social security contributions

New Zealand has no compulsory social security contributions to schemes operated within the government sector (or outside of the government sector for that matter). However, the workplace accident insurance scheme (ACC), which was recently transferred back to the public sector (see Chapter III), is a payroll tax levied at the rate of 1.3 per cent on all employees. It is paid by the employer on behalf of the employees and thus deducted from wages and salaries. The contribution is capped at an annual income of NZ$ 83 017 at which point the levy reaches NZ$ 1 162.24.

III. Corporate income tax[2]

Tax units: corporate taxes are levied on all New Zealand resident companies, local government trading enterprises, unit trusts (including Group Investment Funds, category A income), and superannuation funds. New Zealand resident corporations are taxed on their worldwide income with an allowable credit for tax paid overseas. Non-resident companies operating and investing in New Zealand are taxed only on their income derived from New Zealand. Business profits and interest derived by non-residents with a fixed establishment in New Zealand are subject to corporate taxes. Other interest income and dividends or royalty payments are subject to NRWT.

Income tax rates

National	Local
33 per cent	No local corporate income taxes are levied.

Other key features of the corporate tax system:

Capital gains: no capital gains tax is levied in New Zealand. However, resident companies are taxed on all gains derived from certain types of financial arrangements and from certain property transactions. These gains are subject to tax at the standard corporate tax rate.

Dividends received from other New Zealand resident companies are taxable. However, dividends received from a wholly owned subsidiary resident in New Zealand are exempt as are dividends received from non-resident companies.

Tax credits are allowed for corporate taxes paid to foreign governments. The tax credit is limited to the amount of New Zealand tax payable on that income.

Losses may be carried forward for an unlimited duration, subject to continuity provisions for shareholder ownership (if at all times, from the beginning of the year of the loss to the end of the year of the offset, the same group of persons hold an aggregate minimum voting interest in the company and, in certain circumstances, minimum market value interest of at least 49 per cent). If these provisions are breached, then the losses expire. No carry back is allowed. The so-called loss-attributing qualifying companies (LAQCs) are not allowed to carry losses forward, but must pass on the loss immediately to their shareholders, who can then deduct these losses against other taxable income. Certain criteria must be met to become a LAQC: the company generally must be a qualifying company; it must have five or fewer natural persons as shareholders; all shares in the company must carry the same rights as each other share in the company; a notice in writing electing that the company be a LAQC must be received by the Commissioner of Inland Revenue before the first day of the year for which LAQC status is sought.

Consolidated income reporting: losses incurred within a group of companies may be offset against other group company profits either by election or subvention payments. Subvention payments are inter-corporate payments specifically made to effect the transfer of company losses. They are treated as deductions to the paying (profit) company and as taxable income to the recipient (loss) company. The loss- and profit-making companies must be in the same group of companies throughout the relevant period. The required common ownership is 66 per cent. Wholly owned corporate groups may elect income tax consolidation in which intra-group transactions are largely ignored for tax purposes.

Imputation system: New Zealand's dividend imputation system enables a resident company to allocate to shareholders a credit for New Zealand income tax. This credit can be offset against any tax payable by that shareholder.

Inventories must generally be valued at cost (according to generally accepted accounting principles) or market value (although market value may not be used for shares or "excepted financial arrangements") if it is lower than cost. Simplified rules apply to small taxpayers (annual turnover of less than NZ$ 3 million).

Depreciation: most assets can be depreciated using the declining-balance or straight-line methods (for fixed life intangible property only straight line is available). Assets valued at less than NZ$ 2 000 may be pooled. Property costing less than NZ$ 200 may be expensed immediately. Only economic depreciation rates may be applied to newly acquired buildings, second-hand property bought in New Zealand and imported used cars. An accelerated regime exists ("loading") by which assets can be depreciated by 20 per cent the first year.

Preferential depreciation regimes (immediate deduction of all expenses) exits for forestry, mining, intellectual property rights and certain kinds of R&D. Deduction of R&D expenditures may fall under one of three provisions in the income tax act:

– If the R&D expenditures are not of a "capital nature" (for instance, ongoing modifications of an existing product), the are immediately deductible.

– If the R&D expenditures are of a "capital nature" and classified as expenditures for "scientific research", they are generally immediately deductible, but may also in some circumstances be deductible over the life of the asset.

– If the R&D expenditures are of a "capital nature" and classified as expenditures for "development", they may be deductible over the life of the asset if they result in an intangible, depreciable asset (such as patents and copyrights). If these expenditures do not result in an intangible asset, no deduction is allowed (so-called "black hole" expenditure).

IV. International taxes

Foreign investments by New Zealand companies can be organised as foreign-incorporated entities (subsidiaries) or as branches of the home company. Income earned by a *foreign branch* of a New Zealand company is consolidated with that earned by the parent company and taxed by New Zealand upon accrual. New Zealand provides a tax credit for underlying foreign corporate taxes paid by the branch (limited to the amount of tax that is payable under New Zealand law). Dividend distributions from firms earning profits in foreign branches are taxable to individual recipients in New Zealand, with imputation credits available for New Zealand (but not foreign) taxes paid on the underlying income. Individual resident investors thus effectively pay full New Zealand tax on all after-foreign-tax source income. Individual taxes are not due until income is distributed as dividends, *i.e.* most of the New Zealand tax on income earned by foreign branches is deferred until that date.

In the case of income earned abroad by *subsidiaries*, the New Zealand tax system distinguishes between controlled foreign investment (CFC: "Controlled Foreign Company") and portfolio investment (FIF: "Foreign Investment Fund"). The CFC and FIF regimes were enacted in 1988. These regimes tax the income that residents accumulate in foreign entities that are resident in any other country (except for countries on the grey list). Under the CFC rules, individuals and corporations are subject to tax on their pro-rata share of the annual total income of CFCs in which they own an income interest of 10 per cent or more.[3] Income in such corporations is taxed annually under the same general rules applied to income from domestic corporations and foreign branches. Residents may claim tax credits for foreign income taxes paid by CFCs up to the amount of tax that is payable under New Zealand law. A foreign entity that is not a CFC is by definition a FIF, unless it qualifies for an exception.[4] Under FIF rules, residents are taxed on their net cash receipts from the foreign entity plus the change in the market value of their interests – thereby taxing distributed as well as undistributed income of the foreign entity.

The CFC and FIF regimes do not apply to the so-called "grey-list" countries, *i.e.* the United States, Japan, Germany, the United Kingdom, Canada, Australia and Norway. There are "look through" rules within the CFC regime to prevent grey-list countries from being mere conduits for non-grey-list investment. These look-through rules do not, however, extend to FIFs.

Transfer pricing: transactions between related parties must be made at arms-length prices (assuring fair-market valuation) as determined under OECD principles. Binding rulings with respect to transfer pricing issues are available from the Commissioner of Inland Revenue.

Thin capitalisation: if a non-resident-controlled New Zealand company over-allocates interest expenses to the New Zealand affiliate, the excess interest is disallowed a tax reduction. A safe harbour 3:1 debt/equity ratio is allowed before the clause applies. If the safe harbour is breached, the New Zealand company's debt/equity ratio is compared with that of the non-resident owner's worldwide debt/equity ratio. If the New Zealand ratio is higher (by some percentage), the interest on the excess debt is not deductible.

Foreign investor tax credit. Imputation credits from New Zealand companies may not be used to offset withholding tax on dividends paid to non-residents (generally 15 per cent withholding tax under double tax agreements). However, the New Zealand company may pass on the benefit of such credits to non-resident investors through payments of supplementary dividends. The foreign investor tax credit regime ensures that the sum of the company tax and non-resident withholding tax imposed on distributed earnings cannot exceed the company tax rate of 33 per cent. Hence, it extends the benefits of New Zealand's imputation system to non-resident shareholders of New Zealand companies.

The approved issuer levy. For certain registered securities, resident borrowers are subject to an approved issuer levy (AIL) of 2 per cent on interest payments to non-residents. There is no obligation to deduct the non-resident withholding tax from interest paid to offshore investors in these securities.

The conduit relief regime exempts non-residents from tax on non-domestic income derived by New Zealand companies (except for the 15 per cent non-resident withholding tax).

V. Property, inheritance and gift taxes

The only local taxes on land are the so-called "rates" charged by local and regional authorities. These vary by location but are typically charged on the improved value. There are no central government taxes on holding land or stamp duty on transactions of land. There is no capital gains tax on land *per se*, but the rules that "buttress" land held on revenue account result in the taxation of some gains that would otherwise be capital. If capital gains are held on a firm's revenue account, they are assessable as taxable income. The treatment of individuals is almost the same as the treatment of companies and trusts, although there are some personal exemptions for individuals and businesses from the buttressing rules.

New Zealand does not apply separate inheritance tax or stamp duties. A gift duty is levied at rates ranging from 5 to 25 per cent. The lowest rate applies when the value of the gift exceeds NZ$ 27 000, while the top rate kicks in at NZ$ 72 000.

VI. Consumption taxes

GST (Vat) rate:[5] 12.5 per cent standard rate. For long-term stay in a commercial dwelling GST at standard rate is levied on 60 per cent of the value of the supply (*i.e.* an effective rate of 7.5 per cent). A *zero vat rate* applies to export of goods and services; the supply of fine metal (gold, silver or platinum) from a refiner to a dealer; and the supply of the local authorities' petroleum tax (the distribution of the local authorities' petroleum tax between local authorities).

Exemptions: unlike most other OECD countries, New Zealand *does not* provide a number of "standard exemptions".[6] This means that exemptions are limited to financial services; rental accommodation; life insurance and reinsurance; and unconditional gifts.

Special regimes for small taxpayers:

Basic concession providing relief from VAT registration is given to small traders with annual gross sales up to NZ$ 40 000.

Major excises. Specific excises are levied on alcohol, tobacco and petroleum. A special duty is levied on gambling.

VII. Local taxes:

Almost all revenues stem from the rates (real estate taxes). Rates are generally based on a mixture of land (unimproved) values and/or capital (land plus improvements) values, which are determined by three-yearly valuation cycles. Local governments have full discretion to set the rates, subject to a general balanced budget requirement. Other revenue sources include user charges and fees as well as surpluses from local government enterprises.

Local authorities are required by law to set operating revenues at a level sufficient to cover operating expenses in any financial year (with a few relatively narrow exceptions to run deficits). There is no regular, formal role for central government in reviewing or approving the budgets of local authorities and also no obligation on central government to assist those local authorities which experience financial difficulty: for example, the Local Government Amendment Act (No. 3) 1996 explicitly states that local authority loans are not guaranteed by central government.

Notes

1. Annex Table 1 compares main features of New Zealand's personal income tax system with those of other selected OECD countries.

2. Annex Table 2 compares main features of New Zealand's corporate tax system with those of other selected OECD countries.

3. The act defines a foreign corporation as a CFC if 50 per cent or more of the shares of the corporation are held by five or fewer New Zealand residents or their associates; or one New Zealand corporation owns 40 per cent or more of a foreign affiliate and no single non-resident has a greater ownership interest; or a group of five or fewer New Zealand corporations otherwise control the affiliate.

4. Such as the grey-list country exception, *cf.* below.

5. Annex Table 3 compare main features of New Zealand's GST with VAT systems in other selected OECD countries.

6. These are postal services; dental care; charitable work (other than unconditional gifts); education; non-commercial activities of non-profit making organisations (other than unconditional gifts); cultural services; insurance ad reinsurance (other than life insurance and reinsurance); letting of immovable property (other than rental accommodation); lotteries and gambling; supply of land and buildings (other than land and buildings which have been used for the provision of residential accommodation for five years or more).

References

CCH New Zealand Limited,
   Tax Matters: New Zealand Tax Handbook 1999-2000.

Ernst and Young,
   World Wide Corporate Tax Guide, 1999.

OECD *Tax Database*, 1999.

OECD, *Economic Survey of New Zealand*, 1999.

OECD, *Economic Survey of New Zealand*, 1997/98.

Inland Revenue,
   The New Zealand Tax System: Developments since 1984, 1999, mimeo, Treasury.

Hines, James R.,
   Analysis of "The New Zealand International Tax Regime", 1997, mimeo, Treasury.

Table A1. **Taxation of personal income in selected OECD countries**
1999

	United States	Japan	Germany	United Kingdom	Canada	Australia	Ireland	New Zealand[1]	Sweden
Taxes raised by central government									
Range of statutory rates (per cent)	15-39.6	10-37	0-53.0	20-40	17.5-31.3	20-47	24-46	15-39	20-25
Number of tax schedules[2]	5	4	4	3	4	4	2	4	2
Rates of sub-national taxes (per cent)	0-11.6	5-13	–	–	12.7-22.8	–	–	–	25.2-34.7
Marginal tax rate for top income Earners[3] (per cent)	48.1	50	55.9	40	54.1	48.5	50.3	39	59.6
Effective tax threshold[4] (proportion of APW income)	0.8	0.9	1.0	0.3	0.7	0.2	0.6	0.7	0.04
Highest tax bracket starts at (proportion of APW income)	9.5	4.3	2.0	1.7	1.8	1.2	0.6	1.7	1.7

1. Statutory rates apply for 2000.
2. Excluding zero band or basic allowance.
3. Wage income.
4. For an employee with a non-working spouse and two children (1998 except for Japan (1999) and Korea (2000)). In Japan, one child is between 16 and 22 years of age. APW = average production worker in manufacturing
   In the United States, one child is below 16 years of age.
Source: OECD Tax Data Base, 1999; OECD, Taxing Wages, 1999; Ministry of Finance, Japan (1999).

Table A2. **Taxation of corporations in selected OECD countries**
1999

	Central government basic rate, per cent	Top marginal rate,[1] per cent	Dividend wedge,[2] per cent	Special rates (including small profits rate), per cent	Consolidation of losses within a group of companies	General rules of ownership,[3] per cent	Loss carry forward, in years	Loss carry back, in years
United States	35	39.5	67.7	15	Yes	80	20	2
Japan	30	40.9	70.5	29.3	No	–	7	1
Germany	42.2/30[4]	54[5]	50.2	–	Yes	Several pre-requisites (Organschaft)	Unlimited	1
United Kingdom	31	31	48.3	21	Yes	75	Unlimited	1
Canada	29.1[5]	46.1	73.6	13.1/22.1[5]	No	–	7	3
Australia	34[6]	34	48.5	Pooled development funds; offshore banking units	Yes	100	Unlimited	0
Ireland	28/10[7]	28	56.3	10	Yes	75	Unlimited	1
New Zealand	33	33	39	–	Yes	66	Unlimited	0
Sweden	28	28	49.6	–	No (but income may be distributed within a group of companies)	90	Unlimited	0

1. Including local taxation and surcharges.
2. Differences between the pre-tax profit earned by the distributing company and the net dividend received by a top income shareholder.
3. The ownership rules normally refer to the percentage of ownership of equity (or voting power) that the parent company has over the subsidiary. In some countries the rules may include both direct and indirect ownership. Several countries allow consolidation among resident companies only.
4. Germany and Mexico apply split-rate systems (i.e. different tax rates apply to distribution and retaining of profits).
5. Including surcharges.
6. From FY 2000/2001. The rate will be further reduced to 30 per cent in FY 2001/2002.
7. The higher rate applies to trading income from non-manufacturing activities, the lower the rate for manufacturing activities and certain financial activities. The rate was reduced to 24 per cent from 1 January 2000 and will be reduced to 12½ per cent (25 per cent on non-trading income) from 2003. The 10 per cent rate will then be phased out.
Source: The OECD Tax Data Base, 1999; Ernst and Young, The 1999 World Corporate Tax Guide.

Table A3. **Main features of VAT systems in selected OECD countries**
1998

	Year VAT introduced	Initial standard rate	Current standard VAT rate[1]	Tax-exempt threshold sales for small traders (in thousand 1998 PPP-US$)	Departures from standard exemptions[2]		Zero rate[3]	Coverage of lower rates
					Exemptions other than "standard exemptions"	Taxation of "standard exemptions"		Lower rates
Japan	1989	3	5	183	Social welfare services.	Letting of commercial buildings; postal services; non-commercial activities of non-profit making organisations; cultural services, supply of buildings.	–	–
Germany	1968	10	16	16	–	–	–	Books; food; newspaper; certain cultural events; charitable work if not exempt; transport (applies only to passenger transport by ship and to local public passenger transport). Rate = 7 per cent

Table A3. **Main features of VAT systems in selected OECD countries** (*cont.*)
1998

	Year VAT introduced	Initial standard rate	Current standard VAT rate[1]	Tax-exempt threshold sales for small traders (in thousand 1998 PPP-US$)	Departures from standard exemptions[2]		Coverage of lower rates	
					Exemptions other than "standard exemptions"	Taxation of "standard exemptions"	Zero rate[3]	Lower rates
United Kingdom	1973	10	17.5	76	Burials and cremations; sports competitions; certain luxury hospital care.	The freehold sales of new commercial buildings are standard rated for three years from completion date (furthermore there is an "option to tax" for other supplies of commercial buildings which would ordinarily be exempt from VAT); gaming machines and certain gambling in licensed clubs.	Certain services and goods supplied to charities; children's clothing; food; passenger transport; books; newspapers; domestic sewage and water; prescribed drugs; medicine; certain aids for disabled; new housing; residential and some charity buildings; alterations to listed buildings	Fuel and power for domestic and charity use (5 per cent); certain energy saving materials supplied together with fitting services to recipient of "Passport benefits". Rates = 2.5/5 per cent
Canada	1991	7	15/7	26	Child care; legal aid; ferry; road and bridge tolls; standard municipal services.	Lotteries and gambling; supply and leasing of commercial land and buildings; domestic postal services.	Medicine; basic groceries; exports; certain financial services (usually to non-residents); certain agricultural and fishing products; medical devices; international travel and transportation services; international organisations and officials; agriculture; precious metals (sales of 25 cents or less made through mechanical coin-operated devices).	–

Table A3. **Main features of VAT systems in selected OECD countries** (*cont.*)

1998

	Year VAT introduced	Initial standard rate	Current standard VAT rate[1]	Tax-exempt threshold sales for small traders (in thousand 1998 PPP-US$)	Departures from standard exemptions[2]		Coverage of lower rates	
					Exemptions other than "standard exemptions"	Taxation of "standard exemptions"	Zero rate[3]	Lower rates
Australia	2000	10	10	n.a.	n.a.	n.a.	n.a.	n.a.
Ireland	1982	16.4	21	57	Passenger transport. broadcasting. supply of water by public authorities. admissions to sporting events. funeral undertaking and travel agents/tour operators.	Long-term letting of commercial immovable property. supply of land and buildings.	Books. children's clothing and footwear. oral medicine. certain medical equipment. food products. seeds. fertiliser.	Newspapers and certain periodicals. fuel for certain purposes. electricity. works of art. veterinary services. agriculture services. car and boat hire. driving instruction. photographs. concrete. holiday accommodation. restaurant/hotel meals. building services. immovable goods. repair services. waste disposal. certain foods. tour guide services. admission to cinemas/ certain musical performances and sporting facilities.

Table A3. **Main features of VAT systems in selected OECD countries** (*cont.*)

1998

Year VAT introduced	Initial standard rate	Current standard VAT rate[1]	Tax-exempt threshold sales for small traders (in thousand 1998 PPP-US$)	Departures from standard exemptions[2]		Coverage of lower rates	
				Exemptions other than "standard exemptions"	Taxation of "standard exemptions"	Zero rate[3]	Lower rates
New Zealand[4]	10	12.5	25	Supply of fine metal (gold, silver and platinum).	Postal services; medical care, dental care; charitable work (other than unconditional gifts); education; non-commercial activities of non-profit making organisations (other than unconditional gifts); cultural services; insurance and reinsurance (other than life insurance and reinsurance); letting of immovable property (other than residential accommodation); lotteries and gambling; supply of land and buildings (other than land and buildings which have been used for the provision of residential accommodation for five years or more); transport of sick/injured persons.	The supply of taxable activities (business) as a going concern; the supply of fine metal (gold, silver or platinum) from a refiner in fine metal to a dealer in fine metal; the supply by a local authority of the local authorities petroleum tax (the distribution of the local authorities petroleum tax between local authorities).	For long term stay in a commercial dwelling, certain services, if provided as part of the right to occupancy are subject to tax at the standard rate of 60 per cent of the value of the supply (an effective lower rate on such services of 7.5 per cent).

Table A3. **Main features of VAT systems in selected OECD countries** (*cont.*)

1998

	Year VAT introduced	Initial standard rate	Current standard VAT rate[1]	Tax-exempt threshold sales for small traders (in thousand 1998 PPP-US$)	Departures from standard exemptions[2]		Coverage of lower rates	
					Exemptions other than "standard exemptions"	Taxation of "standard exemptions"	Zero rate[3]	Lower rates
Sweden	1969	11.1	25	–	Public television and radio, certain memberships. Publications, authors' rights, public cemetery services	Postal services, most cultural services	Commercial aircraft and ships, aircraft fuel, prescribed medicine, printing of certain membership publications	Accommodation, food, passenger transport, ski lifts, newspapers, works of art owned by the originator, import of antiques, collectors' items and works of art. Culture (theatre, cinema, etc.) authors' rights, commercial sports events, commercial museums, etc. Rate = 6/12 per cent

1. As of 1 January 1998. For Germany, this rate is applied as of 1 April 1998; for the United Kingdom, the standard rate is applied to a reduced value on imports of certain works of art, antiques and collectors items, resulting in an effective rate of 2.5 per cent. For Canada, 15 per cent Harmonised Sales Tax (HST) applies in those provinces that have harmonised their provincial retail sales tax with the federal GST (the 15 per cent HST is composed of a provincial component of 8 per cent and a federal component of 7 per cent).
2. Standard exemptions are the following: Postal services, transport of sick/injured persons; hospital and medical care; human blood, tissues and organs; dental care; charitable work; education; non-commercial activities of non-profit making organisations; insurance and reinsurance; letting of immovable property; financial services; betting, lotteries and gambling; supply of land and buildings; certain fund-raising events.
3. All countries apply zero rates to exports.
4. 2000 rules.
Source: OECD, Consumption Tax Trends (1999).

Annex II

The foreign investor tax credit and the approved issuer levy

The approved issuer levy (AIL) is charged at 2 per cent on interest payments to non-residents (for certain debt instruments that are registered with the tax department). The liability for AIL rests with the payer of the interest. Since the AIL is a deductible expense, the net tax rate for a company is 1.34 per cent.

The foreign investor tax credit (FITC) results in the combined New Zealand company tax and non-resident withholding tax (NRWT) being a maximum of 33 per cent for non-residents. This regime extends the benefits of New Zealand's imputation regime to non-resident shareholders of New Zealand companies. The FITC effectively implies that New Zealand foregoes the revenue from the non-resident withholding tax. The extent of the shareholders' benefits depend on their home country treatment of dividends received and tax credits. Since most countries allow full tax credit for withholding payments, the majority of revenues foregone by New Zealand accrue to the foreign investor, thereby contributing to a lower cost of capital in New Zealand. This would not be the case if the NRWT was simply abolished: in that case, the tax revenue foregone by New Zealand would mostly accrue to foreign governments, leaving the cost of capital in New Zealand unaffected.

Annex III

Calendar of main economic events

1999

January

The December quarter Consumer Price Index (CPI) was released. It rose by 0.4 per cent in the year ended December 1998. The Reserve Bank's price stability measure, CPIX, which excludes credit services, rose by 1.1 per cent over the same period.

February

The 90-day bank bill rate dipped below 4 per cent to an all time low.

The Crown Financial Statements showed a net surplus of NZ$ 1 173 million for the six months to 31 December 1998.

March

The Reserve Bank changes the way it implements monetary policy. An official Cash (interest) Rate (OCR), of the sort used by most major overseas central banks becomes the primary instrument the Reserve Bank uses to influence overall monetary conditions. The OCR is set at 4.5 per cent. This came with the release of the March 1999 Monetary Policy Statement.

The new state-owned insurer for workplace accident insurance is established and named At Work Insurance.

GDP figures show that the New Zealand economy grew 0.7 per cent in the December 1998 quarter and fell by 0.3 per cent for the year to December 1998, mainly as a result of a drought and the downturn in exports to Asia.

April

The March quarter CPI fell by 0.1 per cent in the year to March 1999. The CPIX rose 1.0 per cent over the year.

May

The sale of the Government owned electricity generation company Contact Energy Limited is completed for NZ$ 2.3 billion. 40 per cent was sold to a cornerstone shareholder (Edison Mission Energy Taupo Limited) and 60 per cent by way of public share float.

The 1999 Budget is delivered. It announces:

- Higher growth forecasts;
- the Governments sixth consecutive operating surplus;
- increases in expenditure on education and health, with particular emphasis on Maori and other disadvantaged groups. Research and development expenditure is boosted;
- a new tax credit for low and middle income families with babies is introduced; and
- the removal of stamp duties and the broadcasting fee, immediately and from 1 July 2000 respectively.

GDP figures show that the New Zealand economy grew 0.7 per cent in the March 1999 quarter and fell by 0.2 per cent for the year to March 1999.

June

APEC Trade Ministers meeting begins.

The Accident Compensation Corporation splits into three new businesses; employers can find private insurance or are signed up to At Work Insurance, the state-owned company, from 1 July 1999.

The United States plan to impose tariffs on Australian and New Zealand lamb.

The current account deficit was NZ$ 6.34 billion in the year ended March.

July

The June 1999 quarter CPI was released – it rose by 0.2 per cent in the June 1999 quarter, while the CPIX increased 0.5 per cent in the quarter and 1.2 per cent over the year.

Government introduces legislation to corporatise the Kiwifruit and Apple and Pear Marketing Boards.

August

The sale of the SOE Vehicle Testing New Zealand is completed.

The Government outlines measures to assist research and development and to reduce compliance costs for business.

September

New Zealand hosts APEC leaders meeting.

New Zealand reaches an understanding with Singapore on negotiating a closer economic partnership.

GDP contracts 0.3 per cent in the June 1999 quarter. The year to June shows growth of 0.6 per cent in economic activity.

The Crown Accounts for the year ended 30 June 1999 show a NZ$ 1.8 billion surplus.

October

The measure of the Reserve Bank's inflation target is changed. The 0 to 3 per cent inflation target is to be calculated in terms the Consumers Price Index (CPI), instead of the earlier underlying inflation and more recent CPIX inflation.

The September quarter of CPI was released. The CPI rose 0.6 per cent in the quarter. The CPIX rose 1.3 per cent in the year to September.

Treasury releases its Pre-election Economic and Fiscal Update (Pre-EFU): average annual growth of around 3 per cent is forecast; the operating balance improves steadily to reach NZ$ 2.3 billion by 2003.

November

The Reserve Bank raises the OCR from 4.5 per cent to 5.0 per cent. This comes with the release of the Reserve Bank's November 1999 Monetary Policy Statement.

The General Election is held resulting in a change of Government. The final allocation of seats allows the Labour and Alliance parties to form a Government with 59 of 120 seats.

December

Statistics New Zealand revised down the September quarter CPI rise from 0.6 per cent to 0.4 per cent.

The Labour and Alliance parties signed a coalition agreement.

The Treasurer and the Governor of the Reserve Bank sign a new Policy Targets Agreement (PTA), this being the statutory contract between the Treasurer and the Governor that sets out specific targets for achieving and maintaining price stability.

GDP increases 2.3 per cent in the September quarter. For the year to September the economy grew by 1.9 per cent.

2000

January

The CPI rose by 0.2 per cent in the December 1999 quarter and 0.5 per cent for the year, while the CPIX rose 1.3 per cent.

The Reserve Bank increases the Official Cash Rate (OCR) to 5.25 per cent. This increase came with the Reserve Bank's scheduled January OCR review.

February

The Ministerial inquiry into the electricity industry begins. The final report is due in June 2000.

Crown Financial Statements for the six months to 31 December 1999 show that the operating surplus was NZ$ 857 million.

March

The Ministerial inquiry into the telecommunications industry begins. The final report is expected in September 2000.

The Budget Policy Statement is released. It establishes the Government's six key goals and sets new fiscal targets for Government. The Government's fiscal policy approach involves:

– Running operating surpluses so that revenue exceeds expenses on average to enable ongoing contributions to pre-fund future New Zealand Superannuation (NZS) costs.

- Keeping net Crown debt below 20 per cent of Gross Domestic Product (GDP), on average.

- Accumulating financial assets to assist with the funding of future NZS costs.

- Keeping expenses around current levels of about 35 per cent of GDP.

It makes a fiscal provision for expenditure of NZ$ 5.9 billion over the next three years. It also outlines the fiscal implications of the Government's pre-funding proposals.

The Reserve Bank increases the Official Cash Rate (OCR) from 5.25 per cent to 5.75 per cent with the release of the March 2000 Monetary Policy Statement.

The current account deficit for the December 1999 quarter was NZ$2.86 billion, which includes NZ$681 million for the frigate HMNZS Te Mana.

GDP increases by 2.2 per cent in the December quarter. The economy grew 3.5 per cent in the year to December 1999.

The Government introduces changes to the industrial relations framework through the Employment Relations Bill.

April

The Reserve Bank increases the OCR to 6 per cent. This increase came with the Reserve Bank's scheduled April OCR review.

The Government announces changes to the Commerce Act that give the Commerce Commission more power and bring New Zealand in line with its key trading partner Australia.

A new tax rate of 39 per cent is introduced for earnings over NZ$ 60 000 (previously 33 per cent).

The Government agrees that tariff will be frozen at existing levels until at least 1 July 2005.

The CPI rose by 0.7 per cent in the March 2000 quarter, and 1.7 per cent for the year.

May

The Government announces increased expenditure on arts, culture and heritage.

The Reserve Bank increased the Official Cash Rate (OCR) by 0.5 per cent to 6.5 per cent. This came with the release of the Reserve Bank's May Monetary Policy Statement.

The New Zealand dollar falls to a 15 year low of US$ 0.4460.

June

The Government delivers its Budget. It announces:

- forecast average growth of around 3 per cent per annum over the next three years;

- the seventh consecutive operating surplus;

- funding for R&D and for industry and regional assistance;

- increased expenditure on education, housing and health;

- measures to reduce the economic and social inequalities that exist in society; and

- an increased policy focus on the environment.

The Ministerial inquiry into the electricity industry makes its final report.

The Ministerial inquiry into the telecommunications releases its draft report.

The current account deficit for the March quarter came in at NZ$ 1.01 billion and NZ$ 8.54 billion for the March year, equivalent to 8.2 per cent of GDP.

National Bank's survey of business confidence falls markedly.

GDP increased in the March quarter by 0.8 per cent. The economy grew by 4.4 per cent for the year ended March 2000.

July

CPI statistics were released for the June quarter, showing that the CPI increased by 0.7 per cent, and by 2.0 per cent for they year to June 2000.

September

The current account deficit for the June quarter was NZ$ 1.18 billion, and the deficit for the year to June 2000 NZ$ 7.5 billion (7.1 per cent of GDP).

Real GDP fell by 0.7 per cent in the June quarter but was still 4.5 per cent higher than a year earlier.

The financial statements for the year ended June 2000 show an operating surplus of NZ$ 1.4 billion.

STATISTICAL ANNEX AND STRUCTURAL INDICATORS

Table A. **Selected background statistics**

	Average 1990-99	1990	1991	1992	1993	1994	1995	1996	1997	1998	1999
A. Percentage change in constant 1991/92 prices											
Private consumption	2.4	-0.3	-1.9	-0.1	2.3	5.6	4.6	4.3	2.8	1.7	2.4
Gross fixed capital formation	4.3	-1.2	-18.6	1.4	14.8	16.7	12.2	7.0	3.8	-1.9	8.4
Public investment	0.3	8.6	-22.7	-16.7	-14.1	17.7	1.3	23.6	21.8	-0.5	3.7
Private investment	5.4	-4.1	-17.2	6.9	21.7	16.6	14.0	4.5	0.6	-2.2	9.4
Residential construction	2.3	2.0	-15.8	3.4	17.0	12.7	2.2	5.4	6.3	-16.9	12.0
Private non-residential	6.6	-6.6	-17.9	8.5	23.8	18.2	18.7	4.2	-1.5	3.3	8.6
GDP	2.4	0.3	-2.3	0.6	4.9	6.1	3.4	2.6	2.9	-0.6	3.7
GDP price deflator	1.5	3.8	1.0	1.7	2.7	1.5	2.7	1.8	0.0	1.7	0.1
Employment	1.9	0.9	-1.3	0.8	2.6	4.7	5.2	3.7	0.4	-0.6	1.4
Compensation of employees (current prices)	3.2	2.0	-1.0	1.4	3.9	6.1	6.1	5.8	4.0	0.7	2.1
Productivity (real GDP/employment)	0.5	-0.5	-1.0	-0.3	2.3	1.4	-1.7	-1.0	2.5	0.0	2.2
Unit labour costs (compensation/real GDP)	0.8	1.6	1.3	0.8	-0.9	-0.1	2.6	3.1	1.1	1.3	-1.6
B. Percentage ratios											
Gross fixed capital formation as per cent of GDP at constant prices	20.2	19.5	16.3	16.4	18.0	19.7	21.4	22.3	22.5	22.2	23.2
Stockbuilding as per cent of GDP at constant prices	0.9	0.7	-0.4	0.8	1.7	2.0	1.3	0.8	0.7	0.0	1.1
Foreign balance as per cent of GDP at current prices	1.5	0.7	3.5	2.4	3.1	2.7	1.8	0.8	0.7	0.6	-1.0
Compensation of employees as per cent of GDP at current prices	44.4	45.8	46.0	45.6	44.0	43.3	43.3	43.8	44.2	44.1	43.4
Direct taxes as per cent of household income	26.4	28.9	25.8	26.7	27.0	27.6	27.5	26.6	26.0	24.3	23.9
Unemployment rate	7.9	7.8	10.3	10.3	9.5	8.1	6.3	6.1	6.6	7.5	6.8
C. Other indicator											
Current balance (billion US dollars)	-2.4	-1.4	-1.2	-1.4	-1.0	-1.9	-3.0	-4.0	-4.4	-2.2	-3.6

Source: Statistics New Zealand and OECD.

Table B. **Gross domestic product and expenditure**
NZ$ million, current prices

Year ending 31 March	1991	1992	1993	1994	1995	1996	1997	1998	1999
Compensation of employees	33 368	33 001	33 785	35 263	37 523	39 753	41 979	43 323	43 388
Operating surplus	21 425	21 795	22 815	26 757	28 997	30 550	30 690	31 689	32 076
Consumption of fixed capital	6 525	6 884	7 403	7 700	8 185	8 661	9 214	9 702	10 125
Indirect taxes	11 135	10 837	10 888	11 408	12 170	12 810	13 371	13 623	13 627
less: subsidies	205	241	313	304	319	313	314	312	302
Gross domestic product	72 248	72 277	74 578	80 824	86 556	91 461	94 940	98 025	98 913
Final consumption expenditure									
Private	45 760	45 810	46 680	49 026	52 943	56 576	59 625	62 124	64 274
General government	12 291	12 269	12 682	12 578	12 535	13 218	13 805	14 769	15 139
Increase in stocks	-116	85	757	1 729	1 438	1 161	689	885	-148
Gross fixed capital formation	13 795	11 536	12 280	14 768	17 607	19 251	20 236	19 821	18 984
Statistical discrepancy	0	0	0	0	0	0	-209	-229	13
Gross national expenditure	71 730	69 700	72 398	78 101	84 522	90 206	94 355	97 599	98 250
Exports of goods and services	19 960	21 680	23 889	25 311	27 173	27 423	27 540	28 459	30 328
less: Imports of goods and services	19 441	19 104	21 709	22 588	25 139	26 169	26 745	27 805	29 677
Expenditure on gross domestic product	72 249	72 277	74 578	80 824	86 556	91 461	95 149	98 253	98 900
Gross domestic product at 1991-92 prices									
Index 1991-92 = 100	101.2	100.0	101.2	107.6	113.3	117.6	120.7	123.1	123.1

Source: Statistics New Zealand.

Table C. **Gross domestic product by kind of activity**
NZ$ million, current prices

Year ending 31st March	1989	1990	1991	1992	1993	1994	1995	1996
Agriculture	4 074	4 491	3 989	4 511	4 344	4 956	4 852	5 008
Fishing and hunting	260	249	233	236	270	272	285	305
Forestry and logging	557	615	701	850	1 052	1 494	1 306	1 298
Mining and quarrying	644	836	1 005	1 082	1 107	1 126	1 080	1 032
Food, beverage and tobacco	3 910	4 015	4 260	4 441	4 389	4 607	4 853	5 060
Textiles, apparel and leather	800	864	817	813	803	840	873	871
Wood and wood products	716	752	720	723	866	970	1 197	1 174
Paper products and printing	1 671	1 827	1 965	1 934	1 886	1 979	2 215	2 446
Chemicals, petroleum, rubber, plastic	1 604	1 776	1 490	1 481	1 574	1 800	2 178	2 075
Non-metallic mineral products	427	413	424	381	417	496	579	604
Basic metal products	255	460	424	477	671	650	613	683
Fabricated metal products	2 693	2 840	2 605	2 534	2 653	3 032	3 356	3 504
Other manufacturing	144	151	142	122	136	156	165	165
Electricity, gas, water	1 992	2 134	2 086	2 107	2 126	2 316	2 383	2 344
Construction	2 997	3 216	2 803	2 389	2 325	2 600	3 048	3 376
Trade, hotels and restaurants	10 524	10 292	11 411	10 244	11 102	12 539	13 783	14 579
Transport, storage	3 470	3 687	3 653	3 633	3 745	4 057	4 480	4 739
Communication	2 148	2 183	2 349	2 677	2 507	2 475	2 622	2 900
Finance, insurance, real estate and business services	10 298	10 771	10 681	10 641	10 693	11 573	12 746	13 451
Dwellings	4 907	5 275	5 914	6 214	6 153	6 265	6 603	7 358
Community, social, personal services	2 584	2 720	2 839	3 121	3 418	3 730	4 034	4 536
Imputed bank service charge	-2 818	-2 996	-3 000	-2 935	-2 581	-2 665	-3 145	-3 429
Total, market production groups	53 854	56 570	57 509	57 676	59 656	65 268	70 104	74 079
Producers of Government services	7 873	8 414	8 606	8 471	8 555	8 716	8 820	9 217
Other producers	644	698	769	852	907	952	1 025	1 082
Total, non-market production groups	8 517	9 112	9 375	9 323	9 462	9 667	9 846	10 299
Total, all production groups	62 372	65 682	66 884	66 998	69 118	74 934	79 950	84 378
Indirect taxes	4 082	5 091	5 364	5 279	5 460	5 889	6 606	7 083
Gross domestic product	66 454	70 773	72 248	72 277	74 578	80 824	86 556	91 461

Source: Statistics New Zealand.

Table D.   **Labour market**
Thousand

Yearly average	1991	1992	1993	1994	1995	1996	1997	1998	1999
Civilian employment, total	1 463	1 475	1 513	1 585	1 668	1 729	1 736	1 725	1 750
of which:									
Agriculture	157	160	159	164	161	164	150	147	166
Industry	343	336	355	396	418	427	414	415	400
Other activities	962	979	999	1 025	1 088	1 138	1 172	1 163	1 184
Unemployment	167	170	159	140	112	112	123	139	128
Unemployment rate									
(per cent of civilian labour force)	10.3	10.3	9.5	8.1	6.3	6.1	6.6	7.5	6.8

Source: Statistics New Zealand.

Table E.   **Prices**

Yearly average	1991	1992	1993	1994	1995	1996	1997	1998	1999
	June quarter 1999 = 1000								
Consumer'price index									
Food	906	907	917	918	929	942	963	994	1 005
Total	886	895	907	923	957	979	991	1 003	1 002
Producer prices (inputs)	922	941	964	977	985	990	994	1 001	1 009
Export prices	975	1 055	1 083	1 039	1 022	986	959	1 005	1 019
Import prices	968	1 032	1 028	992	991	965	954	991	1 012
Terms of trade	1 007	1 022	1 052	1 047	1 031	1 021	1 005	1 014	1 007

Source: Statistics New Zealand.

Table F.　**Monetary aggregates components**
NZ$ million, end quarter

	1998			1999				2000		
	Q2	Q3	Q4	Q1	Q2	Q3	Q4	Q1	Q2	Q3
Notes and coin held by the public	1 516	1 569	1 724	1 682	1 630	1 717	2 077	1 830	1 795	1 858
Total transaction account balances	10 201	10 305	11 195	11 996	12 237	12 820	12 874	13 458	12 866	12 807
Less: Inter-institutional trans balances	45	73	2	9	12	31	9	74	58	27
Less: Government deposit	40	32	29	32	36	34	61	35	32	29
M1	11 632	11 769	12 888	13 638	13 819	14 472	14 880	15 180	14 570	14 609
Total other call funding	14 004	14 896	12 700	15 447	12 831	17 391	14 454	13 667	15 773	14 037
Less: other call inter-institutional funding	1 682	1 818	1 291	1 502	867	1 984	1 181	1 246	1 203	589
M2	34 228	36 794	37 873	40 933	39 626	43 572	40 964	39 930	40 835	39 912
Total term funding	103 294	101 203	102 967	100 664	103 552	108 617	108 909	107 497	107 642	108 376
Less: Inter-institutional term funding	9 563	10 719	11 883	8 402	9 670	10 602	11 721	11 516	10 848	10 419
Less: Government deposit	390	388	425	570	464	497	518	501	544	481
M3	94 856	91 664	92 383	93 374	95 048	99 235	98 748	97 310	98 045	99 333

Source:　Rerserve Bank Bulletin.

Table G.   **Central government revenue and expenditure**
NZ$ million

Year ending June[1]	1996	1997	1998	1999
REVENUE	**35 059**	**34 778**	**35 581**	**36 357**
Levied through the Crown's Sovereign Power	32 468	32 179	33 240	32 456
Direct taxation	21 255	20 489	21 260	20 289
Indirect taxation	10 978	11 427	11 722	11 867
Compulsory fees, fines, penalties and levies	235	263	258	300
Earned through the Crown's Operations	2 591	2 599	2 341	3 901
Unrealised gains/losses arising from revaluation of commercial forests	−87	−48	78	−84
Investment income	1 606	1 596	1 154	2 901
Sales of goods and services	662	664	689	683
Other operational revenue	410	387	420	401
EXPENSES	**31 743**	**32 953**	**34 211**	**35 825**
By functional classification				
Social security and welfare	12 240	12 620	12 509	12 906
GSF pension expenses	..	..	494	1 132
Education	4 949	5 335	5 714	5 899
Health	5 228	5 626	6 001	6 573
Core government services	1 565	1 667	1 562	1 705
Law and order	1 234	1 281	1 345	1 499
Defence	970	946	1 065	1 030
Transport and communications	821	888	948	1 029
Economic and industrial services	997	763	840	858
Primary services	304	351	423	334
Heritage, culture and recreation	247	277	297	316
Housing and community development	40	47	29	41
Other	48	68	167	34
Finance costs	3 703	3 072	2 804	2 516
Net foreign-exchange (gains)/losses	−603	12	13	−47
REVENUE LESS EXPENSES	3 316	1 825	1 370	532
Net surplus/deficit, less distributions attributable to State-owned enterprises and Crown entities	−2	83	1 164	1 245
OPERATING BALANCE	3 314	1 908	2 534	1 777

1. From 1992/93 onward, the reporting entity includes all SOEs and Crown entities, as well as the Reserve Bank of New Zealand.
Source: Financial Statements of the Government of New Zealand.

　　　　　　　　　　　　　　OECD Economic Surveys: New Zealand

Table H. **Balance of payments**[1]
NZ$ million

	1990	1991	1992	1993	1994	1995	1996	1997	1998	1999
Exports	15 408	16 564	18 121	19 354	20 189	20 647	20 849	21 515	22 881	23 809
Imports	13 883	12 976	15 101	16 150	17 880	19 166	20 074	20 228	21 181	24 678
Trade balance	**1 524**	**3 588**	**3 019**	**3 204**	**2 309**	**1 481**	**774**	**1 288**	**1 702**	**–871**
Services, net	–1 395	–1 457	–1 760	–1 187	–552	–307	–375	–931	–1 475	–479
Balance on goods and services	**129**	**2 131**	**1 259**	**2 017**	**1 757**	**1 174**	**399**	**357**	**227**	**–1 350**
Investment income	–2 767	–4 408	–4 057	–4 186	–5 508	–6 033	–6 845	–7 289	–4 882	–5 916
Transfers, net	231	242	240	245	495	303	700	384	537	394
Current balance	**–2 404**	**–2 035**	**–2 557**	**–1 926**	**–3 256**	**–4 556**	**–5 746**	**–6 548**	**–4 122**	**–6 872**
Inflow of capital account	..	..	..	..	..	..	2 684	1 161	961	820
Outflow of capital account	..	..	..	..	..	..	732	813	826	899
Balance on capital account	**354**	**438**	**544**	**1 005**	**1 356**	**1 867**	**1 953**	**348**	**–342**	**–408**
New Zealand investment abroad	..	..	..	..	..	..	3 118	–1 141	–162	3 204
of which: Portfolio investment	..	..	..	..	..	..	..	1 444	666	3 118
Foreign investment in New Zealand	..	..	..	..	..	..	1 819	–1 092	–4 182	–2 009
of which: Portfolio investment	..	..	..	..	..	..	3 515	203	–3 616	–1 134
Net errors and omissions[2]	..	..	..	..	..	..	3 407	5 938	8 864	13 548

1. On an accrual basis.
2. Balancing item.
Source: Statistics New Zealand.

Table I. **Imports: value, volume, prices and commodity groups**
US$ millions

	1990	1991	1992	1993	1994	1995	1996	1997	1998	1999
Value	9 484	8 497	9 205	9 304	11 911	13 946	14 725	14 518	12 499	14 299
Volume index (Year ended June 1989 = 1 000)	1 224	1 224	1 224	1 224	1 224	1 224	1 224	1 224	1 739	1 972
Price index (Year ended June 1989 = 1 000)	1 039	1 039	1 039	1 039	1 039	1 039	1 039	1 039	1 075	1 098
Value of principal commodity groups:										
Live animals, beverages and tobacco	584	605	609	664	833	974	1 051	1 066	982	1 057
Minerals, chemicals and plastic materials	2 082	1 985	2 073	2 155	2 535	2 933	3 199	3 158	2 711	3 029
Manufactured goods	697	656	740	723	880	1 068	1 085	1 118	988	1 076
Textiles and textiles articles	506	502	538	535	679	726	762	789	691	741
Metals and articles of metals	576	536	551	552	696	857	874	812	676	764
Machinery and mechanical appliances	2 243	1 974	2 099	2 215	2 916	3 555	3 733	3 543	2 986	3 241
Vehicles and aircraft	1 477	1 033	1 387	1 200	1 843	2 071	2 131	2 163	1 812	2 697

Source: Statistics New Zealand and OECD.

Table J. **Exports: value, volume, prices and commodity groups**

US$ millions

	1990	1991	1992	1993	1994	1995	1996	1997	1998	1999
Value[1]	8 830	9 177	9 344	9 751	11 660	13 043	13 821	13 708	11 569	11 809
Volume index (Year ending June 1989 = 1 000)	999	1 103	1 131	1 179	1 298	1 336	1 400	1 468	1 464	1 487
Price index (Year ending June 1989 = 1 000)	1 040	996	1 077	1 105	1 060	1 042	1 006	979	1 026	1 041
Value of principal commodity groups:										
Total meat	1 483	1 542	1 599	1 582	1 662	1 751	1 838	1 859	1 553	1 579
Dairy produce	1 260	1 347	1 317	1 470	1 660	1 787	2 307	2 397	2 115	1 993
Fruit, vegetables, prepared food-stuff, beverage and tobacco	920	1 013	1 012	984	1 225	1 429	1 536	1 447	1 302	1 452
Forest products	913	983	1 009	1 292	1 497	1 715	1 670	1 543	1 229	1 391
Minerals, chemicals and plastic materials	937	1 001	926	986	1 334	1 424	1 546	1 613	1 353	1 331
Metals and articles of metals	752	751	683	676	804	1 015	950	1 025	904	869
Manufactured goods	2 298	2 249	2 287	2 550	3 143	3 569	3 488	3 191	2 456	2 493

1. Excludes Re-exports
Source: Statistics New Zealand and OECD.

Table K. **Foreign trade by area**
US$ millions

	1990	1991	1992	1993	1994	1995	1996	1997	1998	1999
Exports, total	9 378	9 759	9 789	10 223	12 184	13 645	14 360	14 220	12 073	12 455
OECD countries	6 452	6 496	6 424	6 564	8 170	8 961	9 327	9 863	8 598	9 019
EC	1 661	1 618	1 599	1 138	1 902	2 127	2 300	2 316	2 168	2 187
of which: United Kingdom	666	606	629	621	735	809	922	871	714	820
United States	1 217	1 247	1 209	1 185	1 342	1 353	1 316	1 470	1 562	1 698
Japan	1 523	1 564	1 436	1 491	1 867	2 230	2 213	2 051	1 588	1 572
Australia	1 797	1 833	1 940	2 043	2 606	2 802	2 932	2 898	2 529	2 706
Republic of Korea	400	423	405	487	586	709	677	646	388	524
Non-OECD countries	2 926	3 262	3 365	3 659	4 014	4 684	5 033	4 357	3 475	3 436
China	389	547	651	709	992	1 160	1 215	1 159	955	968
Other Asia	545	659	781	696	810	1 038	1 164	1 240	808	908
Others	1 993	2 057	1 932	2 254	2 212	2 486	2 654	1 959	1 712	1 560
Imports, total	8 691	7 768	8 493	8 568	11 025	12 938	13 657	13 511	11 606	13 414
OECD countries	6 982	6 174	6 676	6 735	8 720	10 203	10 837	10 796	9 089	10 431
EC	1 673	1 433	1 631	1 059	1 970	2 811	2 781	2 581	2 297	2 503
of which: United Kingdom	641	508	546	506	691	763	719	691	595	548
United States	1 570	1 299	1 667	1 529	2 121	2 407	2 259	2 402	2 264	2 246
Japan	1 309	1 196	1 243	1 391	1 678	1 771	1 915	1 552	1 296	1 617
Australia	1 776	1 731	1 796	1 841	2 382	2 815	3 347	3 450	2 587	3 290
Republic of Korea	142	134	131	136	177	221	251	258	220	312
Non-OECD countries	1 709	1 594	1 816	1 833	2 305	2 735	2 820	2 716	2 517	2 982
China	428	466	562	614	781	941	970	1 071	948	1 084
Other Asia	337	270	427	387	522	778	801	753	785	944
Others	943	859	828	832	1 002	1 016	1 049	892	784	955

Source: Statistics New Zealand and OECD.

Table L. **Production and employment structure**

March ending year	Per cent of GDP[1]					Per cent of total employment				
	1996	1997	1998	1999	2000	1996	1997	1998	1999	2000
Tradeables										
Agriculture, fishing, hunting, forestry and logging	7.1	7.3	7.4	7.2	7.2	9.7	9.2	8.7	8.7	9.3
Mining and quarrying	1.3	1.4	1.3	1.3	1.2	0.3	0.3	0.3	0.2	0.2
Manufacturing	18.4	18.1	18.1	17.4	17.4	17.8	16.8	16.4	16.6	15.8
Non-tradeables										
Electricity, gas and water	2.7	2.6	2.6	2.5	2.3	0.8	0.8	0.6	0.6	0.5
Construction	3.6	3.6	3.5	3.2	3.4	6.2	6.5	6.6	6.3	6.5
Trade, restaurants and hotels	14.7	14.5	14.5	14.6	14.9	21.3	21.2	21.7	21.5	21.3
Transport, storage and communication	10.6	11.0	11.2	11.9	12.6	5.9	5.9	6.0	6.0	6.3
Finance, insurance, real estate and business services	13.8	14.0	14.2	14.6	14.1	10.7	11.5	12.4	12.5	12.6
Community, social and personal services	6.0	6.2	6.2	6.1	6.0	27.1	27.4	27.1	27.3	27.3

1. 1991/92 prices.
Source: Statistics New Zealand.

Table M. **Labour market indicators**

Calendar years	1996	1997	1998	1999
A. Labour market performance				
Unemployment rate: Total	6.1	6.7	7.5	6.8
Male	6.1	6.6	7.6	7
Female	6.1	6.7	7.4	6.6
Youth[1]	11.8	13.1	14.6	13.8
B. Structural or institutional characteristics				
Labour Force (per cent change)	3.5	1.0	0.3	0.8
Participation rate[2]: Total	65.8	65.6	65.2	65.3
Male	74.7	74.4	73.7	73.6
Female	57.5	57.3	57.2	57.4
Employment/population (15 and over)	61.8	61.2	60.3	60.9
Employment shares[3]				
Agriculture	9.5	8.7	8.5	9.5
Industry	24.7	23.8	24.1	22.9
Services	65.5	67.2	67.1	67.5
of which : public sector[4]	15.8	15.5	15.3	. .
Part-time work (as per cent of total employment)[5]	22.4	22.7	23.1	23.4
Wage or salary earners (per cent of total)	78.8	79.9	79.6	78.8

1. 15 to 24 years old.
2. Total labour force as a per cent of population 15 and over.
3. Per cent of total employment.
4. Approximation using QES central and local government non-trading employment as per cent of QES total employment. This excludes agriculture.
5. Part-time is less than 30 hours per week.
Source: Statistics New Zealand, Household Labour Force Survey .

Table N.   **Financial Market**[1]

Year ending December	1994	1995	1996	1997	1998	1999
Sector size						
Credits distributed by financial markets/GDP[2]	93.5	100.6	109.9	116.4	126.1	..
Domestic financial assets/GDP[3]	106.7	112.8	122.1	133.5	140.0	..
Internationalisation of markets						
Foreign business of the banking sector						
Assets[4]	3.9	3.4	3.8	3.1	3.6	4.6
Liabilities[5]	13.3	12.4	12.7	16.3	20.0	24.0
Efficiency of markets						
Developments of interest rate margin[6]	2.96	2.99	2.98	2.85	3.04	2.77

1. All M3 financial institutions.
2. NZ$ claims of registered banks and all M3 financial institutions.
3. Total assets less foreign currency claims.
4. Foreign currency claims/total claims.
5. Foreign currency funding/total funding.
6. Spread between M3 institutions average weighted interest rates for the December quarter for NZ$ funding and claims.
Source: Reserve Bank of New Zealand.

Table O.   **The public sector**[1]
Percentage of GDP

Year ending June	1994	1995	1996	1997	1998	1999
Budget indicators						
Current receipts (excluding interests)	36.1	37.3	37.1	35.6	35.6	37.0
Non-interest expenditures (financial)	31.6	30.2	30.7	31.1	32.0	33.3
Primary budget balance	4.5	7.1	6.4	4.5	3.6	3.7
Net interest (including net capital transfers)	3.6	4.0	2.8	2.6	2.2	1.9
Government budget balance						
(adjusted financial balance/operating balance)	0.9	3.1	3.6	2.0	2.6	1.8
Structure of expenditure and taxation						
General expenditure						
Education	5.6	5.5	5.4	5.6	5.8	5.9
Transportation	1.0	0.9	0.9	0.9	1.0	1.0
Health	5.6	5.5	5.7	5.9	6.1	6.6
Tax receipts						
Personal income tax	16.4	16.9	17.0	16.0	16.0	14.9
Corporate tax	4.1	4.8	5.0	4.3	4.7	4.4
Other indicators						
Income tax as a percentage of total tax	63.5	65.7	65.9	64.2	64.5	63.1
Gross public debt as a percentage of GDP	56.1	50.1	45.0	37.5	38.6	36.7

1. Excluding local government.
Source: New Zealand Treasury.

BASIC STATISTICS:

INTERNATIONAL COMPARISONS

	Units	Reference period [1]	Australia	Austria
Population				
Total	Thousands	1997	18 532	8 (
Inhabitants per sq. km	Number	1997	2	
Net average annual increase over previous 10 years	%	1997	1.3	
Employment				
Total civilian employment (TCE)[2]	Thousands	1997	8 430	3 (
of which:				
Agriculture	% of TCE	1997	5.2	
Industry	% of TCE	1997	22.1	3
Services	% of TCE	1997	72.7	6
Gross domestic product (GDP)				
At current prices and current exchange rates	Bill. US$	1997	392.9	20
Per capita	US$	1997	21 202	25 :
At current prices using current PPPs[3]	Bill. US$	1997	406.8	18
Per capita	US$	1997	21 949	23 (
Average annual volume growth over previous 5 years	%	1997	4.1	
Gross fixed capital formation (GFCF)	% of GDP	1997	21.5	2
of which:				
Machinery and equipment	% of GDP	1997	10.3 (96)	8.8 (
Residential construction	% of GDP	1997	4.4 (96)	6.2 (
Average annual volume growth over previous 5 years	%	1997	7.3	
Gross saving ratio[4]	% of GDP	1997	18.4	
General government				
Current expenditure on goods and services	% of GDP	1997	16.7	]
Current disbursements[5]	% of GDP	1996	34.8	
Current receipts	% of GDP	1996	35.4	4
Net official development assistance	% of GNP	1996	0.28	0
Indicators of living standards				
Private consumption per capita using current PPP's[3]	US$	1997	13 585	12 (
Passenger cars, per 1 000 inhabitants	Number	1995	477	4
Telephones, per 1 000 inhabitants	Number	1995	510	4
Television sets, per 1 000 inhabitants	Number	1994	489	4
Doctors, per 1 000 inhabitants	Number	1996	2.5	
Infant mortality per 1 000 live births	Number	1996	5.8	
Wages and prices (average annual increase over previous 5 years)				
Wages (earnings or rates according to availability)	%	1998	1.5	
Consumer prices	%	1998	2.0	
Foreign trade				
Exports of goods, fob*	Mill. US$	1998	55 882	61
As % of GDP	%	1997	15.6	2
Average annual increase over previous 5 years	%	1998	5.6	
Imports of goods, cif*	Mill. US$	1998	60 821	68 (
As % of GDP	%	1997	15.3	3
Average annual increase over previous 5 years	%	1998	7.5	
Total official reserves[6]	Mill. SDR's	1998	10 942	14 628 (
As ratio of average monthly imports of goods	Ratio	1998	2.2	2.7 (

* At current prices and exchange rates.
1. Unless otherwise stated.
2. According to the definitions used in OECD Labour Force Statistics.
3. PPPs = Purchasing Power Parities.
4. Gross saving = Gross national disposable income minus private and government consumption.

EMPLOYMENT OPPORTUNITIES

Economics Department, OECD

The Economics Department of the OECD offers challenging and rewarding opportunities to economists interested in applied policy analysis in an international environment. The Department's concerns extend across the entire field of economic policy analysis, both macro-economic and microeconomic. Its main task is to provide, for discussion by committees of senior officials from Member countries, documents and papers dealing with current policy concerns. Within this programme of work, three major responsibilities are:

- to prepare regular surveys of the economies of individual Member countries;
- to issue full twice-yearly reviews of the economic situation and prospects of the OECD countries in the context of world economic trends;
- to analyse specific policy issues in a medium-term context for the OECD as a whole, and to a lesser extent for the non-OECD countries.

The documents prepared for these purposes, together with much of the Department's other economic work, appear in published form in the *OECD Economic Outlook, OECD Economic Surveys, OECD Economic Studies* and the Department's *Working Papers* series.

The Department maintains a world econometric model, INTERLINK, which plays an important role in the preparation of the policy analyses and twice-yearly projections. The availability of extensive cross-country data bases and good computer resources facilitates comparative empirical analysis, much of which is incorporated into the model.

The Department is made up of about 80 professional economists from a variety of backgrounds and Member countries. Most projects are carried out by small teams and last from four to eighteen months. Within the Department, ideas and points of view are widely discussed; there is a lively professional interchange, and all professional staff have the opportunity to contribute actively to the programme of work.

Skills the Economics Department is looking for:

a) Solid competence in using the tools of both microeconomic and macroeconomic theory to answer policy questions. Experience indicates that this normally requires the equivalent of a Ph.D. in economics or substantial relevant professional experience to compensate for a lower degree.

b) Solid knowledge of economic statistics and quantitative methods; this includes how to identify data, estimate structural relationships, apply basic techniques of time series analysis, and test hypotheses. It is essential to be able to interpret results sensibly in an economic policy context.

c) A keen interest in and extensive knowledge of policy issues, economic developments and their political/social contexts.

d) Interest and experience in analysing questions posed by policy-makers and presenting the results to them effectively and judiciously. Thus, work experience in government agencies or policy research institutions is an advantage.

e) The ability to write clearly, effectively, and to the point. The OECD is a bilingual organisation with French and English as the official languages. Candidates must have excellent knowledge of one of these languages, and some knowledge of the other. Knowledge of other languages might also be an advantage for certain posts.

f) For some posts, expertise in a particular area may be important, but a successful candidate is expected to be able to work on a broader range of topics relevant to the work of the Department. Thus, except in rare cases, the Department does not recruit narrow specialists.

g) The Department works on a tight time schedule with strict deadlines. Moreover, much of the work in the Department is carried out in small groups. Thus, the ability to work with other economists from a variety of cultural and professional backgrounds, to supervise junior staff, and to produce work on time is important.

General information

The salary for recruits depends on educational and professional background. Positions carry a basic salary from FF 318 660 or FF 393 192 for Administrators (economists) and from FF 456 924 for Principal Administrators (senior economists). This may be supplemented by expatriation and/or family allowances, depending on nationality, residence and family situation. Initial appointments are for a fixed term of two to three years.

Vacancies are open to candidates from OECD Member countries. The Organisation seeks to maintain an appropriate balance between female and male staff and among nationals from Member countries.

For further information on employment opportunities in the Economics Department, contact:

Management Support Unit
Economics Department
OECD
2, rue André-Pascal
75775 PARIS CEDEX 16
FRANCE

E-Mail: eco.contact@oecd.org

Applications citing ''ECSUR'', together with a detailed *curriculum vitae* in English or French, should be sent to the Head of Personnel at the above address.

Did you Know?

This publication is available in electronic form!

Many OECD publications and data sets are now available in electronic form to suit your needs at affordable prices.

CD-ROMs

For our statistical products we use the powerful software platform Beyond 20/20™ produced by Ivation. This allows you to get maximum value from the data. For more details of this and other publications on CD-ROM visit our online bookshop **www.oecd.org/bookshop** or **www.oecdwash.org.**

STATISTICS VIA THE INTERNET

During 2000 we are launching SourceOECD/statistics. Whilst some statistical datasets may become available on the Internet during the second half of 2000 we anticipate that most will not be available until late 2000 or early 2001. For more information visit **www.oecd.org/sourceoecd** or **www.ivation.com.**

BOOKS AND PERIODICALS IN PDF

Most of our printed books are also produced as PDF files and are available from our online bookshop **www.oecd.org/bookshop.** Customers paying for printed books by credit card online can download the PDF file free of charge for immediate access.

We are also developing two new services, SourceOECD/periodicals and SourceOECD/studies, which will deliver online access to all printed publications over the Internet. These services are being developed in partnership with ingenta. For more information visit **www.oecd.org/sourceoecd or www.ingenta.com.**

OECD DIRECT

To stay informed by e-mail about all new OECD publications as they are published, why not register for OECD Direct?

OECD Direct is a free, opt-in, e-mail alerting service designed to help you stay up to date with our new publications. You've a choice of different themes so you can adapt the service to your fields of interest only. Registration is free of charge and there is no obligation. To register, simply follow the instructions at the top of the online bookshop's home page **www.oecd.org/bookshop**. We don't use your e-mail address for any other purpose and we won't give them to anyone else either – you'll just get what you registered for, e-mails announcing new publications as soon as they are released.

Le saviez-vous ?

Cette publication est disponible en version électronique !

Pour répondre aux besoins de ses clients, l'OCDE a décidé de publier un grand nombre d'études et de données sous forme électronique à des prix très abordables.

CD-ROM

Nos bases de données statistiques fonctionnent avec le logiciel Beyond 20/20™ produit par Ivation. Ce logiciel, convivial et très simple d'utilisation, vous permet d'utiliser au mieux les données.
Pour plus de détails et pour consulter la liste des publications sur CD-ROM, visitez notre librairie en ligne : **www.oecd.org/bookshop.**

STATISTIQUES SUR INTERNET

SourceOECD/statitics sera lancé au cours de l'an 2000. Ce nouveau service commencera à être opérationnel à partir du second semestre de l'an 2000 et nous envisageons de diffuser la totalité de notre catalogue de statistiques pour la fin de l'an 2000/début 2001.
Pour plus d'information : **www.oecd.org/sourceoecd** ou **www.ivation.com.**

LIVRES ET PÉRIODIQUES EN VERSION PDF

La plupart de nos publications sont également disponibles en format PDF. Vous pouvez les trouver dans notre librairie en ligne : **www.oecd.org/bookshop.**
Les clients de notre librairie en ligne, qui font l'acquisition d'un ouvrage imprimé en utilisant une carte de crédit, peuvent télécharger gratuitement la version électronique, pour une lecture immédiate.

Nous développons actuellement deux nouveaux services, SourceOECD/periodicals et SourceOECD/studies, qui vous permettront d'accéder en ligne à toutes nos publications. Ces services, qui sont actuellement en voie de développement en association avec ingenta, ne seront dans un premier temps disponibles que pour les versions en langue anglaise. Une étude est en cours pour élargir ce service aux publications en langue française. Pour plus d'information, visitez les deux sites **www.oecd.org/sourceoecd** ou **www.ingenta.com.**

OECD DIRECT

Pour être informé par e-mail de la parution de nos toutes dernières publications, enregistrez dès maintenant votre nom sur **www.oecd.org/bookshop.**
OECD Direct est notre service « Alerte » gratuit qui permet aux lecteurs qui le souhaitent de recevoir par e-mail des informations sur la sortie de nos nouvelles publications. Une série de thèmes est proposée et chacun pourra choisir en fonction de ses propres centres d'intérêt. L'inscription est gratuite et sans obligation. Pour enregistrer votre nom, il vous suffit de suivre les instructions figurant en haut de la page d'accueil de notre librairie en ligne **www.oecd.org/bookshop.** Soyez assurés que nous n'utiliserons pas votre adresse e-mail à d'autres fins et ne la transmettrons en aucun cas. Vous ne recevrez par e-mail que des informations vous annonçant nos nouvelles publications dès lors qu'elles sont parues.

www.oecd.org/sourceoecd

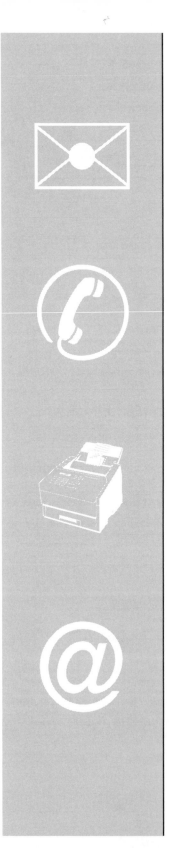

For more information about all OECD publications
contact your nearest OECD Centre, or visit
www.oecd.org/bookshop

Pour plus d'informations sur les publications de l'OCDE,
contactez votre Centre OCDE le plus proche
ou visitez notre librairie en ligne :
www.oecd.org/bookshop

Where to send your request:
Où passer commande :

In Central and Latin America / En Amérique centrale et en Amérique du Sud

OECD MEXICO CENTRE / CENTRE OCDE DE MEXICO
Edificio INFOTEC
Av. San Fernando No. 37 Col. Toriello Guerra
Tlalpan C.P. 14050, Mexico D.F.
Tel.: +525 281 38 10   Fax: + 525 606 13 07
E-mail: mexico.contact@oecd.org   Internet: www.rtn.net.mx/ocde

In North America / En Amérique du Nord

OECD WASHINGTON CENTER / CENTRE OCDE DE WASHINGTON
2001 L Street N.W., Suite 650
Washington, DC 20036-4922
Tel.: +1 202 785-6323
Toll free / Numéro vert : +1 800 456-6323   Fax: +1 202 785-0350
E-mail: washington.contact@oecd.org   Internet: www.oecdwash.org

In Japan / Au Japon

OECD TOKYO CENTRE / CENTRE OCDE DE TOKYO
Landic Akasaka Bldg.
2-3-4 Akasaka, Minato-ku
Tokyo 107-0052
Tel.: +81 3 3586 2016   Fax: +81 3 3584 7929
E-mail : center@oecdtokyo.org   Internet: www.oecdtokyo.org

In the rest of the world / Dans le reste du monde
DVGmbH
Birkenmaarsstrasse 8
D-53340 Meckenheim
Germany
Tel.: +49 22 25 9 26 166/7/8   Fax: +49 22 25 9 26 169
E-mail: oecd@dvg.dsb.net

OECD Information Centre and Bookshop/
Centre d'information de l'OCDE et Librairie
OECD PARIS CENTRE / CENTRE OCDE DE PARIS
2 rue André-Pascal, 75775 Paris Cedex 16, France
Enquiries / Renseignements : Tel: +33 (0) 1 45 24 81 67
E-mail: sales@oecd.org

ONLINE BOOKSHOP / LIBRAIRIE EN LIGNE : **www.oecd.org/bookshop**

(secure payment with credit card / paiement sécurisé par carte de crédit)

OECD PUBLICATIONS, 2, rue André-Pascal, 75775 PARIS CEDEX 16
PRINTED IN FRANCE
(10 2000 05 1 P) ISBN 92-64-17505-9 – No. 51599 2000
ISSN 0376-6438